Absent
Mandate

Canadian Electoral Politics
In an Era of Restructuring

Harold D. Clarke
Jane Jenson
Lawrence LeDuc
Jon H. Pammett

THIRD EDITION

gage EDUCATIONAL PUBLISHING COMPANY
A DIVISION OF CANADA PUBLISHING CORPORATION
Vancouver·Calgary·Toronto·London·Halifax

Canadian Cataloguing in Publication Data

Main entry under title:

Absent mandate
3rd ed.
Includes index.
ISBN 0-7715-5116-9

1. Elections – Canada – History – 20th century.
2. Voting – Canada. 3. Political participation – Canada. I. Clarke, Harold D., 1943-

JL193.A27 1995   324.971'064   C95–931796–1

Cover and text design: First Image
Page makeup: First Image
Editor: Gail Copeland

ISBN 0-7715-**5116-9**
1 2 3 4 5 WC 98 97 96 95
Written, Printed, and Bound in Canada

TABLE OF CONTENTS

Preface

In 1993, Canadian voters handed the fledgling Conservative government of Kim Campbell a crushing defeat. Although the results of the 1993 election were dramatic, big losses by an incumbent government have been relatively common in Canada. In fact, the first sentence of this paragraph is similar to the introductory sentence of the preface to the previous edition of this book. In that instance, the reference was to 1984 and the "crushing defeat" had been rendered to the "fledgling Liberal government of John Turner." In each case the electorate had become disenchanted with those in power, and was not restrained in the slightest by residual party loyalties from throwing them out. Volatility, potential and actual, is a prime characteristic of the Canadian electorate and has been a consistent theme of our studies of past elections in this country.

What instructions did the voters give to the Liberals when they entrusted them with the reins of power once again? As on previous occasions, the search in the details of the 1993 election for a policy mandate of substance and depth is a frustrating enterprise. Despite an extraordinarily specific Liberal program, the most that can be said is that voters gave the nod to the expenditure of money for short-term job creation and the cancellation of a contract to purchase helicopters. Those supporting the Liberal Party in 1993 were not asked to endorse massive budget cutting and reductions in social programs, or to give the final seal of approval to NAFTA. Once again, the country's electoral institutions seemed almost peripheral to the real policy-making activities of government.

While "absent mandates" have been the rule from the voters in the past two decades, an extraordinary change in the political landscape has nevertheless taken place. Both Conservative and Liberal governments have put in place basic elements of the restructuring of the country in a neo-conservative direction, embodying principles of free trade, globalization, and the withdrawal of the state from responsibility for establishing distinct national economic goals and priorities. Similarly, without public approval, political elites have embarked on several rounds of constitutional change, mostly designed to devolve power to the provinces in the Canadian federation. The negative public verdict on both the economic and constitutional restructuring projects is visible in virtually every public opinion poll, and also was reflected in the 1992 referendum, in which the Canadian electorate decisively rejected the Charlottetown constitutional proposals.

This edition of *Absent Mandate* explores the way in which this situation has come about. Despite the fact that Canada possesses a democratic ideology rooted in the philosophy that the people should decide the directions of their government, there is a wide gulf between public views on policy and the actions that governments have taken. The result has been an angry electorate, ready and willing to try new parties and leaders. Whether 1993's new faces will last longer than the old ones is an open question.

The analyses in this book are based on many different kinds of large nationwide surveys of the Canadian public that have been conducted by us and by other researchers over the last 30 years. A detailed description of the surveys utilized here may be found in the appendix on Data Sources (p. 188). In conducting the extensive analyses that have formed the basis for this book and for its predecessors, we have acquired debts to many individuals and organizations. The National Election Studies, on which some of our analyses of elections prior to 1988 are based, were funded by the Social Sciences and Humanities Research Council of Canada, whose continued support for this valuable series of studies is gratefully acknowledged. Harold Clarke and his co-principal investigator, Allan Kornberg (Duke University), also wish to thank the U.S. National Science Foundation for the grants that provided the principal funding for the 1993 and earlier Political Support in Canada studies, which are also utilized extensively in the analyses reported in this book. The advice and encouragement offered by the NSF's Political Science Program Director, Dr. Frank Scioli, is gratefully acknowledged. Thanks are also due to the Canadian Embassy (Washington, D.C.), Duke University, and the University of North Texas, for providing additional financial assistance for these studies. The field work for the Political Support in Canada surveys, and for all of the National Election Studies prior to 1988, was conducted by Canadian Facts (Toronto) under the direction of Senior Project Director, Mary Auvinen. Mary's sage advice and her many efforts on behalf of electoral research in Canada through these and other projects are appreciated by all of us who have worked with her over many years.

A number of other surveys are also utilized in the analyses reported in this book. A 1988 reinterview of respondents from the 1984 National Election Study, and a 1992 study of the constitutional referendum, both conducted by the Carleton University Survey Centre under the direction of Alan Frizzell, also provided us with important sources of data. The support of Carleton University for this research, and the contribution of the University of Toronto, the NSF, and SSHRCC to these studies is gratefully acknowledged. We also were fortunate to have access to a 1993 survey conducted by Insight Canada Research, and the advice and assistance provided by Michael and Angela Marzolini was greatly appreciated. We have also made occasional use of surveys conducted by Gallup Canada and by other polling organizations. Neither the principal investigators of any of these studies, the various granting agencies, nor the survey units, are responsible for the specific analyses or interpretations of the data presented here.

In preparing this third edition of *Absent Mandate*, our universities have provided essential research facilities and support—the University of North Texas, the Université de Montréal, the University of Toronto, and Carleton University. We are likewise grateful to the many students from these universities and others whose work on these projects has been essential to their success, and especially to Jon Rapkin for his work in connection with this edition of the book. Thanks are also due to the many skilled and enthusiastic people at Gage with whom we have worked on all three editions, and particularly to Tim Johnston and Darleen Rotozinski for their work in bringing this third edition into print. And finally, we acknowledge the contribution of thousands of Canadians whose responses to our questions and to those of other researchers provided the raw material for our work. This book is about them, and the many changes that continue to take place in the political world in which they live.

1

The Electorate Wants In

On election day 1993 the electorate spoke loudly. Whether or not its voice was clearly heard or its preferences were clearly expressed is the subject of this book. The election result was more dramatic than anyone had anticipated. Losing all but two seats, the governing Progressive Conservative Party almost disappeared from the House of Commons. According to the rules of the House, both the Conservative Party and the New Democratic Party lost their standing as official parties, as neither had won the minimum 12 seats needed to claim that status (and the considerable resources accompanying it). At the same time, two new parties—the Bloc Québécois and the Reform Party—competed to form the official opposition, with the Bloc Québécois eventually outdistancing the Reform Party by a mere two seats. The familiar three-party system exploded on 25 October 1993.

The electorate exhibited its volatility to an even greater extent than usual. It vented its dissatisfaction with the politicians and parties who had brought about not only a disastrously deep recession and soaring rates of unemployment, but also several years of unresolved and divisive constitutional debate about citizens' rights, the future design of democratic institutions, and the status of Quebec and Aboriginal peoples in Canada. Change, even angry change, does not necessarily produce a clear mandate for a new program, however. The election's meaning and consequences for government action in the future remain uncertain. Will the Liberals in power embark on a different social, economic, and constitutional agenda, or will they continue along the same path as their predecessors?

1

Both the dramatic election result and the uncertainty about its eventual consequences are in many ways a logical result of the two decades of politics, including six elections, analysed in this book. The governing parties and their opponents have long pursued a strategy of brokerage politics, reinforcing a party system that often lacks the capacity to generate innovative responses to new or ongoing problems, to debate alternative projects, and to translate such broad alternatives into programs and policies. They have avoided presenting alternative projects to the electorate, choosing instead to focus on leadership capacities. Once in office they have made policy decisions that have received little discussion in the campaign. Given these practices, the party system's ability to generate mandates for action, as commonly understood in liberal democracies, remains limited.

Elections have never been irrelevant events, of course. They have provided an opportunity for the expression of public discontent as well as the designation of the governing team and the prime minister. Nonetheless the election outcomes have been quite imperfect guides to eventual policy choices, including the hugely important decisions made in the last decade about the country's economic, social, and constitutional future. This absence of fit between electoral politics and policy in turn encourages a volatile electorate to expect easy solutions to complicated problems, to focus on leaders and their images rather than policy alternatives, and to develop a deep suspicion of political elites. In recent years there have been some signs that the voters may no longer stand for the old ways of doing politics. Indeed, citizens have demanded, and received, several opportunities for some involvement in policy discussion. New mechanisms of consultation (for example, commissions of inquiry, roving televised weekend-long conferences, and the 1992 referendum) have been extended to previously closed policy realms such as constitutional reform, budget making, and social policy. All of these exercises have, however, helped to reveal the inadequacies of partisan politics, which rarely uses elections and campaigns as moments for consultation about future policy direction, preferring instead to focus on style, image, and generalities. A theme of this book is how the intersection of party actions and electoral behaviour results in parties taking office with no clear mandate for policy choices. Not feeling bound by promises given or programs outlined in the campaign, the government proceeds nonetheless to make the crucial decisions about Canadians' future.

The Major Political Projects of the 1990s

The existence of brokerage politics and ambiguous mandates does not mean that a project for restructuring the Canadian economy and redesigning its place in the global order does not exist. It would also be an error to ignore

2

the importance of controversy over alternative constitutional projects. Even if these issue areas have rarely been successfully and seriously debated in the forum supposedly available for considering them—party and electoral politics—governments have been active, and political controversy has broken out in other institutional forums.

For well over two decades, economic actors in all of the advanced industrial economies have struggled to come to grips with new economic conditions. By the mid-1970s inflation, unemployment, and low rates of growth already seemed intractable, refusing to respond to the traditional postwar economic instruments. Governments everywhere floundered in their search for workable programs. The 1980s opened with a deep recession, which many likened to the Great Depression of the 1930s, and ended with an equally serious downturn. This was the context in which businesses began to restructure, taking advantage of innovative technologies, and redesigning management techniques and employment practices. The goal was to increase productivity, which sometimes meant moving to new locations and sometimes hiring new types of workers, especially part-time and other atypical ones. At the same time, governments revamped their relationships with business, by deregulating, lowering corporate taxes, and seeking ways to help companies compete in international markets. Governments also changed their own economic behaviour, both by privatizing many activities and services that the state had performed, and by seeking to reduce state spending, even as the fixed costs of unemployment and other social programs mounted during hard times.

In these years, a high level of consensus about problems and their solutions emerged, nurtured by large international bodies like the Organization for Economic Co-operation and Development (OECD). Beliefs about the role of the state began to change, as did the actions of governments. Support grew for business-led restructuring and for shifting the relationship between citizens and the state. The economic project promoted for three decades after 1945 had been based on the theoretical position that governments could intervene in the economy, deploying Keynesian macroeconomic policies and welfare state expenditures in order to maintain both economic equilibrium and social solidarity. Current tenets of economic thinking are quite different. We can, indeed, speak of another economic restructuring project—titled the "neoconservative agenda" by its critics and the "best response to the needs of international competition" by its proponents. This project has been going forward apace for at least a decade.

Neoconservatism implies acceptance of the discipline of market forces by individuals as well as for the economy as a whole. This reasoning follows from an interpretation of the global economy as being increasingly interdependent, competitive, and beyond the control of national governments. Stressing the ways in which their hands are tied by this international competition and by their inability to count on adequate levels of tax revenues, politicians have begun to give priority to deficit reduction over job creation, to free trade over state-promoted development strategies, to spending restraints over social programs, and to fostering the competitive capacities of companies for trade and individuals for jobs. Those state activities that *are* supported must all fit into this market-celebrating worldview. So, for example, individuals would be induced to "invest in their human capital" by enrolling in training and retraining programs, while the programs themselves are often "privatized," that is, provided by firms rather than by the state. Under neoconservatism, the state retains some responsibility, but its actions must be consistent with what is best for global competition and the needs of domestic companies.

In Canada's case, neoconservatism arose in a particular context. Canada is a small open economy with a single large trading partner—the United States. Economic difficulties in the last two decades have contributed to the breakdown of a certain policy consensus which characterized Canadian politics for the first 25 years after World War II. This consensus was founded on a commitment to macroeconomic policy inspired by Keynesian economic theory and on a belief that "continentalism" was the basis for the country's economic well-being. Moreover, an important institutional locale for resolving conflicts about economic and social policy was federal-provincial negotiations. The effect was to create close ties between constitutional politics and economic strategy. By the mid-1970s that consensus had shattered.

The confluence of high inflation, high unemployment, and low rates of economic growth, which marked the 1970s, confounded Keynesians (see Figure 1.1). Policy makers searched for new tools to relieve the economic malaise. At the same time, processes of restructuring in the global order began to reveal some of the limits to traditional forms of continentalism based on foreign investment. Disputes about whether to pursue a state-led industrial strategy, resource-based megaprojects, or free trade marked the 1970s and early 1980s, crosscutting party politics and shaking federal-provincial relations. The decision to go with the third of these options, free trade, was quickly linked by its proponents to growing enthusiasm for markets over states. The Bank of Canada, supported by the Liberal government as early as 1975, had begun to introduce monetarism as an alternative to Keynesianism, and to put the fight against inflation well ahead of job creation. This battle was won, as Figure 1.1 documents, but at the cost of double-digit unemployment rates, and without generating the growth that was theoretically supposed to accompany it.

4

Figure 1.1

**Inflation, Unemployment, and Changes
in Real Gross Domestic Product: 1965–93**

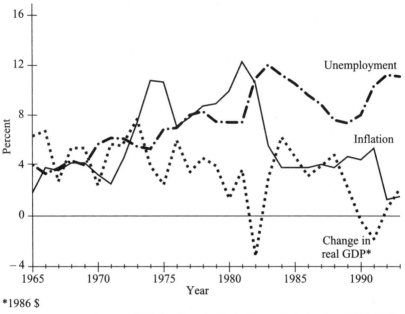

*1986 $

Source: Statistics Canada, *Main Economic Indicators*, 1993, 1994.

By the 1980s the postwar consensus was merely a memory. The new language was one of risk-taking, restraint on government spending, and retrenchment of state responsibility for fostering equality, whether across social groups or across regions. Spurred on by a rising tide of protectionist sentiment in the United States and the recommendations of the 1985 Report of the Royal Commission on the Economic Union and Development Prospects for Canada (Macdonald Commission), worried business people and government officials opted for the Canada-U.S. Free Trade Agreement (FTA) in 1988. Subsequently, Canada joined the United States and Mexico's negotiations for the North American Free Trade Agreement (NAFTA), which concluded just before the 1993 election. At the same time, governments were already introducing restraints on social spending, which had produced a fundamental redesign of the federal government's role and the types of support available to the most vulnerable groups in society.[1]

Economic restructuring has been closely related to constitutional politics. Provinces have sought greater room for initiating their own preferred forms of restructuring. Since the 1960s, Quebec had already been claiming greater space within federal-provincial programs for doing those things considered essential to its economic and social development. Then, the sudden increase in energy and other resource prices in the 1970s, brought new development dreams to the Prairies and some other parts of the country. Fearing that they would not be able to reap the potential benefits of these windfalls, provincial governments became more aggressive in asserting their rights in the federal division of power. Alberta in particular joined Quebec in efforts to create or capture levers of control over their local economies. This new assertiveness led to major conflicts within federalism and meant that constitutional questions would remain squarely on the political agenda. As the effects of further changes in the international economy became clear, all provinces moved to develop their own responses, often seeking control over programs considered especially crucial to the new conditions. The call for provincial authority over labour force training by Quebec was one example of this. Another was the effort of some provinces such as New Brunswick, for example, to redesign their own social programs in advance of any overhaul led by the federal government.

Although economic restructuring projects have dominated the political agenda in many countries, in Canada they have also been accompanied by efforts at constitutional and institutional change. In part as a result of pressure from social movements that advocate alternative politics, regional governments, along with regional economies, have expanded. New agencies, very often recognizing the advantages of public consultation, have been created. Reforms of electoral systems, arrangements for public funding of parties and elections, as well as the balance of powers between courts and parliaments, constitutional rights of individuals (to abortion, for example) and groups (religious minorities, for example), are all topics hotly debated recently in several Western European countries as well as in the United States. Many of the forces at work generate a political agenda that is reminiscent of Canada's. This country is not alone in putting its constitution and democratic institutions under scrutiny at the same time as economic restructuring proceeds apace.

Canada's particularity, of course, is that much of the debate is about the proper way to accommodate linguistic and cultural duality and the claims of Aboriginal peoples. Therefore, calls for reform have focussed on constitutionally recognized rights and the institutions of federalism, although senate and electoral law reform have also attracted their share of attention. In contrast to the economic restructuring project just described, however, there has been much less consensus among major actors about constitutional change. Alternatives abound. People differ, for example, over whether to identify Canada as a bilingual country (as the 1969 Official Languages Act did) or to grant Quebec distinct standing as the homeland of a French-speaking people. There are also differences over whether federalism should be decentralized, with more powers going to the provinces, or made more centralized. Debates also occur about whether all provinces should have the same powers or whether some asymmetry among provinces is preferable. Until recently such matters were, at least in federal politics, more the subject

Figure 1.2

Evaluations of Federal Government's Handling of Inflation and Unemployment: 1979, 1988, 1993

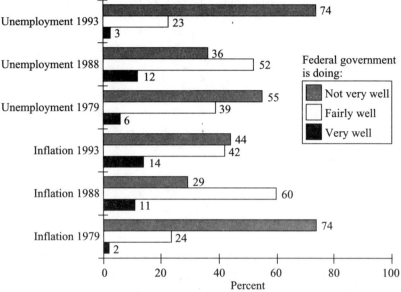

Federal government is doing:

- ■ Not very well
- □ Fairly well
- ■ Very well

Source: 1979 – CNES, 1988 – PSC; 1993 – PSC. Please see the appendix "Data Sources" for an explanation of the source abbreviations used in the figures and tables.

of controversy among elites than mass publics. More and more, however, Canadians have demanded the right to be heard in constitutional debates. Indeed, they have claimed that this issue area, previously dealt with behind the closed doors of federal-provincial negotiations, must be open to democratic discussion. From the mobilizations of the women's movement and Aboriginal peoples in 1982 to the pressure to use a referendum to make any decision in 1992, calls have multiplied for opening up constitutional politics to democratic consultation.

Canadian citizens have been affected by worldwide and world-shaking processes of economic restructuring and constitutional change. This does not mean that they approve of what is going on. Voters have been particularly critical of the economic restructuring projects, while the overwhelming rejection of the Charlottetown Accord exposed high levels of opposition to the proposed constitutional project. Surveys reveal that public opinion is reluctant to grant high approval ratings to any political party, and especially the governing one, for its handling of the economy. Most Canadians felt that the federal government had not done well in dealing with inflation when it was considered the principal economic problem facing the country in the late 1970s (Figure 1.2). And few believed that different governments had done any better in handling the unemployment problem a decade later.

Election campaigns, which provide an opportunity to express this dissatisfaction, have frequently focussed on economic questions. At first in the 1970s this discontent was manifested in specific, short-term formulations of "grievances." Voters rarely understood, nor did the parties describe, such grievances as arising from long-term patterns or structural relationships in the economy. Rather, problems tended to be attributed to dislocations that could be fixed if only the "right" formula or leadership were found. The 1974 election, for example, focussed on inflation, with the Progressive Conservatives proposing to combat the evil with wage and price controls, and the Liberals retorting that the cure might prove worse than the ailment. A year later, the Liberal government imposed wage controls, without much success in solving the fundamental problems, however.

After several years and several governments lurching from one quick fix to another, the government transferred responsibility for sorting out Canada's economic prospects to the Macdonald Commission, established in 1982. Well before the Commission's report was in, however, both the Liberals and the Conservatives had already decided that the new economic conditions called for leaders whose private-sector experience clearly attuned them to business concerns. The Progressive Conservatives chose Brian Mulroney, who had had a successful corporate career before entering politics. The Liberals brought back John Turner, who had retired from Parliament to Bay Street in 1975, to replace Pierre Trudeau, who had dominated Canadian politics for a decade and a half.

Despite public distress at the consequences of the economic recession, the 1984 election provided few choices. With their new leaders the Liberals and Tories looked very much alike. Voters were asked to choose between two men who advocated better management of the economy, some trade liberalization, more jobs, and more cordial federal-provincial relations. In the campaign, media attention focussed on controversies over patronage appointments made by the Liberal government just before the election, and on the campaign behaviour of the two leaders. There was minimal discussion of a project that would be central to the future of the country in the next century—free trade with the United States. During the leadership campaign, Mulroney had declared his opposition to a free trade agreement with the United States. However, the Conservatives readily learned from the Liberals that one could reject a policy in the campaign and then proceed to implement it soon after the election. The Mulroney government took the advice of the 1985 Macdonald Commission Report and moved ahead in search of a trade agreement. Months of negotiations produced an agreement, presented to Parliament in the summer of 1988. When the Liberal-dominated Senate blocked the bill that would have ratified the FTA, the issue was pushed to the forefront in the November election.

Even in this election the character of the three parties continued to mitigate against posing clear alternative projects or programs. Both the Tories and the NDP attempted to offer only vague positions, to avoid discussing the Agreement in depth, and to run on their overall image or that of their leader. The Conservatives initially refused to ask for a specific mandate for free trade, while the NDP carefully avoided seeming to want one. Even the Liberals' conversion to anti-FTA campaigning was based on a last-ditch strategic calculation that their original plan was not paying off. Their stance on the issue of free trade was actually quite similar to that of the Conservatives. John Turner never opposed free trade in principle; he just did not like the specific agreement negotiated by the Mulroney government.

In this election, the free trade issue was engaged to a major extent by non-party groups such as the Coalition for Jobs and the Pro-Canada Network. Both groups spent massive amounts of money advocating the FTA in the first case and opposing in the second one.[2] The parties, in particular the NDP, often gave the impression of running to catch up with the debate being conducted in this "parallel campaign."

In the inter-election years of 1988-93, the other major issue in Canadian politics—the constitutional project—again came to the fore, with the Meech Lake Accord. Despite its inherent importance and the amount of attention given it by the media, the constitutional project has not been any more clearly debated in electoral politics than has the economic restructuring project. Neither the conflict over the 1982 Constitution Act nor that over Meech Lake followed party lines. All three parties initially supported the redesigned constitution and were stunned by the outpouring of opposition from social movements, especially women's groups and Aboriginal peoples. Similarly, all parties endorsed the Meech Lake Accord, despite some grumbling within their ranks. For Liberals in particular, linking up with the Tories to recognize Quebec as a distinct society was seen by many as a reversal of former Prime Minister Trudeau's constitutional positions, which had been accepted by that party for almost two decades.

Given this inter-party consensus, opposition to the Meech Lake Accord was again organized largely by non-party groups, who added to their criticisms of the specifics of the agreement the way it had been negotiated by "11 white men in suits" behind closed doors. As the Accord unravelled during 1990, the spectacle of the first ministers locked up in Ottawa hotels negotiating to save the deal in a final "roll of the dice" did little to assuage concerns about conditions of democratic representation. The Spicer Commission (the Citizens' Forum on Canada's Future), the Beaudoin-Dobbie parliamentary committee, and the five weekend conferences all provided evidence not only of citizens' dissatisfaction with the way that constitutional politics had been conducted, but also of the public's demand to be more involved.[3] Calls for a constitutional convention, for a referendum, and for other mechanisms of popular consultation were as much a part of the debate as were the specifics of the constitutional design, which themselves included demands for more democratic institutions.

If the style of the 1991-92 Canada Round of constitutional debate demonstrated that the principal players had appreciated the need to be more open and inclusive, it did not signal that the parties would lead the debate around alternative projects. Just as there had been all-party support for the Meech Lake Accord, the Liberals and NDP provided no clear alternatives to the positions proposed by the federal government or those emerging from negotiations, despite the fact that their traditional constituencies were often in the lead in criticizing the government and proposing other options. The NDP was strangely silent over the months in which women's groups, the labour movement, and Aboriginal associations had a great deal to say about constitutional issues. All of these were groups whose electoral support the NDP had long cultivated. Nor were the Liberals willing to say much, recognizing that movement away from the constitutional positions long advocated by Trudeau had the potential to split the party.

With the outcome of the referendum of October 1992 demonstrating conclusively that a cranky and volatile electorate was disinclined to take the advice of the vast majority of opinion leaders, it became evident that "politics as usual" was in for a hard time. New political parties stepped in to take advantage of this situation. The Bloc Québécois was clearly willing to offer a choice to the voters of Quebec. There was no ambiguity about its stance on constitutional matters even if the position of a mélange of ex-Tories, Péquistes, and even ex-Liberals on questions of economic restructuring was hard to pin down. The Reform Party too, even if its economic and social positions owed a great deal to the neoconservative agenda also favoured by many Tories, had a clear vision of the future and was pressing a populist agenda for democratizing institutions. The Liberal Party joined in, proposing institutional adjustments and better government. The party issued its Red Book, titled *Creating Opportunity: The Liberal Plan for Canada*. This document was quite specific and the leader cited it frequently, committing himself and his party to enacting its provisions if elected.[4] In this context we might well ask whether party politics has fundamentally changed, whether the years of Tweedledum and Tweedledee had been left behind, and whether the 1993 election did generate a policy mandate for the Liberal government.

Finding answers to these large questions is the goal of subsequent chapters, in which we examine the behaviour of voters and seek evidence that they have provided such a policy mandate and have given up their well-learned responses to decades of brokerage politics. In order to begin answering these questions, we need to consider in a more general way the history and characteristics of the form of party competition and its consequences for electoral behaviour, assessing it against some of the basic principles of democratic theory and recent Canadian history.

Political Parties and Liberal Democracy

Theorists differ widely in their prescriptions for institutional arrangements to maximize democracy, and thereby achieve self-government, self-development, and equality for individuals. Some emphasize reducing the size of decision making units to enhance the public's participation in decisions affecting it. Other theorists are more concerned about how information moves from leaders to citizens, how equality of access can be assured, and how the agenda of political decision making is set. Still others, less Utopian in their prescriptions, simply seek to improve existing institutions. Nevertheless, despite theoretical debates and a variety of prescribed reforms, almost everyone accepts that, in the contemporary world, the political party will serve as a bridge between state actions and the interests and demands of society. Parties have done so since the invention of liberal democracy founded on mass suffrage. Although challenged by other actors competing for the right to represent interests, they nevertheless seem to be here to stay.

Given this history, many people have turned to an examination of party democracy, attempting to determine how a party system helps or hinders decision making and governance in capitalist democracies. With the development of models of party democracy, the very concept of "party" has been revalued. Previously party often had a negative connotation. For example, at the beginning of the 20th century, students of politics sometimes criticized parties as self-interested groups subverting the constitutional process and perverting the representational system.[5] But by mid-century many observers saw the political party in a more positive light. It was regarded as an institution capable of integrating a divided society for united political action, the embodiment of democratic society in many ways.[6]

Joseph Schumpeter, writing in the gloomy years between two world wars, advanced a theory of party democracy that has had a major impact on the way that people now regard democracy and its possibilities.[7] Schumpeter sought to explain and evaluate the process by which elites organize political choice. According to his "realistic theory," democracy is the competition among rival leaders of political parties for a mandate to rule. Even this quite limited view of democracy nevertheless states that choice among at least two broadly different party platforms is crucial to avoiding tyranny and achieving good government. Schumpeter's thesis that parties can generate teams of experts in governance, trusted by the people, has spawned elite and elite-pluralist theories of democracy. These theories seek to identify the conditions under which more democracy, rather than less, can be achieved.[8]

Students of party politics have incorporated Schumpeter's notion of the role of parties into their own models of party behaviour. Thus, the "responsible party" model expects parties to provide clear choices between rival approaches to policy making, and to change their positions only incrementally, to avoid confusing or alienating an electorate that has developed ongoing perceptions of where the parties stand. Other analysts assume that differentiated parties work best for all concerned. This type of "economic" model, based on notions of consumer sovereignty borrowed from economics, posits that parties will normally not adopt widely divergent ideological positions. Party leaders will then "sell" their programs to an electorate that wants similar, yet differentiated, positions. This second model incorporates a strong assumption that parties are the captive of their electorates.[9] It depicts voters as choosing parties either prospectively on the basis of expectations of their likely behaviour in office, or judging them retrospectively on the basis of past performance.[10]

Although both the "responsible party" and the "economic" models recognize that choices among parties might become blurred because of party competition, they both define the election process as one in which mandates to rule are at issue. Therefore, elections are times for meaningful evaluation by the voters. The notion of *mandate* is quite simple. All parties should present a project describing their intentions for dealing with the problems facing the country, and voters can choose among the projects. Once victorious, the party of choice will enact what it has proposed. Then the process will begin again, with the next election. A slightly modified version of this notion of mandate is that voters might judge after the fact, with an election providing an opportunity to evaluate how well a party has done since the last one. Nevertheless, even these discussions of retrospective voting indicate that governing parties seek a mandate to continue, while the opposition seeks a mandate to modify the direction.

The Royal Commission on Electoral Reform and Party Financing (RCERPF), which was established by the government after the 1988 election to propose solutions to some of the ongoing problems of Canada's parties, reflects these positions. The Commission accepted the idea shared by both Schumpeterian and Utopian democrats, that elections could (and should) be moments of meaningful choice among alternative programs for the future. Therefore, it advanced a detailed definition of political parties to serve as a foundation for its far-reaching reform recommendations. The Commission described parties as primary political organizations whose purposes are:

> ... nominating candidates for election to Parliament; mobilizing electoral support for their candidates; engaging their members in discussion of democratic governance; providing forums for the development of alternative policies and programs; preparing their elected members for their parliamentary responsibilities; and organizing the processes of representative and responsible government, ...[11]

In other words, the task of a political party is not simply to get its candidates elected; it should also be the locale for the development of alternative policies and programs.

All such analyses have implied that parties will present general *projects* for the future.[12] From these they will derive a program and policies to address problems of concern to the country. For some people, such projects are based on the differing worldviews of parties (for example, those with class-based or nationalist projects). For others they are general projects created by competing teams of leaders in order to win elections. Such projects represent general statements of alternatives that leaders can clearly communicate to voters. The electors will then decide which party is closest to their own preferences. Moreover, such democratic theory anticipates a correspondance between the promises embedded in the projects and the actual policy decisions taken; consistency is a central element of the equation. Finally, the voters are expected to demand that parties address and solve problems and that they take the lead in finding innovative responses. Only if parties, subject to periodic review by the electorate in ways that other state institutions are not, play this role will the electorate actually have a choice about alternative futures.

Canada's parties, especially the three that have historically dominated electoral politics, have rarely provided such alternatives, nor have they performed all the tasks assigned to parties in the RCERPF's definition. Even the last years of intense controversy on many political fronts have not provided clear evidence of the parties' willingness to seek clear mandates or their capacity to win one. The 1988 election did not reveal parties seeking policy mandates. Instead, all parties in the initial weeks of the campaign attempted to avoid the free trade issue. The Tories highlighted their government's supposedly proven abilities to "manage change." Following the advice of its pollsters, the NDP focussed its campaign on its leader, Ed Broadbent, because the polls showed him to be popular and also indicated that voters feared the way in which the NDP framed its long-standing opposition to free trade. Therefore, in opening the campaign Broadbent did not mention the issue. Even the Liberals started the election campaign, following Liberal senators' refusal to pass the Agreement, with a series of specific proposals on other policy matters that attracted little interest. Only when the leaders' debates revealed an impassioned John Turner opposed to the FTA negotiated by the Conservative government did the parties' campaigns begin to focus on the issue. But Turner's opposition was, as we have noted, to the "Mulroney deal," not to free trade per se.

Nor did the 1993 election provide much evidence that these three parties had greatly changed. Certainly the Progressive Conservatives explicitly sought to avoid any specific programmatic discussion.[13] They could not run on their record because of its association with the exceedingly

13

unpopular Brian Mulroney and his finance minister, Michael Wilson, and because of the fall-out from the failed Charlottetown Accord. As the new party leader, Kim Campbell spent much of her time trying to distance herself from the past of her own party and the Mulroney team, by suggesting that she would be "doing politics differently." Advised by their election strategists, candidates were encouraged to run as members of the "Campbell team" rather than as Progressive Conservatives. The hope was that a new female leader would be enough to alter the image of the party. In all of this, preparation and mastery of policy positions received very little attention. Policy documents often simply did not exist, and Campbell herself seemed not to miss them. In what might have been a very honest, albeit perhaps electorally unfortunate characterization of many politicians' views on policy development she said, "an election is no time to talk about social policy."[14]

The Liberals followed a different strategy than they had in 1988. Rather than introducing policy piecemeal, they launched their Red Book, brandishing it at every opportunity. The party at last seemed to realize that voters wanted some substance to their nightly election media doses. The program itself was a careful effort to balance divergent tendencies within the party. It promised to reduce the deficit, to be sure, but to do so by having the country grow its way out of its unfavourable competitive position. As Stephen Clarkson described it, "... the platform positioned the Liberal party flexibly on a middle ground."[15] Despite all the attention to policy and promises in the campaign, however, the Liberals, once in government, did not eschew the familiar practice of unveiling major policy initiatives that had not been elaborated during the campaign. By the time of the first budget in February 1994, a complete overhaul of social programs was at the top of the government's agenda, although the Red Book was "remarkably silent on the issue of income security and welfare reform."[16] Nor had many voters been led to expect the deep cuts in Unemployment Insurance, which the Tories had also targeted in earlier budgets, and expenditure reductions that "bear a strong resemblance to those made in the Conservatives' last budget, although these are much bigger cuts than the former government ever attempted."[17] Indeed, such actions led political columnist Jeffrey Simpson to tag the Liberal finance minister, "Michael Wilson Martin, sometimes called Paul J."[18]

This is, then, more a story of continuity than one of change, of similarity than of difference, and of opportunism than of political principle. The reasons for its familiarity can be found in the ongoing effects, both for the political parties and the electorate, of ways the Canadian party system has operated for decades and its limited capacity for producing policy mandates.

Parties As Brokers

It is important, in the beginning, not to exaggerate the possibilities for elections to produce mandates. As many students of party democracy have noted, the periodic consultation of voters by teams of party leaders is not a perfect formula for choice. Voters have little opportunity to nuance their selections or to send a complicated message to the parties. Nevertheless, there are signs that voters use even such limited opportunities to evaluate party performance. For such evaluation to work in more than a short-term, volatile fashion, however, the parties themselves must provide a relatively fixed point of reference, some predictability to their behaviour, and some consistency between words and deeds. As the Citizens' Forum on Canada's Future (the Spicer Commission) wrote in 1991:

> ... the actions of government, once in power, seem to bear little resemblance to the party platform in an election campaign. Major government policies are developed and enacted during a mandate which either were never mentioned or received little attention during a campaign.[19]

It is the absence of this fixity, predictability, and consistency in Canadian political parties that had led observers for decades to characterize them as brokers. This means that in each election, the parties canvass and delineate the varied interests of the electorate, seeking to broker a coalition of supporters. Political parties in such a situation have a number of characteristics, all of which limit the prospect that elections and inter-party debates will deliver a mandate for policy innovation designed to cope with fundamental problems. When new political projects are considered and promoted, debate over alternative futures occurs among actors other than the political parties. Thus, the long-term strategic adjustments to new economic and constitutional circumstances over the past two decades have been developed in institutions relatively isolated from federal elections. The Progressive Conservatives' original notion in 1988 that an election was an unnecessary stage in instituting free trade was simply a reflection of the norms of brokerage politics, as was Prime Minister Campbell's scorn for elections as a time to debate policy more generally. This is not to say that in either economic or social policy there was not a project for economic restructuring to which the leaders of the Progressive Conservative Party were profoundly committed. It is rather to say that the party in government was willing to act without having sought a clear mandate for that project from the voters. In behaving this way, Tory governments were not significantly different from their Liberal predecessors or successors, who also reversed policy or announced major programmatic initiatives once in office, after conducting election campaigns around other themes or other promises.

Canada's brokerage parties differ in several ways from those in most other advanced industrial societies.[20] Rather than having well-defined

15

support from one election to the next, based on long-term loyalties of social groups, brokerage parties re-create coalitions at each election. Rather than dividing the electorate among themselves along clear and relatively stable lines of social cleavage, such parties constantly compete for the same policy space and the same votes. Rather than mobilizing support along a limited number of cleavages, Canadian parties are most comfortable multiplying the number of politically relevant divisions. Voters are rarely presented with a clear choice between worldviews and the political projects that follow from them. More commonly, they receive appeals to narrow interests, and proposals that tinker with existing arrangements. Rather than following through on the logic of stances adopted in the past, brokerage parties practise inconsistency as they search for electorally successful formulae or respond to new versions of old problems. They organize around leaders rather than around political principles and ideologies. Then, they expect the leader to work out the multitude of compromises required for such a party to enjoy electoral success. Therefore, a wide variety of conflicting and contradictory policy stances may co-exist inside each brokerage party.

Students of Canadian politics have always been struck by these aspects of party competition.[21] They have emphasized the lack of principled difference between parties, the inconsistencies of policies over very short periods of time, and the parochialism of partisan organizational structures. The reasons for brokerage politics of this kind were often attributed to the Canadian social structure, supposedly characterized by an unusually large variety of politically important cleavages. The continuing ethnic and linguistic conflicts and the importance of regional inequalities have seemed to contribute to a situation in which any party would fail if it tried to mobilize the electorate around a single cleavage or difference. Moreover, the very existence of so many cleavages forced the parties to take responsibility for integrating the nation by finding a combination of electoral support that would prevent the pieces from flying apart. Responsibility for this delicate task supposedly falls to the party leader, who is expected to symbolize the country's current image of itself. Canadian history has therefore often been depicted as a story of long-lived leaderships—those of Macdonald, Laurier, King, and Trudeau—rather than party projects for governing society. As the leader changes, so, too, do party projects and programs. Moreover, as the leader's popularity declines, so too does that of the party. Therefore, a party that cannot win elections most often blames the leader, not the program, and pins its hopes on a new leader who promises to guide it out of the political wilderness.

The job of the leader is to "make the party" after winning a leadership contest in which widely divergent candidates seek the highest post. Anyone, from "red Tories" to free-marketers, can run for the Conservative leadership. Similarly for the Liberals, candidates have often ranged from left-wing nationalists who might have been quite at home in the NDP, to "business Liberals" who could have led the Conservatives. Leadership and policy conventions send mixed messages to an electorate seeking to understand where a party stands. A new leader must forge a coalition of supporters within the party and calm the ruffled feathers of those whose policy and personal proclivities are at variance with their own. Stephen Clarkson succinctly describes the dilemmas that Jean Chrétien faced immediately after winning the Liberal leadership:

> How to square Trudeau's hard line on the constitution with Quebec's demands for greater powers was far from being Chrétien's only policy dilemma. The question of free trade had left the party deeply divided ... . Equally difficult was bridging the gap between the party's business Liberals, whose top priority was reducing the federal deficit, and its welfare Liberals, who wanted to maintain universal social-welfare programs, whatever their budgetary cost.[22]

Not surprisingly, such umbrella-like bodies frequently appear to outsiders and voters as a babble of competing voices.

This kind of brokerage politics has identifiable consequences for party competition and policy making, as well as for electoral behaviour. One consequence is that the party system has no dynamic that will reliably generate innovation or identify solutions for new problems.[23] Responsibility for innovation has often rested with new or "third" parties. Such parties have emerged at times of severe economic or social strain, and promoted innovative, even radical, strategies. As the two major parties recognized the validity of critiques developed by third parties or were frightened by their vote-getting potential, they moved to minimize the discontent by modifying their own programs. While third parties were a major source of innovation before World War II, the 1940s brought a virtual displacement of policy innovation from the party system. The arena of policy controversy and innovation shifted in general toward the public service and federal-provincial relations. Then, in the major controversies of the 1980s— constitutional reform and economic restructuring—a royal commission and autonomously mobilized popular movements became additional engines of innovation.[24]

As the public service began to serve as a locale for policy generation and debate, agenda setting for both alternative projects and policy was insulated from electoral politics. This trend accelerated after World War II as the Liberals' organization encouraged a blurring of boundaries between party and government.[25] As the state became more interventionist in social and economic areas, citizen-state relationships became more bureau-cratized. This meshed with the ministerialism of the Liberals. Ministers increasingly had difficulty separating their departmental responsibilities for administration from their partisan tasks of keeping the party at campaign readiness. The party merged into the government, relying on the bureaucracy for policy innovation.

In the current era of economic restructuring, as Canada began facing new economic realities, alternative projects were heatedly and even publicly debated among various departments and ministries, whose considerations frequently established the terms of public discourse on the issues. Two distinct examples of bureaucratic agenda setting illustrate the role of the bureaucracy in policy debate and formulation. In the 1970s the Economic Council of Canada faced off against the Science Council in a contest to define an economic future for Canada. At issue was whether an industrial strategy could be found that would push the country toward more autonomous development. Since both these bodies were part of the federal bureaucracy, the debate, while animated, was also necessarily quite isolated from the realm of partisan politics.[26] The experience of the contemporary women's movement provides the second example. When women mobilized to demand greater equality and recognition by Canadian society, the demands were acknowledged much more quickly and innovatively by institutions like the Secretary of State than by the parties. Moreover, it was the bureaucracy that nurtured and shaped the movement. It provided not only funding but also public recognition, a role that in many other countries belonged to political parties.[27]

Under the Mulroney Conservatives, the bureaucracy may have lost some of its influence to organize debate about policy, for several reasons. First, efforts to reduce public spending have brought the privatization of much policy development to research companies and policy institutes. Second, the government has abolished some of the very think tanks within the public sector in which this discussion occurred. Both the Economic Council and the Science Council have been eliminated.

These changes do not mean that the influence of state-based experts on policy has disappeared; it is simply less visible. Observers attribute a good deal of the post-electoral backtracking from the Liberals' Red Book to ministers' encounters with a bureaucracy whose preferences for neoconservative-style solutions are entrenched. Thus, Finance Minister Paul Martin dramatically altered his analysis of the route to economic well-being, from one which privileged fostering growth to one stressing deficit reduction before anything else. As he said, "nothing so wonderfully concentrates your mind ... as the feeling that the department of finance is slowly tightening around your neck."[28]

Another reason why policy innovation and debate were located outside the party system came with the growth of the institutions of executive federalism. As more provinces embarked on "province building," which granted greater autonomy for provincial decision making, the institutions of federalism decentralized.[29] At the same time, the power to establish the national agenda shifted from the federal Cabinet and Parliament to federal-provincial conferences. The compromises over the new constitution and the Meech Lake Accord, two crucial moments of constitutional politics in the 1980s, were forged in such conferences, thus minimizing the partisan content of the decisions. In addition to providing a locale for these spectacular events, federal-provincial negoitations took up the more mundane issues of social and economic development. Decisions taken there resulted from coalitions that were much less connected with the partisan labels of governments, and more concerned with their long-standing strategic differences over how to advance their own provinces' interests. As a result, the role of the federal party system as an arena for meaningful policy discussion or direction continued to decline. The negotiations leading to the Charlottetown Accord by-passed parties while budget making, the traditional opportunity to debate economic policy, is now preceded by non-partisan public consultations in which the terms of debate are set.[30]

These general trends are supplemented by two other locales for policy innovation—royal commissions and social movement politics. The impact of the Macdonald Commission was clearly to create a blueprint for the future of the economy, thereby establishing an agenda in a process necessarily stripped of much partisan content. This royal commission, as any other, was charged with eliminating a direct party role and "discovering" the range of possible solutions that fit with the national interest. It seemed to identify an alternative project for the future conceived, not in the hurly-burly of partisan politics, but in the supposedly calmer environment of research and extensive public consultation.[31]

The group that crystallized opposition to the Macdonald Commission's primary recommendation of free trade with the United States was one first mobilized by participation in such public consultations, the so-called "popular sector."[32] During the 1988 election the groups that rejected free trade altogether felt compelled to band together in ad hoc organizations like the Pro-Canada Network, which later became Action Canada.[33] These were composed of representatives of women's organizations, labour unions, churches, Aboriginal peoples' groups, and other bodies concerned about the potential impact of free trade. The coalition of the "popular sector" first emerged with the mobilization of women's and Aboriginal groups when the new constitution was being debated in 1981-82. It then gained strength from its interventions and several years of opposition to the recommendations of the Macdonald Commission and the Meech Lake Accord. But such a coalition, never designed to serve partisan purposes, had difficulty translating its opposition to free trade into partisan terms. In 1988, it divided over whether to call on its supporters to vote Liberal or NDP.

The first consequence of a system of brokerage politics is that very few mechanisms exist for policy innovation and debate within the party system. Instead, innovation has been displaced to the bureaucracy or royal commissions, both of which are arenas constitutionally isolated and protected from electoral politics. Moreover, to the extent that alternatives are mobilized more by social movements and the institutions of federalism, party labels and party politics lose relevance. Elections have reflected this displacement, being events in which clear policy choices are rarely presented, and where the range of choices is limited. Moreover, even when a clear position is expressed in the campaign, policy reversals immediately after an election are quite common. A recent example is the Liberals' campaign promise to sign NAFTA only if significant changes were made to it and then subsequently signing it without any meaningful modifications.

As a result, political issues have played a quite particular role in election campaigns. Despite forming the substance of debate and providing a focus for attention, issues are usually vaguely defined and changeable in their meaning. Frequently, issues are phrased in terms of code word labels that mask a multitude of meanings. As Chapter 2 shows, any election issue, despite seeming to have captured the attention of many voters, can fall into oblivion in the next election, without solving the problem it represented.[34] Nor are specific issues inserted into or linked to a more general framework of party principles. The very weight of the existing system of brokerage parties discourages long-term position taking. Parties feel compelled to remain flexible, to take advantage of the shifting short-term preferences of potential voters. In fact, they possess few guaranteed support bases that can be counted on from election to election. Even the Liberals' seemingly solid Quebec base melted away with the arrival of Brian Mulroney. And in turn, Conservative support in Quebec has been displaced by the rise of the Bloc Québécois.

Indeed, a second consequence of a system of brokerage parties is the instability of party loyalty, or "partisanship," documented in Chapter 3. The first election studies in the 1960s found levels of partisan instability greater in Canada than in many other advanced industrial societies.[35] Voters could not identify fundamental differences among the parties, differences that might have encouraged long-term loyalties.[36] Nor were people likely to see consistencies in the parties' policy goals, which might have led them to maintain a long-standing identification with a single party for most of their lives.[37] Therefore, studies of electoral behaviour have consistently revealed high rates of partisan instability in Canada.

A third consequence of a system of brokerage parties is the strong emphasis on leadership discussed in Chapters 4 and 5. Lacking ideological or even continuing policy differences, the parties take on, in a sense, the personalities of their leaders. The role of leaders in creating and sustaining

20

an electoral coalition has always been recognized in Canada. Throughout Canadian history, party leaders have been crucially important to the creation of their parties (Macdonald and Laurier), or have pulled them back from the abyss and led them to electoral victory (King) or taken them down a new and experimental road (Diefenbaker). The trend toward leader-oriented politics has been encouraged by changes in communication technology and the organizational evolution toward executive dominance after World War II. Nonetheless, such trends have been hastened in Canada by the characteristics of brokerage politics.

Canadian federal elections since 1974 have occurred in this fluid context. Most campaigns provided an occasion for voicing concerns and grievances, rather than for offering fundamentally different long-term strategies to ease economic troubles. Indeed, voters' decision making, as Chapters 5 and 6 demonstrate, provides very little evidence that the electorate awards a mandate to any government. There is, indeed, a tendency to see elections as an opportunity to "throw the rascals out" more than one of directing the future. Electoral politics of this sort are ill equipped to deal with the dramatic intensification of economic difficulties and constitutional controversy of the last two decades.

Conclusion

Recent years have been marked by restructuring of the Canadian economy, of the relationship between citizens and the state, and of federalism. Profound questions have been raised about development strategies, the role of the state, and the future identity of the country. Public trust in political elites has been shaken by fears that economic conditions would worsen and by a general dissatisfaction with elites' performance as decision makers. Nonetheless, elections have been conducted as if voters had little to say about the major decisions taken to implement economic restructuring projects or reform constitutional arrangements. Rather, such innovations were discussed within the non-partisan world of the bureaucracy or the paid consultant, the expert world of the royal commission, the quasi-diplomatic world of federal-provincial negotiations, or the extra-party world of social movements.

The voters have expressed their displeasure at being ignored. Yet, all the parties must now confront voters whose habits and behaviour display the consequences of decades of brokerage politics. These effects also constrain party behaviour; the relationship is not one way. There are three major effects of past practices discernible in the electorate. The first is high levels of volatility; voters move about in search of solutions or follow a new leader. They may even, as in 1993, abandon the familiar parties and install completely new ones. A second effect is that voters display disillusionment with electoral politics and politicians. The displacement of policy discussion from the electoral arena dampens voters' hopes for satisfaction from elections. Moreover, their experiences with failed promises leads to scepticism, cynicism, and disbelief that politicians can do much. Some voters turn against the familiar, seeking those persons, groups, and institutions, even outside the party system, that appear more inclusive and open. A third effect is to foster loose ties of partisanship, which, in turn, may well contribute to flux in electoral politics. Brokerage parties are not able to call on well-established and relatively insulated electorates; rather, many voters are available to any party, old or new. The voters move among the parties in response to short-term appeals, deciding during campaigns for whom they will vote. The rest of this book examines these effects by dissecting Canadian voters' reactions to their political worlds and the ways they make their choices within them.

Notes

1.   James R. Rice and Michael J. Prince, "Lowering the Safety Net and Weakening the Bonds of Nationhood: Social Policy in the Mulroney Years," in Susan D. Phillips, ed., *How Ottawa Spends: 1993-94: A More Democratic Canada?* (Ottawa: Carleton University Press, 1993), pp. 381ff.

2.   Janet Hiebert, "Interest Groups and Canadian Federal Elections," in F. Leslie Seidle, ed., *Interest Groups and Elections in Canada*, vol. 2 of the Research Studies of the Royal Commission on Electoral Reform and Party Financing (Toronto: Dundurn Press, 1991), pp. 20-29.

3.   Leslie A. Pal and F. Leslie Seidle, "Constitutional Politics 1990-92: The Paradox of Participation," in Susan D. Phillips, ed., *How Ottawa Spends: 1993-94*, pp. 143ff.

4.   For a summary of most important provisions see Susan D. Phillips, "Making Change: The Potential for Innovation under the Liberals," in Susan D. Phillips, ed., *Making Change: How Ottawa Spends 1994-95* (Ottawa: Carleton University Press, 1994), pp. 14ff.

5.   The best example of writing from this perspective is the classic work of M. Ostrogorski, *Democracy and the Party System in the United States: A Study in Extra-Constitutional Government* (New York: Macmillan, 1910). The opposition was expressed in political practice by Progressives who feared the effects of giving over representation to parties and who worked to establish an alternative representational system. See, for example, the classic study by W.L. Morton, *The Progressive Party in Canada* (Toronto: University of Toronto Press, 1950). The Reform Party's program rehabilitates some of these demands in the 1990s. See A. Brian Tanguay, "The Transformation of Canada's Party System in the 1990s," in James P. Bickerton and Alain-G. Gagnon, eds., *Canadian Politics*, 2nd ed. (Toronto: Broadview, 1994), pp. 125ff.

6. This theme of parties' contribution to social stability was expressed in both structural-functional analyses and in the work of the advocates of "creative politics." For a discussion see Janine Brodie and Jane Jenson, "Piercing the Smokescreen: Brokerage Parties and Class Politics," in A.-G. Gagnon and A.B. Tanguay, eds., *Canadian Parties in Transition: Discourse, Organization, Representation* (Toronto: Nelson, 1988), pp. 31-32.

7. *Capitalism, Socialism and Democracy* was published in 1942 but written in response to the rise of totalitarianism in Europe, as well as to the achievement of the universal franchise, which was accomplished almost everywhere in Europe and North America by the end of World War I. For a recent discussion of Schumpeter's ideas see David Held, *Models of Democracy* (Stanford, CA: Stanford University Press, 1987), pp. 164-85. For another classic discussion of democracy, more Utopian than that of Schumpeter, see C.B. Macpherson, *The Life and Times of Liberal Democracy* (London: Oxford University Press, 1977).

8. Robert Dahl is best known as a proponent of this position. See his *A Preface to Economic Democracy* (Cambrdge, England: Polity, 1985). For a discussion of elite theories of democracy more generally see Held, *Models of Democracy*, Chapters 5 and 6.

9. An alternative view, that parties actually shape the preferences of voters, has been discussed less by the heirs of Schumpeterian democratic theory. For one such formulation, and a critique of the "economic" model see Brodie and Jenson, "Piercing the Smokescreen."

10. For a description of these models see Patrick Dunleavy and C.T. Husbands, *British Democracy at the Crossroads: Voting and Party Competition in the 1980s* (London: Allen and Unwin, 1985), Chapter 2. The classic statement of the "prospective" position is Anthony Downs, *An Economic Theory of Democracy* (New York: Harper and Row, 1957). The "retrospective" notion has been developed in Morris Fiorina, *Retrospective Voting in American National Elections* (New Haven, CT: Yale University Press, 1981).

11. Royal Commission on Electoral Reform and Party Financing, *Reforming Electoral Democracy* (Ottawa: Supply and Services, 1991), vol. 1, p. 246.

12. For a summary of the RCERPF's proposals for overcoming some of the weaknesses of brokerage politics, see Alexandra Dobrowolsky and Jane Jenson, "Reforming the Parties: Prescriptions for Democracy," in Susan D. Phillips, ed., *How Ottawa Spends: 1993-94*, pp. 43-81.

13. This description is based on Peter Woolstencroft, "Doing Politics Differently: The Conservative Party and the Campaign of 1993," in Alan Frizzell, Jon H. Pammett, and Anthony Westell, eds., *The Canadian General Election of 1993* (Ottawa: Carleton University Press, 1994), pp. 13-23.

14. Woolstencroft, "Doing Politics Differently," p. 18.

15. Stephen Clarkson, "Yesterday's Man and His Blue Grits: Backward into the Future," in Frizzell et al., *The Canadian General Election of 1993*, p. 34. He also describes the flexibility in the Liberals' presentation of self, by examining the story of the policy conference convened in November 1991. While the "overall policy message lay somewhere to the Left of centre," the media spin put on it by the leadership was that the Liberals had changed. "The Chrétien party was not going to resist globalization but embrace it, and such Left-leaning nationalists as Lloyd Axworthy would have to concur," p. 30.

16. Phillips, "Making Change," p. 15.

17. Ibid., p. 25.

18. Jeffrey Simpson, "All political wisdom can be found in the Liberals' little red book," *The Globe and Mail*, 20 Spetember 1994, p. A18.

19. Quoted in Tanguay, "The Transformation of Canada's Party System," p. 114.

20. For this comparison, see Maureen Covell, "Parties as Institutions of National Governance," in Herman Bakvis, ed., *Representation, Integration and Political Parties in Canada*, vol. 14 of the Research Studies for the Royal Commission on Electoral Reform and Party Financing (Toronto: Dundurn Press, 1992), pp. 63-127.

21. For two quite different discussions of the brokerage model see Brodie and Jenson, "Piercing the Smokescreen" and David E. Smith, "Party Government, Representation, and National Integration in Canada," in *The Royal Commission on the Economic Union and Development Prospects for Canada* (Toronto: University of Toronto Press, 1985), vol. 36, 1:54.

22. Clarkson, "Yesterday's Man," p. 28.

23. For one version of the "failure of innovation" thesis see Frank H. Underhill, "The Party System in Canada," in *In Search of Canadian Liberalism* (Toronto: Macmillan, 1960). Later debates focussed more on the lack of "creative politics" due to the blurring of class cleavages. See, for example, Gad Horowitz, "Toward the Democratic Class Struggle," in Trevor Lloyd and Jack McLeod, eds., *Agenda 1970* (Toronto: University of Toronto Press, 1968).

24. For a discussion of the political system's reliance on royal commissions for representational tasks see Neil Bradford, "Ideas, Institutions and Innovation: Economic Policy in Canada and Sweden," in Stephen Brooks and Alain-G. Gagnon, eds., *Social Scientists, Policy Communities and the State* (New York: Praeger, 1994).

25. Reginald Whitaker, *The Government Party: Organizing and Financing the Liberal Party of Canada 1930-58* (Toronto: University of Toronto Press, 1977).

26. For a discussion of this debate see Rianne Mahon, *The Politics of Industrial Restructuring* (Toronto: University of Toronto Press, 1984), Conclusion.

27. Sue Findlay, "Facing the State: The Politics of the Women's Movement Reconsidered," in Heather Jon Maroney and Meg Luxton, eds., *Feminism and Political Economy* (Toronto: Methuen, 1987), pp. 42ff.

28. Quoted in Edward Greenspon, "Encounter with debt leads to conversion," *The Globe and Mail*, 17 October 1994, p. A1. Immigration Minister Sergio Marchi may have been equally subject to and succumbed to the preference of departmental staff for cutting immigration, despite the Liberals' election promise. See Jeffrey Simpson, "Rethinking the bromides, homilies and vagaries of the Liberal Red Book," *The Globe and Mail*, 2 November 1994, p. A18.

29. For an expansion of this analysis for the whole postwar period see Jane Jenson, "'Different' But Not 'Exceptional': Canada's Permeable Fordism," *Canadian Review of Sociology and Anthropology*, 26 (1989): 69-94.

30. On these consultations see Pal and Seidle, "Constitutional Politics 1990-92."

31. Jane Jenson, "Commissioning Ideas: Representation and Royal Commissions," in Susan D. Phillips, ed., *Making Change*, pp. 39-69.

32. Daniel Drache and Duncan Cameron, eds., *The Other Macdonald Report: The Consensus on Canada's Future that the Macdonald Commission Left Out* (Toronto: Lorimer, 1985).

33. Peter Bleyer, "Coalitions of Social Movements as Agents for Social Change: The Action Canada Network," in W.K. Carroll, ed., *Organizing Dissent: Contemporary Social Movements in Theory and Practice* (Toronto: Garamond, 1992), pp. 102-18.

34. For example, despite the Liberals' blatant reversal on the issue of wage and price controls after the 1974 election, no one in the 1979 CNES study mentioned that matter as an important issue.

35. For an overview of these debates see H. Michael Stevenson, "Ideology and Unstable Party Identification in Canada: Limited Rationality in a Brokerage Party System," *Canadian Journal of Political Science*, 24 (1987): 813-50.

36. As the RCERPF reports, one in every two voters felt that there is no difference among the parties. See *Reforming Electoral Democracy*, vol. 1, p. 226.

37. The effects of such characteristics of the party system and partisanship were not felt in the same way everywhere, of course. In some parts of the country traditional religious and ethnic differences still seemed to anchor party loyalties. Nor were the effects probably as strong in earlier elections, when the glue of patronage politics could have contributed to the creation of more stable party ties.

2

Making an Issue of It

Much of the dislocation in the world economy that began in the 1970s has been translated into election issues. Large problems have pushed themselves to the forefront of public consciousness through their sheer dimensions, and the political parties have responded by identifying these as subjects that need immediate attention. But in election campaigns these problems are usually formulated as issues on which everyone agrees. The principal disagreements are over who can best solve the problems, and at times about the speed and direction of that solution. This process started with inflation in the early 1970s, continued with unemployment, and was joined by deficit reduction toward the end of the 1980s. Unemployment, debt reduction, spending restraint, and establishing competitiveness promise to be the staples of political discussion for the rest of the 20th century and beyond.

All of these issues are consequences of the market-driven restructuring project outlined in Chapter 1. Elite consensus on the desirability of this project has meant that the major political parties avoid discussion of the basics, and instead proceed as if the mass public's doubts are of minor importance. The fundamental policies used to implement the project are to be accepted as the baselines for the future because the global economy is assumed to be guided by market forces throughout the world. Independent action by individual states to counteract international trends is not thought possible or desirable under the assumptions of neoconservatism. In particular, the level of unemployment will be dictated by the market and can only be affected in a minor way by government policies intended to create employment or foster economic growth. It is taken as a given that government debt is bad, that high deficits are worse, and that social programs must be cut back to sustainable levels.

Political parties, particularly the brokerage parties that dominate the Canadian system, are understandably nervous about dealing with "big" issues in any other way than identifying them as general societal problems. This hesitancy also applies, however, to suggestions for the draconian implementation of the economic project. Strong medicine, such as the Reform Party's stated intention in the 1993 campaign to eliminate the deficit in three years through drastic cutbacks in social programs, or the Conservatives' 1974 plan to bring in wage and price controls to get rid of inflation, immediately becomes the focus of criticism and is likely to lose that party as many votes as it gains. When deciding which issues to emphasize in a campaign, and how to present them, parties employ strategists such as pollsters, consultants, or advertising firms to maximize their electoral prospects. As a result, they generally prefer to emphasize their leaders' determination to "do politics differently"[1] or their ability to "manage change"[2] instead of asking for a public verdict on the way in which that change is to be addressed or initiated.

Political parties also find it in their interest to change the issue focus from one election to the next. Parties in government seeking re-election do not wish to remind voters of the problems they pledged to solve in the previous campaign, or to emphasize their record in office. Opposition parties do so, but they risk cynical commentary that they probably would not have done any better. Voters soon tire of empty promises about solving the same old problems, but their memories nevertheless may constrain the parties to some degree. Massive problems like unemployment move in and out of the electoral arena, as we will show in this chapter, but cannot be avoided forever.

The Issue Shuffle

Any subject, large or small, discussed during an election campaign gets translated into an "issue." The peril of nuclear destruction can be an issue, and so can the colour of the uniforms of the armed forces. The way in which taxes are collected can be an issue, as can the level of taxation on such things as alcohol or gasoline. Global warming is a potential issue, and so is the provision of recycling boxes. Trade policy with other nations is an issue, as is the promise of a grant to establish a small business in a specific location. The appearance, dress, conduct, or perceived capability of political leaders or candidates can also be issues.

The ubiquitous use of the word "issue" disguises the fact that these subjects of political discussion take very different forms. Political issues fought over in elections can and sometimes do reflect the major questions of our times. Although the threat of nuclear war or nuclear proliferation rarely have sufficient domestic consequences to be important in elections, the reliance on nuclear power stations, the deployment or testing of nuclear weapons, or a commitment to disarmament have generated controversy in various countries. Environmental protection is a plank in almost every political party's platform. Small numbers of citizens in most elections consider these types of issues to be of primary importance to their voting decisions. However, these "big issues" are hardly ever discussed in elections in a manner that allows the general public to have an impact on their resolution. Political parties or candidates are often in agreement in identifying the subject's importance, while the specific methods of accomplishing such things as environmental protection are often difficult for the public to evaluate in the midst of an election campaign in which many other subjects are getting more attention.

Table 2.1 displays the revolving issue agendas in recent Canadian federal election campaigns. It shows the movement of the electorate as a whole from issue to issue in different campaigns between 1974 and 1993 by presenting the answers of all respondents to each survey's invitation to name the most important issues in an election. Issues have been grouped into broad categories such as economic, constitutional, and social, but the table also retains detailed information about the specific issues in each category across time.

Inflation, the issue that dominated the 1974 scene, was injected into the political arena largely because of public concern about rising prices (see Figure 1.1, p. 5). These were visible with every visit to the grocery store, or the arrival of every winter heating bill. The media were quick to respond to this public preoccupation with the skyrocketing cost of living; newspaper articles pointed to potential causes of the phenomenon and described the worldwide nature of the inflationary spiral. Then, during the election campaign, the parties were compelled to respond. Despite their unreadiness to provide long-term solutions to such a complicated economic phenomenon, the election context demanded that the parties promise that solutions were available, and declare that they could provide them. But by the next election, these proposed solutions had been discarded. Despite the consistently high rate of inflation, and continued poll results indicating that inflation was seen by the public as the most important problem facing the country through the early 1980s,[3] it declined sharply as an election issue after 1974.

In 1979, the Liberals attempted to reshuffle the issue agenda. A repetition of the inflation theme, or a close examination of the country's economic situation, would not likely produce a second favourable result for them. Moreover, the public had become extremely pessimistic about the intractable nature of Canadian economic problems. Political authorities were regarded as incompetent to deal with the twin evils of inflation and unemployment; stagflation continued regardless of efforts undertaken to eliminate it. While the Conservative and New Democratic parties criticized

Table 2.1

Most Important Election Issues: 1974–93

	1974	1979	1980	1984	1988	1993
Economic Issues						
Economy in general	5%	11%	9%	17%	2%	23%
Inflation, cost of living, wage and price controls	46	14	14	2	–	–
Taxes	3	8	3	3	4	2
Government spending, deficit, budget	3	4	17	12	7	21
Unemployment, jobs	3	10	4	36	2	34
Free trade	–	–	–	–	88	2
Other economic issues	3	1	1	3	–	–
Constitutional Issues						
National unity, inter-governmental relations	2	10	7	2	6	3
Bilingualism, language	3	3	–	1	–	–
Quebec, separatism, referendum	1	15	6	2	–	–
Resource Issues						
Oil prices, energy policy, development	2	4	31	1	–	–
Environment, pollution	–	5	1	1	9	1
Social Issues						
Housing, health, medicare, pensions, women's issues	12	5	2	11	14	5
Other Issues						
Foreign policy, defence	2	2	3	3	1	1
Leadership, leaders	6	14	15	8	5	3
Change, parties, retrospective evaluations	1	8	8	14	1	3
Trust, patronage, majority government, the polls	7	1	4	4	1	4
All other issues	3	2	2	4	3	2
None, No important issues, Don't know	30	28	22	25	5	7

Source: 1974–84 – CNES; 1988 – CPS; 1993 – PSC.

the Liberal government's performance in the economic arena, the Liberals declared that the real election issue was not economic at all but one of "national unity." Quebec was to be kept in Confederation, and the upcoming referendum in that province defeated. The notion that this was a priority was scoffed at by the opposition and by some of the media, but was accepted by a significant portion of the public, as Table 2.1 shows.[4]

The 1980 election, held only nine months later, was fought over another issue, this time a program to raise the level of energy prices to world levels, thus financing expansion of the private energy sector. To do this, the Conservative government proposed a budget featuring a major rise in energy taxation, particularly on gasoline at the pump. This budget, which embodied elements of economic restructuring undertaken by the PCs as soon as they formed a government in 1979, was tagged with the slogan "short-term pain for long-term gain." It was never designed to be the centrepiece of an election campaign; the Tories were genuinely surprised to be defeated in a House of Commons vote over its provisions. The ensuing campaign did, however, enable the government to seek a mandate for its budget. The media and the public were also given the chance to examine closely the plans for the price rises on gasoline. The devastating result of the election for the Conservatives may have further inhibited political parties from revealing extensive plans to the electorate.

Here we see an example of the way in which a general issue like inflation can take on different forms. In the 1980 election, the main economic issue was phrased in terms of gasoline taxation, not price increases. The potential contribution to inflation of the budgeted tax increases was part of the latter issue; however, other elements were involved as well, such as the government's desire to privatize Petro-Canada and the lack of progress in negotiating an oil-pricing agreement with Alberta. The broad problem of inflation was discussed in the 1980 campaign in far different terms than it had been during 1974. It was regarded as an extra blow to the weary motorist rather than an indicator of rising prices in general. After the 1984 election, inflation disappeared from campaign discussion. This occurred even though its prevention still dominated the monetary policy being pursued by the Bank of Canada. The wisdom of the Bank's tight-money, high-interest-rate policy was debated among elites, especially in financial circles, but no mandate from the public for this controversial economic policy was ever sought.

By 1984, a new issue had risen to the top of the agenda. The problem of unemployment, with high rates for much of the decade, had suddenly become the dominant focus of media commentary. This arose from the severe economic recession of the early 1980s, which saw the unemployment rate soar to the 12% mark (Figure 1.1, p. 5). Efforts to curb inflation were in part responsible for this development. The PCs also charged that the policies of the Liberal government, such as the National Energy Program, had adversely affected economic conditions in the Western provinces. During the campaign, the public's concern with unemployment was fanned to crisis proportions by the media. The opposition parties, delighted with this focus, agreed wholeheartedly that the Liberals had failed to deal with the jobs problem.

With a modest, if regionally differentiated, decline in joblessness after 1984, the parties, the public, and much of the media abandoned the unemployment issue in the 1988 federal election. The centrepiece of that Conservative campaign was not originally intended to be the implementation of the Free Trade Agreement with the United States; rather, this treaty was to be an example of their general competence to "manage change" for the future. But soon the FTA was at the front and centre of the campaign. Advocacy groups mobilized on both sides of the issue, and the media stepped up their examination of the Agreement. The Liberals sensed a strategic advantage in the public's hesitant reaction to free trade, the overwhelming sense that inadequate information on the deal had been provided, and Canadians' fears of the potential consequences of closer links with the United States. They therefore brought the issue to the forefront of their campaign, and John Turner declared it to be the cause of his life. The difficulties of managing the electoral agenda meant that, for the second time in the decade, a major Conservative government project would be placed before the public for a potential mandate.

By 1993, free trade was forgotten, if not gone. The government was moving forward with NAFTA. However, the only party interested in talking about trade issues in 1993 was the NDP, and the status of this party in the estimation of the media or the public was such that they were unable to set the agenda for discussion. The focus was back on the unemployment rate and the importance of job creation. The Liberal strategy was to make it the first priority in their campaign manifesto, *Creating Opportunity*. These economic growth issues dominated the agenda in 1993. They were joined by the need for deficit reduction and cuts in government spending, issues that had received modest numbers of mentions in previous elections. This time, however, there was widespread pessimism about the ability of any government to restore the jobs that had been lost in recent years due to the globalization of production and the effects of the Free Trade Agreement, a pessimism only matched by those viewing the mounting debt situation.

So the shelf life of issues is short. Public concern about issues is substantial, but the actual object of attention changes readily from one election context to the next. Both citizens and politicians create an issue agenda anew at each opportunity, and both seem to prefer not to immediately revisit the subjects that were prominent in the previous election.

Figure 2.1

**Stability of Types of Issue Concerns
Across Successive Elections: 1974–93**

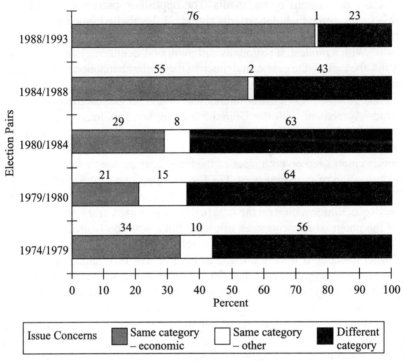

Note: Issue categories are: economic, constitutional, social, other. See Table 2.1 for details.
Source: 1974–79, 1979–80 – CNES; 1980–84, 1984–88, 1988–93 – PSC.

We have seen in Table 2.1 patterns of aggregate variability across the electorate in the choice of important election issues. A series of panel studies allows us to determine the extent to which individuals shifted their issue agendas from one election to the next.[5] Figure 2.1 shows that up until the 1984 election, there was a lot of individual volatility in this regard. For example, in the 1979 and 1980 elections, held only nine months apart, only 36% of respondents chose the same type of issue (economic, constitutional, resource, social, or other) as the most important in both. As the figure also indicates, over half of those showing continuity of issue choice picked economic issues as important both times. Much more common, however, were people who moved among different categories of issues, selecting one type as important in one election, and another in the next. In the case of 1979 and 1980, substantial numbers moved between constitutional, economic, resource, and other issues.

The dominance of Canadian elections by economic issues has solidified in recent times. Figure 2.1 shows that between the 1984 and 1988 elections, over half the panel respondents felt the important issues were of the same type, mostly economic. And between the "free trade election" of 1988 and the "unemployment" election of 1993, over three-quarters of the people felt that economic issues were the important ones on both occasions. We have already noted, however, that these are frequently not the *same* economic issues. In each election context, there is a distinct tendency to move on to another way of defining the economic problems facing the country.

The issues that form the basis of discussion during election campaigns spring from no single source. Chapter 1 points out that the party system in Canada is not geared toward electoral debate on long-term projects, even if parties do have such plans. Commonly, an economic or constitutional problem is identified at election time, and the parties react with short-term policy suggestions drawn from wherever they can find them. Sources of such innovation can include the bureaucracy, interest groups, academia, royal commissions, and even the media. Policy experiments of provincial governments or other national governments are watched closely for evidence of success or popularity. An example of this occurred during the 1993 campaign when Jean Chrétien picked up the idea of "workfare" as a way of reforming the welfare system from experiments being contemplated by the province of New Brunswick, which in turn had gotten the idea from Denmark.[6]

Long-term projects, particularly those of an ideological nature, are not often directly acknowledged by the parties during election campaigns. Potentially attractive elements derived from them are, however, introduced as election issues. The common pattern is for the more important elements to be ignored during elections and brought forward immediately afterward. The National Energy Program (NEP), the Free Trade Agreement (FTA), and the Goods and Services Tax (GST) are three examples of very controversial programs about which electoral discussion was muted at best prior to their introduction. Free trade became the paramount issue in 1988 because of the delays in negotiating the Canada–U.S. Free Trade Agreement and passing the enabling legislation; Conservative Party strategists had expected the FTA to be in place long before they would be called to account.

The 1993 campaign and the Liberal government's activities in the months subsequent to its taking office provide an excellent example of the operation of this process. The Liberals emphasized job creation during the campaign and took a very low-key and moderate position on the issues of deficit reduction and changes to social programs, issues on which the Conservative and Reform parties advocated tougher measures. Once the election was over, the Liberals brought deficit reduction to the forefront of their economic program, and launched a social-policy review designed to develop strategies to cut such programs. The document made public in the fall of 1994 targets Unemployment Insurance, health, and education for reductions, despite the fact that the Red Book made no mention of cuts to the last two areas and said only that UI funds should be better spent.[7] Such cutbacks are likely to be finished before the Liberals must seek re-election in 1997/98, allowing other issues to be introduced for a future campaign.

Issues, then, in the last three decades, moved onto the electoral stage in every way *except* that which democratic theory implies is the most appropriate. In no case did any of the established parties deliberately announce an important project as a lead-up to an election campaign and seek a mandate to carry it out. These parties either reacted to crises with concern and short-term solutions, announced a series of "goodies" for particular areas of the country, or relied on the qualities of their leadership. Only the cases of the Reform Party and the Bloc Québécois provided a partial exception to this pattern in 1993. Both of these parties promoted projects, involving the cutting of government expenditure and the separation of Quebec respectively, during the campaign. However, their appeals were also pitched more broadly than these policies might imply and contained many elements of traditional brokerage politics.

The Different Faces of the Economic Issue

Free Trade

Free trade between Canada and the United States, a perennial theme through Canadian history, moved to the top of the political agenda in 1985 when the release of the report of the Macdonald Commission gave the idea a renewed respectability in the policy community. Initially, Conservative leader Brian Mulroney was opposed to a free trade agreement, but, as often happens in a brokerage party system, even a position taken with seeming conviction fell to expediency, and was soon reversed. The idea fitted well with the neoconservative philosophy of key Tories like Finance Minister Michael Wilson and many of the other influential members of the party, all of whom were dedicated to implementing the new economic agenda. By late 1985, Prime Minister Mulroney was writing to U.S. President Reagan proposing that negotiations begin for a comprehensive treaty to reduce trade barriers between the two countries.[8]

Prior to 1988, public opinion in Canada had been generally supportive of the concept of free trade. Figure 2.2 reports the trend since 1953 in public response to the Gallup Poll question: "Do you think Canada would be better off, or worse off, if U.S. goods were allowed in here without tariff or customs charges, and Canadian goods were allowed in the U.S. free?" Public opinion on this question was remarkably stable until the Macdonald Commission placed concrete proposals for such a free trade treaty on the public agenda and negotiations started. From that point on, strong opposing

Figure 2.2

Public Opinion on Free Trade: 1953–90

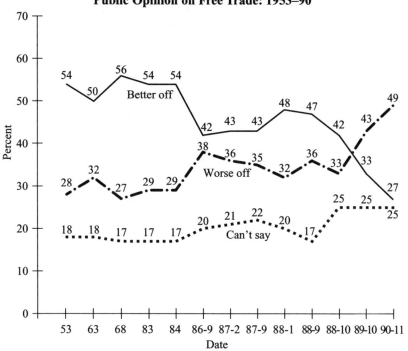

Source: Canadian Institute for Public Opinion (CIPO), *Gallup Report.*

views began to be expressed by a series of groups, and the country became more sceptical about the desirability of free trade. However, Canadians were still more likely to think that the country would be better off with the free movement of goods back and forth across the border right up until the 1988 election campaign. During that campaign, attention shifted to the specific question of the adequacy of the FTA; however, the Gallup Poll continued to ask the more general question about free trade on two occasions in subsequent years. The public's verdict on free trade in general clearly shifted; by November 1990, with the FTA in place and the recession being felt, the previous pattern of public opinion had been reversed and almost half of Canadians were sceptical of free trade (Figure 2.2).

Those favouring the actual Free Trade Agreement during the 1988 campaign were far fewer than those favouring free trade in general (Figure 2.3). Data from surveys conducted at the time of the election show substantial public wariness about the FTA. Majorities of Canadians, even of those favouring the Agreement, felt it would hurt some regions of the

Figure 2.3

**Public Opinion on Canada–U.S. Free Trade Agreement:
October–November 1988, and 1989–93**

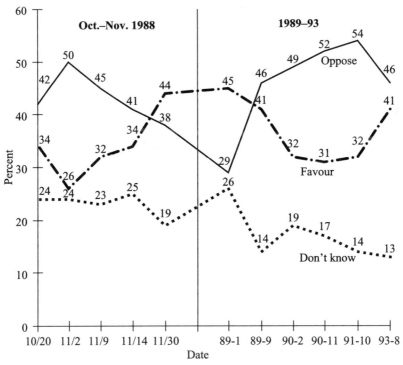

Source: CIPO, *Gallup Report.*

country and some sectors of the economy.[9] There was also a strong minority opinion that the FTA was a threat to Canadian sovereignty and culture, and over 40% in the post-election survey felt that Canadian social programs would be harmed under free trade. Realizing that the FTA was less popular than the more general concept of free trade, the Liberals strategically concentrated their criticism on the specific deal negotiated by the Conservatives.

Currents of public opinion on the Free Trade Agreement have followed an interesting path in the period since the 1988 election. As measured by the identical Gallup Poll question, the verdict on the FTA became more positive for a brief period following the Conservative victory, an effect likely produced by the election outcome. After the result became known, the re-elected Conservative government was able to secure the final passage of its FTA legislation through the Senate. Some former opponents became resigned to the inevitability of a new relationship with the United

36

States. By mid-1989, however, the public had once again turned negative on the FTA. For example, a poll in October 1991 found that 54% opposed the Agreement, while only 32% were in favour (Figure 2.3). An earlier Gallup Poll, done in September 1990, asked the question: "Since the policy of free or freer trade between the U.S. and Canada was adopted in January, 1989, who in your opinion has gained more—Canada or the United States?" Responses to this question were overwhelmingly negative; 71% of the Canadian public thought the U.S. had gained more, with only 5% picking their own country as free trade winners. Despite the electoral battle on the Free Trade Agreement in 1988, then, Canadians are now stuck with a policy many opposed at the time, and more have come to dislike in subsequent years.

By 1993, criticism of the FTA had become passé, and was seen as carping. The Conservatives had extended their trade policy project further south, and had participated in negotiations for a North American Free Trade Agreement (NAFTA) involving not only Canada and the United States, but also Mexico. This time, the verdict of the Canadian public was clear from the start; neither the general idea of North American free trade, nor the NAFTA treaty, was widely supported. Figure 2.4 shows that for much of the 1990s, roughly twice as many people disliked the idea of North American free trade as were favourable to it.

However, neither trade issue emerged as a major one in the 1993 election. Only the NDP took an unequivocal position in opposition to NAFTA. The Liberals pledged to renegotiate both the FTA and NAFTA to improve them, but stated that "abrogating trade agreements should be only a last resort if satisfactory changes cannot be negotiated."[10] The party knew that the Canadian public really did not want the confrontation that would come with "ripping up" the trade pacts, as John Turner and Sheila Copps had pledged to do in 1988. A Gallup Poll in November 1990 had shown that only 21% of Canadians surveyed were in favour of abolishing the FTA, whereas 61% felt that "the Agreement should be retained but improvements made to it." After the 1993 election, the Liberals completed passage of the NAFTA legislation without having obtained anything except a weak American promise to talk about some of the matters that were supposed to be "renegotiated." With their new position, the Liberals effectively confirmed their acceptance of the trade policy component of the global free-market economic project. Since then, they have embraced free trade even more enthusiastically.

As the political stratum united in its acceptance of the global economic project, divisions in society began to open up on the project's major components. The free trade issue divided Canadians along regional, class, and gender lines as a perception developed that the economy was operating in the interests of certain parts of the country, of the moneyed classes, and of males. The "have" sectors of society can assemble the

Figure 2.4

**Public Opinion on North American Free Trade Agreement (NAFTA):
1990–93**

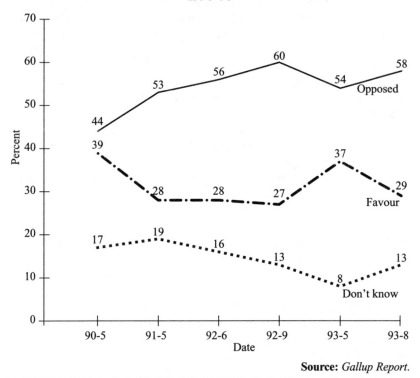

Source: *Gallup Report.*

resources to compete in the global economy: the "have nots" are left to struggle with minimal state assistance. These societal divisions are illustrated in Table 2.2, which identifies those respondents who were in favour of free trade as embodied in the specific FTA and NAFTA policies in the electoral contexts of 1988 and 1993. As we have already noted, the overall level of support for free trade decreased substantially in the period between the two elections, but the socio-demographic patterns in that support remained basically similar.

In 1988, free trade captured the imagination of two regions of the country, Quebec and the West, for some similar and some different reasons. For the West, a commitment to free trade represented both an ideological reaffirmation of the free-enterprise spirit prevalent in the culture of that region, as well as an opportunity to shake off the restraints of the federal government, long seen as encouraging inefficient central Canadian industries at the expense of higher costs to Westerners. The 1988 spirit in

38

Table 2.2

Percentages Favouring Free Trade Agreements, FTA and NAFTA: 1988, 1993

	Favour FTA			Favour NAFTA
	1988 Pre*	**1988 Post†**	**1993**	**1993**
Canada	46	56	40	28
Gender				
Men	53	63	48	35
Women	38	48	30	20
Income				
< $20,000 per year	36	42	27	18
$20,000–39,999	43	53	31	19
$40,000–59,999	51	62	39	25
$60,000–69,999	49	63	55	43
$70,000 or more	66	73	62	50
Region				
Atlantic	39	46	31	17
Quebec	55	69	45	34
Ontario	40	49	39	25
Prairies	55	59	40	29
British Columbia	43	51	38	28

* 1988 pre-election survey
† 1988 post-election survey

Source: 1988, 1993 – PSC.

the West was such that free trade meant freedom to compete, and many Westerners felt local business would do well in such a climate and that consumers would be able to enjoy lower-priced goods from the United States. In Quebec, confidence in the ability of francophone business to compete internationally was very high, both among the business elite and the general public. The provincial government of Robert Bourassa was also strongly supportive of the free trade policy.

The other regions of Canada were much more hesitant about the implications of free trade. For the Atlantic provinces, any diminution of Canadian government power meant fewer national resources to be allocated for industrial development in that impoverished area of the country. Table 2.2 shows that support for free trade at all time points was lowest in the Atlantic region. Ontario too has expressed consistent doubts about this policy. Its industries were likely to be hardest hit in the overall rationalization of the economy that would inevitably follow the lifting of tariffs on items produced there. Opinion in Ontario was never very favourable to free trade in 1988, and had become increasingly negative to the FTA by 1993. The decline in the overall popularity of the FTA in the years between 1988 and 1993 has had the effect of reducing the regional disparities in public attitudes toward it. By 1993, the West was just as negative to the FTA as Ontario was, and even the public in Quebec had turned more sceptical. With regard to NAFTA, support was quite low across the country, with the Atlantic region still more negative than anywhere else, and Quebec somewhat less negative.

If a regional cleavage in support for free trade had diminished between 1988 and 1993, the same is not true for class and gender differences in the population. Table 2.2 shows that the relationship between income level and support for free trade, present at both times, became stronger in 1993. In 1988, the highest-income Canadians were about twice as likely as the lowest income group to want free trade; by 1993, they were three times more likely to favour it. As free trade became established policy, and public opinion became more negative toward it, support for it became more concentrated among the well-off sector of society.

Table 2.2 also reveals a gender gap in public attitudes toward free trade. Support is generally 15% higher among men than women, and this difference is remarkably consistent across the surveys. A number of reasons may combine to explain the hesitancy of women to embrace the new economic project. The deleterious effects of greater reliance on the market are perceived more acutely by women. Women are particularly concerned with social policy preservation and extension, threatened under the provisions of free trade.[11] A final reason is that as government relinquishes its policy-making authority, the chance of implementing policies to promote employment equity for women recedes.

Unemployment

The last six federal elections have exhibited a curious pattern, in which unemployment has been a prime issue in every *second* election. The public reaction to the decreased inflation rate between 1974 and 1979 was to turn to unemployment as one of the major issues in the latter campaign (10% did so). The official unemployment rate in 1979, 7%, was higher than the 5% registered in 1974. Attention turned to other issues in 1980, however, despite the fact that the unemployment rate remained steady (see Figure 1.1, p. 5). In 1984, a much higher unemployment rate of 11% was emphasized in a Conservative campaign promising "jobs, jobs, jobs," and this issue reached dominant proportions. In 1988, the unemployment rate dropped to 8%, and the issue virtually disappeared during the election campaign, only to re-emerge in 1993 as the dominant issue in the campaign when the jobless rate again climbed over 11%.

The above patterns suggest that the identification of unemployment as a prominent election issue is relatively sensitive to rises in the jobless rate rather than to the level of unemployment. In 1988, the rate was lower than it had been four years previously, but was still substantially higher than it had been during the 1970s or any decade since the Great Depression of the 1930s. The reaction of those who felt unemployment was a major issue in 1984 was, however, to abandon discussion of it during the election of 1988. A mere half a percent of these voters regarded the jobless rate as the major question for political debate four years later. Even if this result is understandable given the overwhelming attention accorded free trade in 1988, it is something of a puzzle why unemployment-minded voters from 1984 did not respond to the follow-up survey question asking about "any other important issue" in 1988 by again bringing up that subject. Only 2.3% did so, fewer than the percentage who talked about the importance of unemployment as an election issue in 1974, when the election rhetoric was dominated by inflation, and when the rate of joblessness was substantially lower.

Incumbent governments seeking re-election have an incentive to change the focus of discussion, at least in such a way that their failures are not showcased. Any relative improvement in the economy, such as that which occurred between 1984 and 1988, allows a government to claim that its policies are working, and that jobs are being created, even if not as quickly as everyone would have liked. However, the lack of issue continuity on something so basic as job creation inhibits governments being called to account for their past promises, and hence provides a deterrent to electoral results being interpreted as mandates for policy implementation.

The 1993 federal election campaign returned to the themes of jobs and joblessness. The discussion was more specific than that during previous elections, largely because the Liberals campaigned on a platform of spending $6 billion on an infrastructure program to create jobs and stimulate the economy. Even a not-so-close inspection of this proposal revealed that the Liberals were actually promising to have the federal government spend only $2 billion on this program, since the money would have to be matched by provincial and municipal governments. Nevertheless, the proposal was popular, and efforts by the other parties to label it evidence of the "politics of the past" were not successful. The past, the Liberals pointed out, had more people working than the present.

Concern about unemployment was widespread throughout the electorate, both in 1984 and 1993. Nevertheless, some groups were more likely to cite this as an important election issue than others. Table 2.3 shows that in both years, the regions of Canada were differentially concerned with the jobs issue. The two years differed, however, in the regional patterns displayed. In 1984, Quebec was the lone province out of step with the

Table 2.3

Percentages Mentioning Unemployment As Most Important Issue*:
1984, 1993

	1984	1993
Canada	36	34
Gender		
Men	36	30
Women	36	38
Income†		
< $20,000 per year	35	36
$20,000–39,999	38	41
$40,000–59,999	37	33
$60,000–69,999	36	30
$70,000 or more	23	24
Region		
Atlantic	40	51
Quebec	28	35
Ontario	37	36
Prairies	38	28
British Columbia	48	22

* multiple mentions
† 1993 income categories; 1984 categories are:
   < $15,000 per year, $15,000–29,999, $30,000–49,999,
   $50,000–99,999, $100,000 and over

Source: 1984 – CNES; 1993 – PSC.

others, in the sense that it was considerably less likely to identify the unemployment issue as most important. In 1993, Quebec was very close to the national percentage (34%) of residents picking this issue as most important. Given the high jobless rate in the Atlantic region, it is not surprising that residents of these provinces were dramatically more concerned with the issue; 51% cited jobs as the primary issue focus of the election. It was Westerners who were more likely to cite other issues (primarily the deficit) rather than unemployment.

Social class factors were also related to the identification of unemployment as the most important election issue in 1984 and 1993. In both years, lower income people and those without a university education were more concerned with joblessness. In occupational terms, however, the threat of losing work has shifted. In 1984, it was skilled workers who were more concerned with unemployment, whereas in 1993 it was the clerical category. The threat to white-collar jobs in the 1990s had outstripped the prospective blue-collar job losses. To some extent, this relationship must reflect personal fears of being thrown out of work, and indeed in the 1984 survey a question was included that asked whether respondents were fearful about being laid off. Those having such fears were more likely to cite unemployment as an issue in the election. However, the relationship between respondents actually being unemployed and the degree to which they specified unemployment as the most important election issue is quite muted in both 1984 and 1993. For example, of those in the 1984 study who had themselves lost their jobs in the past year, 40% cited this issue as primary in the election, only 4% higher than those who had not been put out of work. Similar small differences are present between those reporting friends or family members being unemployed in the past year, and those who did not. In 1993, the difference is greater, with 44% of those currently jobless picking this as the central election issue, as opposed to the average of 34%.

Table 2.3 also shows that a difference has emerged between men and women on this issue. In 1984, there was no gender gap in the designation of the importance of jobs in the election. In 1993, women were more likely than men by 8% to pick unemployment as the most important issue. When considering the occupation of respondents, it is also noteworthy that homemakers, primarily women, were more likely to be concerned about the unemployment rate. As we have seen with free trade, women are less attracted to the neoconservative business agenda than are men. They are averse to the risks associated with trade policies, which may have dramatic affects on traditional jobs. Women in the work force have also been heavily affected by the loss of jobs throughout the economy.

The Deficit

Public concern about the level of the yearly deficit run by the federal government, and the accumulated amount of the public debt, has been building for the last decade. Conservative economists, and politicians of most parties have expressed increasing degrees of alarm over the amount of government revenue (currently over 30%) being used to service past debt. With the implementation of free trade, the economic policy agenda-setters turned, therefore, to the task of raising consciousness on the question of the deficit, and marshalling public opinion behind the policies of cutting public services in order to reduce or eliminate it.

During the 1993 campaign, deficit elimination and cutting government spending were the major planks in the platform of the Reform Party. Graphs illustrating the recent rise in the deficit were a prominent part of the party's advertising in the print media and on brochures—the graphs were then extended into the future to show the precipitous drop in the deficit with the hypothetical implementation of Reform's plan to eliminate it in three years. Party leader Preston Manning was fond of displaying these

Table 2.4

**Percentages Mentioning Deficit As Most Important Election Issue
and Most Important Issue Facing Canada: 1993**

	Issue in Election*	Issue Facing Canada
Canada	21	18
Gender		
Men	23	20
Women	18	15
Income†		
< $20,000 per year	13	11
$20,000–39,999	18	17
$40,000–59,999	22	19
$60,000–69,999	17	24
$70,000 or more	30	25
Region		
Atlantic	13	11
Quebec	20	13
Ontario	17	15
Prairies	29	25
British Columbia	26	30

* multiple mentions
† PSC categories; INS categories are: < $25,000, $25,000–44,000, $45,000–54,000, $55,000–74,000, $75,000 or more

Source: election issue – 1993 – PSC; issue facing Canada – INS.

graphs on occasions when television cameras offered free opportunities for additional publicity, such as during the leaders' debates. The Conservative Party, in government for the years since 1984 during which the most dramatic rise in the deficit had occurred, also campaigned for its swift reduction, and proposed elimination within five years. This longer time period was promoted by Prime Minister Campbell and her associates as a more realistic timetable, which would not disrupt social programs to the same degree as that proposed by the Reform Party. The Liberals committed themselves to a "realistic" approach to reducing the deficit, one that would shrink it to 3% of GDP by the end of three years in office.[12] The Bloc Québécois, as well as the other parties, thought the Liberals were not serious about tackling the deficit, and proposed swifter reductions. Even the NDP expressed concern about the extent of the deficit and debt problems.

This virtual consensus on the desirability of deficit reduction didn't fool the electorate, as we shall soon see. Those voters who were particularly concerned with the issue overwhelmingly preferred the Reform and Conservative positions on it. Table 2.4 shows, however, that the agenda of spending reduction was favoured by those less likely to be directly hurt by the cuts being proposed. High-income Canadians (as well as those with university degrees and those in managerial and self-employed occupations) were most likely to identify the deficit as the most important issue in the election. Just as men were more favourable to free trade than were women, they were also more likely to favour action on the deficit. In addition, the priority of deficit reduction varied considerably from one end of the country to the other. In the Western provinces, 28% thought it was the most important election issue. The number drops to 20% in Quebec, 17% in Ontario, and only 13% in the Atlantic region, an area much more concerned with the potential results of cutbacks to government services and welfare programs on which they depend. As with the other issue offshoots of the economic restructuring project, deficit reduction opens up divisions within Canadian society.

The Links to Party

A key goal of a party's election campaign is to achieve a positive linkage in the public's mind between important election issues and its capacity to take action on them.

In the last two elections, those of 1988 and 1993, there has been a close connection between public opinion on the most important election issues, free trade and unemployment respectively, and the parties that have ended up winning the elections. Figure 2.5 shows that 65% of those who favoured the Free Trade Agreement in 1988 voted Conservative, as against only 6% who disliked the Agreement. The main questions during the campaign, therefore, were whether or not public opinion on free trade, divided coming into the election, could be nudged in a positive or negative direction, as well as whether negative opinion could be united behind one of the two parties opposing the Agreement. We will discuss the outcome in detail in Chapter 6 of this book.

While the Free Trade Agreement was a specific policy directly connected with the party that introduced it, unemployment is a different sort of issue. In 1993, as in 1984, it was a major problem that all parties defined as important, and to which they all claimed to have the solutions (except for possibly the Conservatives, who struggled to overcome Prime Minister Campbell's statement that the solutions to the unemployment situation would not come until the next century). Figure 2.5 illustrates, however, that it was the Liberals who were able to establish a linkage with their policies and credibility on the unemployment issue. People who defined the most important election issue as that of unemployment were substantially more likely to vote Liberal than those for whom another issue was most important.

45

Figure 2.5

Percent Voting Conservative in 1988 by Opinion on Free Trade Agreement, and Percent Voting Liberal in 1993 by Unemployment as Most Important Issue

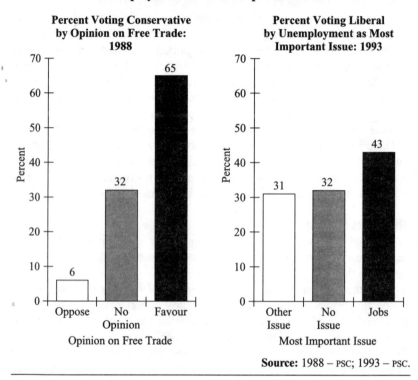

Percent Voting Conservative by Opinion on Free Trade: 1988

Percent Voting Liberal by Unemployment as Most Important Issue: 1993

Source: 1988 – PSC; 1993 – PSC.

In the last three federal elections, the party seen as "closest" to a plurality of respondents on economic issues has ended up the election winner. Table 2.5 shows, however, that this has not always been the case. The 1980 election saw the PCs as closer to more people on economic issues, despite their defeat. And in the preceding elections of 1979 and 1974, the election winner received fewer designations of closeness on economic issues than has been the case more recently. Thus, the ambitious elements of the project of global economic restructuring have focussed discussion of the issues in Canadian elections on some of the resulting economic plans and problems, even if these roots are not specifically addressed in the campaign rhetoric.

Table 2.5 also shows party popularity on constitutional issues, variously defined in terms of national unity, bilingualism, Quebec independence, and relations between federal and provincial governments.

Table 2.5

**Party Closest on Most Important Issue:
1974–93 Elections**

Issue	Party Closest					
	Liberal	**PC**	**NDP**	**Other**	**None**	**(N)**
Economic						
1974	37%	25	13	3	22	(1146)
1979	22%	36	21	2	20	(786)
1980	30%	39	20	1	11	(557)
1984	12%	57	16	1	15	(1390)
1988	27%	48	16	2	6	(950)
1993	45%	13	5	26*	11	(945)
Constitution						
1974	55%	16	7	9	13	(64)
1979	58%	16	7	9	13	(430)
1980	51%	23	5	3	19	(74)
1984	21%	64	1	1	13	(30)
1988	32%	29	–	29	9	(13)
1993	12%	14	5	48**	2	(42)

*   includes 18% Reform and 7% Bloc Québécois
** includes 3% Reform and 42% Bloc Québécois

Source: 1974–84 – CNES; 1988 – CPS; 1993 – PSC.

Traditionally, these issues had been strengths of the Liberals, helping that party win majorities in the elections of 1980 and 1974, and staving off a greater defeat in 1979. In 1984, this issue area, as every other, became the preserve of the Mulroney Conservatives. But the failure of the Meech Lake Accord, and the defeat of the referendum on the Charlottetown agreement discredited the major parties, all of whom had endorsed these initiatives. Accordingly, the Bloc Québécois captured the attention of many of those identifying constitutional issues as important in 1993. The ability of the traditional parties to reassert their dominance on this sort of issue is problematic for the future. However, this, as with every other category of election issues, has taken a back seat to the economy in the last decade, and there are few portents for change in the immediate future unless a constitutional crisis erupts. The parties must therefore jockey for position on the issues of public concern in each election. They cannot rely on linkages with past issues nor, as we will soon see, can they rely on any general feelings of loyalty toward them.

Conclusion

The major feature of the Canadian public's concern with issues in the last 25 years has been a propensity to change the "important" issue from one election to another. Issues are presented and discarded with remarkable rapidity. What sells, and not what's needed, remains the guiding principle. In its continuing search for solutions to pressing problems, the electorate has accepted these altered issue agendas quite readily. Thus, parties have been able to implement elements of a new economic system emphasizing free markets and a reduced role for the state without sustained scrutiny of their actions. The public, and the media, have tended to abandon the definitions of problems sanctioned in previous elections for new policy suggestions or new claims of expertise in dealing with threatening economic consequences of global trends.

The fact that some of the issues in recent elections stem from efforts to implement the new economic agenda does not reflect an alteration in the familiar "patchwork approach" to problem solving long characteristic of Canada's brokerage parties. Rather, these patterns represent an extension and exaggeration of previous tendencies. Parties rarely present issues in ways derived from more general analyses of the country's economic difficulties. Rather, they display a marked predilection for the quick-fix approach, exemplified most recently by the Liberal plan to spend several billion dollars on short-term job creation. Even free trade, an issue with enormous long-term potential, assumed some of these characteristics in the course of the 1988 campaign. In their scramble for immediate electoral advantage, parties try to assess the state of the public mind at the moment and tailor their issue agendas accordingly.

Notes

1. See Peter Woolstencroft, "Doing Politics Differently: The Conservative Party and the Campaign of 1993," in Alan Frizzell, Jon H. Pammett, and Anthony Westell, eds., *The Canadian General Election of 1993* (Ottawa: Carleton University Press, 1994), pp. 9-26.

2. See Robert Krause, "The Progressive Conservative Campaign: Mission Accomplished," in Alan Frizzell, Jon H. Pammett, and Anthony Westell, eds., *The Canadian General Election of 1988* (Ottawa: Carleton University Press, 1989), pp. 15-25.

3. See Harold D. Clarke et al., *Absent Mandate: The Politics of Discontent*, 1st ed. (Toronto: Gage Educational Publishing Company, 1984), p. 23.

4. For a model of elections in which parties declare subjects on which they have an advantage to be issues, see Ian Budge and Dennis J. Farlie, *Explaining and Predicting Elections* (London: George Allen and Unwin, 1983). See also Harold D. Clarke, Euel Elliott, and Barry Seldon, "Key Assumptions Reconsidered: A Utility Function Analysis of Competing Models of Party Support," *Journal of Theoretical Politics* 6 (1994): 289-305.

5. These and other surveys analysed here are described in more detail in the appendix, "Data Sources."

6. Jack Aubrey, "Chrétien favours experiment to link welfare to work," *The Ottawa Citizen*, 21 September 1993.

7. Mark Kennedy, "The surprise social policy agenda," *The Ottawa Citizen*, 14 October 1994, p. A3.

8. For a comprehensive account of the negotiation of the Free Trade Agreement between the United States and Canada, see G. Bruce Doern and Brian W. Tomlin, *Faith and Fear: The Free Trade Story* (Toronto: Stoddart, 1991). A critical analysis of trade policy can be found in Glen Williams, *Not For Export*, 3rd ed. (Toronto: McClelland and Stewart, 1994).

9. Harold D. Clarke and Allan Kornberg, "Risky Business: Partisan Volatility and Electoral Choice in Canada, 1988," *Electoral Studies* 6 (1992): 138-56.

10. Liberal Party of Canada, *Creating Opportunity: The Liberal Plan for Canada* (Ottawa: Supply and Services, 1993), p. 24.

11. See Janine Brodie, "Women and the Electoral Process in Canada," in Kathy Megyery, ed., *Women and Canadian Politics: Toward Equity in Representation*, vol. 6 of the Research Studies of the Royal Commission on Electoral Reform and Party Financing (Toronto: Dundurn Press, 1991), pp. 23-24 (esp. Table 1.7). See also Sylvia Bashevkin, *True Patriot Love: The Politics of Canadian Nationalism* (Toronto: Oxford University Press, 1991), esp. Chapter 6.

12. Liberal Party of Canada, *Creating Opportunity*, p. 20.

Party (Dis)Loyalties

A major consequence of decades of brokerage politics is that no party has been able to count on a stable base of supporters who will remain loyal to it through the bad times as well as the good. Uncertain about where the parties *really* stand on the implications of the major restructuring projects of recent decades, individuals have been willing to desert one party, to seek out another, and in general exhibit very little partisan loyalty. Rather than having a strong, stable commitment to a political party, for both provincial and federal elections, a voter is much more likely to be weakly committed, to swing from one party to another, and to prefer different parties in different elections. Such flexible partisanship helps to account for volatility in electoral choice and provides fertile ground for the rapid rise of new parties and political actors.

Flexible Partisanship
Parties have adopted more or less the same pragmatic approach to problem solving and are not readily distinguishable by their ties to strong social or ideological cleavages in the population. In consequence, the events, personalities, or issues of the day serve to guide their choices, and attachments to political parties are highly flexible.

The proposition that people develop psychological attachments to political parties has played an important role in studies of voting and elections.[1] In Canada, national surveys conducted since the mid-1960s consistently reveal that large majorities of people think of themselves as supporters of a political party. However, these surveys demonstrate an additional important point, namely that Canadian voters' commitments to parties are often limited and contingent.

Figure 3.1

Federal Party Identification: 1965–93

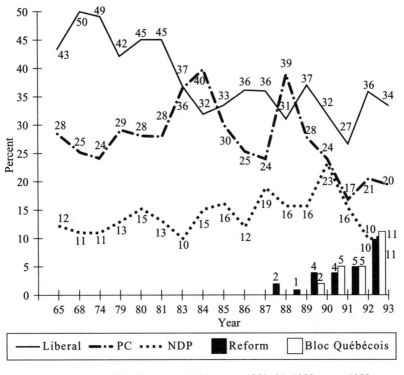

Source: 1974–80 – CNES; 1981 – QOL; 1983–91, 1993 – PSC; 1992 – CRS.

Partisan attachments in Canada can exhibit considerable change between successive elections. To a large extent, such change parallels the fortunes of the parties in these contests. As Figure 3.1 illustrates, the dramatic success of the Reform Party and the Bloc Québécois in attracting votes in 1993 was accompanied by the presence of substantial numbers of identifiers with these parties (10% and 11%, respectively). Five years earlier, the percentage of Reform partisans had been less than 1%, and the BQ did not even exist. The growth of identification with the new parties contrasts with the situation for the Conservatives, whose cohort of partisans fell precipitously from 39% in 1988 to 20% in 1993. Similarly, the NDP share fell from 16% to 11%. For their part, the Liberals enjoyed a modest resurgence in the early 1990s, with their group of partisans rising from 27% in 1991 to 34% in 1993. Thus, changes in the vote share for various parties are accompanied by parallel movements in the patterns of more general support for them.

These changes in the direction of party identification in recent years are not unique. As Figure 3.1 also shows, the Liberals enjoyed a considerable advantage over their rivals during the 1960s and 1970s, but this evaporated in the early 1980s. Between 1980 and 1984, the Liberal partisan share fell from 45% to 33%, and the Conservative one moved sharply upward from 28% to 40%. At that time, one might have speculated that these figures signalled an important, enduring shift in the relative strength of these parties. The change proved transitory, however, and although the Conservatives were able to rally a large number of their 1984 supporters again in 1988, many of these 1984 and 1988 Tory partisans proved to be "fair-weather friends" who quickly abandoned their PC identifications after the party won these elections.

The propensity to change partisan attachments is not confined to particular regional or other groups in the population. Rather, ties between parties and various social groups are easily severed, and relationships between socio-demographic cleavages and party support tend to be weak and changeable.[2] For example, as Table 3.1 shows, large decreases in the percentage of Conservative partisans between 1988 and 1993 were evident in all areas of the country, including Quebec and the West—the two regions that had provided the foundation for the Tory electoral victories of 1984 and 1988. In 1993, these regions were the ones that opted strongly for the two new parties, Reform and the Bloc Québécois. Nor is partisanship firmly anchored by other attributes such as gender or social class. In this respect, the erosion of Conservative and NDP partisan attachments between 1988 and 1993 among both men and women and all income categories (see Table 3.1) is illustrative of more general tendencies. Large-scale movements in the direction of partisanship across a wide variety of socio-demographic categories from one election to the next are not unusual, and the observation that a party currently is enjoying strong support from a particular group of voters is not a reliable indicator that it will continue to do so.

It is evident that when the times seem to call for change, many people find their partisan attachments are sufficiently flexible to allow them to shift to another party. This helps to account for the high level of volatility that characterizes Canadian electoral politics. The massive repudiation of the governing Progressive Conservatives in 1993 in the wake of widespread discontent with how they had handled the country's economic and constitutional problems is a striking example of this volatility, but it is not unique. Dissatisfaction with how governments were handling these issues in the 1970s and early 1980s was sufficient to motivate substantial changes in party support at those times as well. Before the Mulroney-led Conservatives were returned to power in the turbulent election of 1988, three successive governing parties went down to defeat—the Liberals in 1979, the Conservatives in 1980, and the Liberals in 1984. Indeed, prior to the Tories'

Table 3.1

Federal Party Identification by Gender, Income, and Region: 1993, 1988

A. 1993 **Party Identification**

	Liberal	PC	NDP	Reform	BQ	Other	None
Canada	34%	20	11	10	11	1	14
Gender							
Men	30%	20	9	13	13	1	15
Women	38%	20	12	7	9	X	13
Income							
< $20,000 per year	39%	14	12	8	12	X	15
$20,000–39,999	33%	19	11	11	16	X	10
$40,000–59,999	34%	21	10	13	7	1	15
$60,000–69,999	36%	15	11	8	9	2	20
$70,000 or more	32%	26	9	9	11	0	14
Region							
Atlantic	48%	21	7	2	0	1	21
Quebec	29%	12	1	0	42	0	17
Ontario	43%	22	12	10	0	X	13
Prairies	27%	25	13	24	0	X	11
British Columbia	22%	23	26	18	0	2	8

B. 1988 **Party Identification**

	Liberal	PC	NDP	Reform	Other	None
Canada	31%	39	16	1	2	11
Gender						
Men	29%	42	15	1	2	12
Women	33%	36	17	1	3	10
Income						
< $20,000 per year	26%	36	21	1	3	13
$20,000–39,999	32%	38	16	1	3	11
$40,000–59,999	29%	41	17	1	1	12
$60,000–69,999	38%	41	14	0	2	5
$70,000 or more	33%	47	9	0	3	7
Region						
Atlantic	43%	36	12	0	X	10
Quebec	28%	37	13	0	3	18
Ontario	37%	37	15	0	2	10
Prairies	24%	49	15	2	2	8
British Columbia	22%	40	30	1	4	4

X less than .5%

Source: 1988, 1993 – PSC.

1988 success, the last post-World War II federal government to achieve consecutive parliamentary majorities was that of Louis St. Laurent, who led the Liberals to victory in 1949 and 1953. Election outcomes thus reinforce the story that the survey evidence tells us; the hallmark of partisanship in Canada is its flexibility.[3]

Just how flexible *is* the Canadian electorate? To answer this question, it is useful to assess partisan attachments in terms of three properties: (1) stability over time, (2) intensity, and (3) consistency across the federal and provincial levels of the political system.[4] For a large segment of the electorate, one or more of these properties of partisanship undergo change over relatively brief periods of time. Depending upon which survey is consulted, from about one-third to slightly over one-half of those identifying with a party recall that they previously supported another one, and repeated interviews with the same people indicate that the actual amount of change is even greater. Moreover, at any given time, a sizable minority of those who claim to identify with a party do not exhibit intense partisan feelings; rather they describe their party attachments as "not very strong." Variations in levels and patterns of support for federal and provincial parties are noteworthy as well. Differences in partisanship in federal and provincial politics affect the nature of party attachments at *both* levels. All three characteristics of partisanship—stability, intensity, and consistency—need to be taken into account to understand how voters relate to political parties, and how this relationship affects their electoral behaviour.

Using these three properties of partisanship, we divide the electorate into two categories. *Durable partisans* are those who identify with the same party in federal and provincial politics, and whose federal partisan attachments are stable over time and at least moderately intense. *Flexible partisans*, in contrast, include those who either: (1) identify with different federal and provincial parties, or (2) have a weak attachment to a federal party, or (3) have changed their federal party identification over time. Using this classification scheme, analyses of data from national surveys conducted since the late 1960s consistently reveal the presence of large numbers of flexible partisans. For example, as Figure 3.2 shows, fully 74% and 76%, respectively, of those interviewed in 1988 and 1993 are flexible partisans. Although these percentages are larger than that for 1984 (66%), the differences are not dramatic. Since 1965, surveys have revealed that from three-fifths to two-thirds of the electorate falls into the flexible partisan category.

The presence of many flexible partisans is related to the brokerage strategies pursued by the parties that have long dominated the electoral arena. Since such strategies are seen as *the* recipe for electoral success, the parties have had little incentive to discuss basic and potentially divisive issues. Although the dynamics of an election campaign may occasionally

Figure 3.2

**Flexible Partisanship and Political Interest
in the Canadian Electorate: 1984–93**

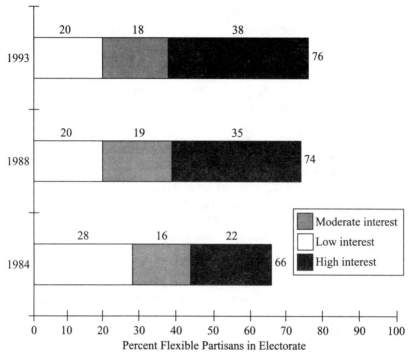

Source: 1984 – CNES; 1988 – CPS; 1993 – PSC.

force discussion of some elements of the major projects to the forefront, as happened in 1988 with free trade, this is very much the exception. Recognizing that voters are accustomed to appeals cast in terms of quick and painless relief for national ailments, parties readily provide them. This mutually reinforcing relationship between parties and voters perpetuates high levels of instability in a system where parties lack a firm basis of support in a volatile and oftentimes dissatisfied electorate.

Figure 3.2 also shows that many flexible partisans have high levels of political interest[5] and that the number of such persons is greater now than it was in 1984. However, flexible partisans with high levels of political interest, together with those less interested in politics, have always been present in substantial numbers. As we will see in Chapter 5, these combinations of partisanship and political interest condition how various long- and short-term forces affect voting behaviour and election outcomes.

Changing Parties, Changing Votes

One important indicator of the high level of partisan flexibility in the Canadian electorate is found in the changes in its attitudes and behaviour over relatively short periods of time. A change in partisanship may or may not be reflected in a switch in vote from one election to another. In certain circumstances, voters may decide to opt for a rival party's candidate in a particular election without abandoning their partisan attachments. For example, not all Liberals who voted for the Conservatives in the 1984 election thought of themselves as Tories, and not all Conservatives who voted Reform in 1993 thought of themselves as Reformers. More generally, in some countries, notably the United States with its frequent elections and long ballots, voters' ability to detach their preferences for particular candidates from their party identification is well documented.[6] In 1988, for example, some American voters sported bumper stickers proclaiming themselves "Democrats for Bush," and in 1992, some Democratic and Republican partisans were attracted by independent presidential candidate Ross Perot. In parliamentary systems such as Britain, partisan ties are more likely to change in tandem with changes in voting behaviour, but the distinction between partisanship and electoral choice is nevertheless important.

In Canada, panel surveys in which the same voters are reinterviewed two or more times enable us to study the degree of change in both partisanship and vote. In studies spanning the period between successive elections (1984-88 and 1988-93), fewer than half of all panel respondents maintained the same party identification *and* vote (see Table 3.2). Consistent with the larger difference between the 1988 and 1993 election outcomes, as compared to the difference between the 1984 and 1988 ones, the percentage of panel respondents with both stable partisan attachments and stable votes for the 1988-93 panel is smaller (30%) than that for the 1984-88 panel (48%). Nevertheless, the latter figure indicates considerable instability in partisanship and voting, and it is identical to that for an earlier (1974-79) panel study.[7] Moreover, the magnitude of change in both partisanship and vote is impressive over shorter time intervals. Thus, a 1979-80 panel shows that only 58% maintained the same party identification and vote in two federal elections separated by only nine months. These figures take into account *all* types of change, including non-identification and non-voting. Both of the latter are as important for understanding partisanship and voting behaviour as are direct switches between parties.

The overall similarity of the results of the several panel studies conducted over a 20-year span suggests that the patterns of change observed in them reflect a fundamental quality of the relationship between voters and parties in Canada. These patterns are not specific to any particular set of

Table 3.2

Turnover in Partisanship and Vote: 1984–88 and 1988–93 Panels

1984–88 Panel   **Partisanship**

	Same Party	Different Parties	Moving to or from non-identification	Total
Voting for same party in 1984 and 1988 elections	48	5	5	58
Voting for different parties in 1984 and 1988 elections	12	10	5	27
Moving to or from non-voting	8	3	4	15
Total	68	18	14	100

1988–93 Panel   **Partisanship**

	Same Party	Different Parties	Moving to or from non-identification	Total
Voting for same party in 1988 and 1993 elections	30	5	4	39
Voting for different parties in 1988 and 1993 elections	17	24	9	50
Moving to or from non-voting	4	5	2	11
Total	51	34	15	100

Source: 1984–88 – CPS; 1988–93 – PSC.

issues, personalities, or events. To be sure, the many important political events that occurred between 1988 and 1993 (the failure of the Meech Lake and Charlottetown constitutional accords, the birth of the Bloc Québécois, the implementation of the Canada-U.S. Free Trade Agreement, and the GST), and a serious economic downturn set the stage for a dramatic reversal in the fortunes of the Conservative government, and the electoral successes of the Liberals, Reform, and the BQ. But, as noted above, the basic patterns of change in partisanship and voting between 1988 and 1993 were simply exaggerated versions of those occurring between earlier pairs of elections. The 1988-93 period, then, witnessed an amplification of the kind of instability in political attitudes and behaviour that has long been characteristic of the Canadian electorate. Regardless of the specific directions of such movements or their aggregate effects in particular elections, the total amount of individual-level instability in partisanship and voting has been substantial for some time.

The 1988-93, 1984-88, and earlier panel studies alert us to another source of political change, namely the entry and exit of *transient* voters, persons who cast ballots in one election, but not in another. The potential impact of such "turnout" effects on election outcomes is considerable. This depends, of course, on the relative success of the parties in getting their supporters to the polls, and on how voters and non-voters are distributed across various ridings, some of which may be characterized by very close contests. As shown in Table 3.2, there are also small groups who do change partisan attachments, but who fail to vote in an election. Taken together, the groups of stable and unstable partisans moving into or out of the active electorate can make significant contributions to an election outcome, although at any given time, the groups are not large. The panel studies indicate that for most Canadians, non-voting and non-partisanship are temporary conditions associated with the circumstances of particular elections, rather than enduring expressions of disaffection from all parties or the political process more generally.

Both the 1984-88 and 1988-93 panels show that there are people who change their vote from one election to another, but not their party identification. In the 1984-88 panel, 12% fell into this category; in the 1988-93 panel, 17% did so (Table 3.2). There is, then, a sizable cadre of voters whose party commitments can survive the effects of the short-term forces that caused them to choose another party's candidate in a particular election. For such persons, partisanship is both more stable than vote, and able to withstand changes in it. However, there also are sizable contingents of people in the two panels who changed both their party attachments *and* their votes. In the 1984-88 panel, 10% exhibited this pattern of attitudes and behaviour, a figure that is quite similar to that for earlier panels. In the 1988-93 panel, the figure moved sharply upward to 24%, reflecting the movement of many Conservatives to the two new parties, along with the shift of a large number of previous NDP supporters to other parties. The fact that a change in partisanship frequently accompanies a change in vote represents an important aspect of the flexibility of partisanship in the Canadian electorate.

In addition to those who either retain or change their partisanship between elections, the surveys disclose a group of people who do not identify with *any* party at one or more times. For example, 11% of those participating in the 1988 cross-sectional survey said they did not identify with any of the federal parties. However, the 1988-93 panel study shows that a much smaller percentage (5%) continued to report being a non-identifier when interviewed in two surveys conducted five years apart. The notion of being a political "independent" does not have wide currency in Canada, and most people without a partisan attachment at a given time do not consistently reject a party affiliation. Instead, they are flexible partisans caught at a given moment in the process of moving from one party to another.

Like a single frame clipped from a strip of movie film, non-partisanship in Canada is a static fragment of a dynamic process. Although the number of true non-partisans is very small, the incidence of occasional non-identification is much more widespread than it appears in any cross-sectional survey. For example, in a three-wave panel study conducted in 1974, 1979, and 1980, 22% of the respondents said that they lacked a party identification at one of the three times they were interviewed. However, only 2% reported being non-identifiers at all three times. Persons participating in the 1988-90-93 three-wave panel tell almost exactly the same story; 23% said they were non-identifiers during one of the three interviews, but only 3% did so on all three occasions. Movements toward and away from non-partisanship can be as important a source of flexibility as directional change.

Flexibility is woven into the very fabric of partisanship in Canada. Because it is, the mix of short-term forces in the political arena at a given time has large effects on the distribution of party identification, and the balance of party strength is often highly volatile. Since most voters lack durable partisan attachments, parties cannot count on those who supported them in previous elections to see them through difficult times. Each election is a new ball game, and parties must assiduously practise the arts of brokerage politics to rebuild their fragile electoral bases. Even if the parties were not inclined to employ brokerage strategies, the necessity of putting together at least a partially new coalition for each election would encourage this kind of behaviour, and the political outlook that goes with it. Although new parties such as the Bloc Québécois and Reform may claim that they are "pas comme les autres" and eschew the strategies practised by their old-line antagonists, doing so runs counter to well-established realities of Canadian electoral politics. There is no evidence that the new parties' partisan bases are immune to the strong and frequently volatile short-term forces that can quickly turn "winners" into "losers" or vice versa.

Strength of Party Feeling

Moving from one party to another is the most dramatic expression of discontinuities in partisanship over time. But partisan feelings also might vary in intensity without necessarily being accompanied by a change from one party to another or from partisanship to non-partisanship. In fact, changes in intensity are quite common; about half of all directionally stable partisans in the 1984-88 and 1988-93 panels (47% and 52%, respectively) reported a change in the intensity of their party feelings (see Table 3.3). These figures are very similar to those for the earlier 1974-79 panel, and they suggest that changes in intensity are a normal feature of Canadians' partisan attitudes; they are not idiosyncratic reactions to a particular set of political events, personalities, or issues.

Table 3.3

Changes in Intensity of Party Identification by Stability of Party Identification: 1984–88 and 1988–93 Panels

Directional Stability of Party Identification

Intensity of Party Identification	1984–88		1988–93	
	Same Party	Different Party	Same Party	Different Party
Intensity Strengthening	27%	39%	21%	30%
Intensity Weakening	20	22	31	21
Intensity Unchanged	53	39	48	49

Source: 1984–88 – CPS; 1988–93 – PSC.

The panel surveys also do not suggest any overall weakening of partisanship, even for those reporting a change in party attachments. In fact, changers in the 1984-88 and 1988-93 panels display a stronger attachment to their "new" parties than to the ones they abandoned (see Table 3.3); and for the earlier 1974-79 panel, the percentages reporting stronger and weaker attachments to new parties are virtually identical. Thus, despite the relatively high degree of individual-level dynamism in both direction and intensity of party attachments, surveys taken at the time of elections do not show any trend toward weaker partisanship. Also, as measured by the series of national cross-sectional election surveys, the intensity of partisanship and the incidence of non-identifiers has been quite stable in the aggregate over the entire period for which such data are available.

It is important to note that these studies have been conducted in the immediate aftermath of national election campaigns in which voters were exposed to a barrage of media reports about the parties and their leaders and candidates, and a multitude of messages from the parties themselves. This information activates partisan sentiments and mobilizes party support and, because it does, data about partisanship generated by a series of post-election surveys may not enable one to discern trends that would be apparent if surveys for *non-election* years were also considered. The latter kind of data are available for every year but one (1982) since 1981, and they clearly indicate that the strength of partisanship does ebb and flow with the occurrence of elections. Across the 1979-93 period, the average percentage of "very strong" party identifiers is 26% in election years and 18% in non-election ones (see Figure 3.3). Similarly, the average percentages of non-identifiers in election and non-election years during this time span are 12% and 19%, respectively (see Figure 3.4).

Figure 3.3

Percentages of "Very Strong" Federal Party Identifiers: 1979–93

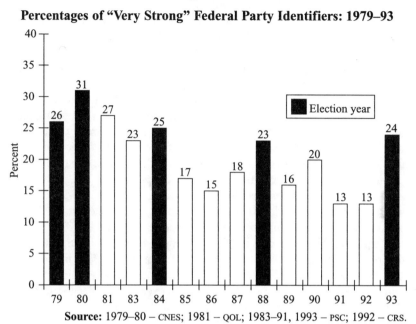

Source: 1979–80 – CNES; 1981 – QOL; 1983–91, 1993 – PSC; 1992 – CRS.

Figure 3.4

Percentages of Federal Party Non-Identifiers: 1979–93

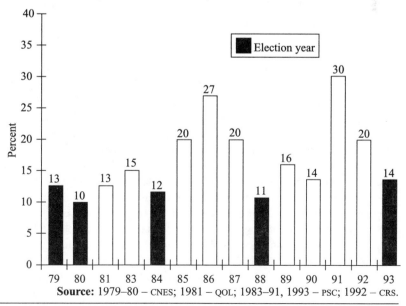

Source: 1979–80 – CNES; 1981 – QOL; 1983–91, 1993 – PSC; 1992 – CRS.

But there is another story too. As Figures 3.3 and 3.4 document, differences in the percentages of very strong identifiers and non-identifiers in election and non-election years have tended to be larger over the past decade than was the case in the early 1980s. This pattern, in turn, suggests the presence of a general downward trend in the percentage of very strong identifiers and an upward one in the percentage of non-identifiers. Time series analyses designed to detect such trends confirm their existence.[8] Controlling for the mobilizing effects of elections, which, on average, are associated with an increase of over 5% in the number of very strong party identifiers, and a nearly 6% drop in non-identifiers, very strong partisanship has decreased by approximately seven-tenths of a percent per year. The upward trend in non-identifiers is weaker, but the number of such persons has increased by about four-tenths of a percent per year.

These trends in the incidence and strength of partisan attachments suggest that aggregate levels of party support have eroded since the late 1970s. Undoubtedly, this facilitates large-scale changes in party support such as that which occurred in 1993. However, it is important to note that this tendency toward a loosening of party ties has taken place in a political context where many voters did not have strong partisan allegiances to begin with. As such, the weakening of partisanship over the past decade amplifies an already high potential for short-term forces to influence party fortunes.

Federal and Provincial Loyalties

The powerful role exercised by the provinces in the Canadian political system requires that an examination of the nature of partisanship must consider the provincial level, as well as the federal one. Parties' federal and provincial organizations maintain distinct identities and, in some provinces, party systems at the two levels differ markedly. These federal-provincial differences affect partisan attachments in a direct and meaningful way. Only a minority of people interviewed since the mid-1960s report feeling the same degree of attachment to the same party at both the federal and provincial levels. The 1988 and 1993 survey data are illustrative. In the former year, 38% were fully consistent (direction and strength) across both levels. In 1993, depending upon the classification of Bloc Québécois partisans, the figure is 42%[9] (see Figure 3.5). Ignoring the variations in intensity of feeling, 64% in 1988 and 62% in 1993 are classified as directionally consistent identifiers. These levels of directional consistency are similar to those for four election surveys conducted between 1974 and 1984—the average percentage of such persons in those studies is 62%.

Two other points about federal-provincial partisan consistency are noteworthy. First, substantial minorities actually identify with different parties in federal and provincial politics. In 1993, 21% did so[10] (Figure 3.5).

Figure 3.5

Variations in Federal and Provincial
Partisanship: 1988, 1993

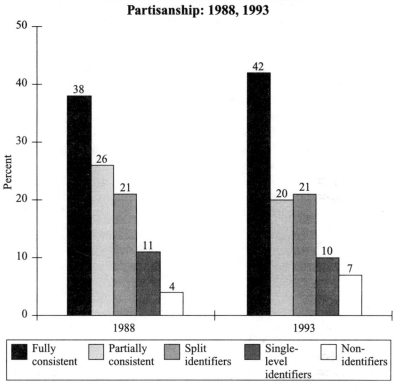

Source: 1988 – PSC; 1993 – PSC.

This figure is quite typical of those for earlier years, with the percentage of split identifiers varying from 18% in 1974 to 21% in 1988. Second, although the incidence of split identifiers and partisan inconsistency is greater in British Columbia and Quebec, where federal and provincial party systems historically have been very different, it is not confined to these provinces. Inconsistent partisans may be found in all parts of the country. Thus, in 1993, the percentage of split identifiers in British Columbia was 44%, whereas the figures for the Atlantic provinces, Ontario, and the Prairies were 11%, 15%, and 28%, respectively. In Quebec, if the BQ and PQ are treated as the same party, the percentage of split identifiers in 1993 (13%) is considerably lower than in earlier years. However, if these parties are considered as separate entities, the figure climbs to fully 52%, just 3% more than in 1988 when the BQ was not a player on the Quebec political stage.[11]

Inconsistency across levels of the federal system is a well-established feature of partisanship in Canada. It is not merely an artifact of the peculiarities of the party systems of one or two provinces, a result of a transitional phase of changes in party systems in some provinces, or a general rejection of federal parties in favour of provincial ones or vice versa. Moreover, partisan inconsistency influences electoral behaviour at both levels of government; persons with inconsistent partisan ties are more likely to switch their votes in federal and provincial elections than are those whose partisan attachments are consistent across levels.[12] Whatever one's federal or provincial party, the absence of a reinforcing attachment at the other level makes a vote switch in any given election more likely than it would be otherwise. However, inconsistent partisan ties in federal and provincial politics do not prompt voters to try to reconcile these differences by moving toward consistency or by abandoning a party at one level. Like those with consistent partisan attachments, inconsistent partisans react primarily to the forces at work in the federal or provincial political arenas at particular times.

Tracking Partisan Instability

Each of the components of partisanship examined in this chapter is related in some degree to the others. Each also contributes to the overall instability of partisanship over time and to the continuing volatility of Canadian elections. Persons whose partisan attachments are weak or inconsistent are more likely, for example, to report a change in the direction of their party identification over the course of any one of the panel studies. Similarly, those who changed or abandoned their party identification at sometime in the recent past are more likely to do so again. Although a number of these variations in partisanship can occur together, they should not necessarily be considered to be of the same magnitude. Looking at two of the components of partisanship, one may think of them in terms of a hierarchy of partisan instability. Foremost in this hierarchy is a switch in the direction of one's federal partisanship, followed by any movement toward or away from non-identification, and finally, by variations in the intensity of partisan feelings. The different types of federal partisan change in the 1984-88 and 1988-93 panels are summarized in terms of this hierarchy in Figure 3.6. Here, a person who reports more than one type of change in federal party identification is classified in terms of the higher type only. This produces an ordering of the degree of change.

Some degree of change in federal partisanship was widespread between 1988 and 1993. Only 24% of those interviewed in 1988 and 1993 reported that they identified with the same party at the same level of intensity. Over this period, 26% stayed with their party but changed the intensity of their identifications, and another 18% either acquired or abandoned an identification. Fully 33% actually switched their

64

Figure 3.6

Summary of Changes in Federal Partisanship:
1984–88, 1988–93

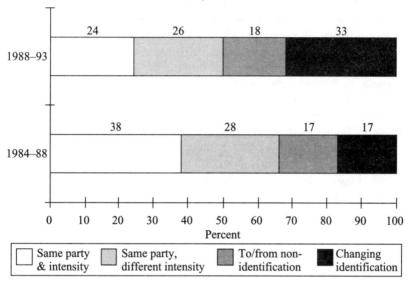

Source: 1984–88 – CPS; 1988–93 – PSC.

identifications from one party to another. Although undoubtedly impressive, these levels of change are not different in kind from those in earlier periods including the 1984-88 one, which witnessed the re-election of an incumbent federal government. Between 1984 and 1988, only 38% maintained the same party identification with the same level of intensity, 45% either varied the intensity of their partisanship or moved to or from a party, and 17% changed direction. Nor are the 1980s atypical; data from panel studies conducted in the 1970s tell much the same story.[13] Substantial levels of all types of partisan change are always apparent, and the cohort of fully stable partisans is always a distinct minority. Again, the high levels of instability in recent years represent simply an exaggerated version of long-standing tendencies in a volatile electorate.

Feelings About the Parties

Evidence concerning the instability in the electorate's feelings about the national parties is not confined to the data on partisan attachments. It is also apparent if one examines over-time movements in average scores for the parties on 100-point thermometer scales that measure levels of voters' "warmth" or "coolness" toward them. Feelings about the Liberals and

Conservatives have cooled since the late 1960s (Figure 3.7). Thus, for example, the Liberal thermometer scores have varied from a high of 65 in 1968, when Trudeaumania was at its height, to a low of 44 in 1984, the year when the "Tory tide" swept across the electoral landscape. Similarly, Conservative scores have varied from a high of 60 in 1984 to a low of 35 at the time of the party's disastrous defeat in 1993. Large-scale movements in feelings about the Liberals and Conservatives have occurred between successive elections. For the Conservatives, for example, their 1993 score is fully 19 points lower than that recorded in 1988, and their 1984 score is 9 points higher than that in 1980. Feelings about the NDP have been less volatile, but consistently below the neutral point (50) on the thermometer scale. Like the Tories, the New Democrats received their lowest score in 1993, dropping 8 points from that registered in 1988. Further, the average thermometer scores for all three of the old parties show a general downward trend over time.[14] Although this trend was quite modest prior to 1993, with average scores for the three parties decreasing from 56 points in 1968 to 50 points in 1984 and 1988, the average for these fell to 43 points in 1993. If all five parties' scores are included in the 1993 computation, the average is only 39 points.

The average thermometer scores accorded the two new parties in 1993 were also quite low when measured across the electorate as a whole—39 for Reform and 27 for the Bloc Québécois. Although the former party's score remains unimpressive (43) when only non-Quebeckers are considered, the BQ's score among that segment of the electorate that mattered for the party's success (that is, Quebeckers) was much higher (59). Indeed, the Bloc's score in 1993 was the fourth highest recorded for any party in any year.

Enhanced disaffection with the parties in 1993 is readily apparent, but it should not be interpreted as representing a marked departure from the past. Rather, the dominant message conveyed by the "feeling" thermometer data is that the reception accorded the parties by the public has been lukewarm at best. Indeed, since the late 1960s, the parties' thermometer scores have exceeded the 60-point mark on the 100-point scale on only two of 23 occasions, and the last time this occurred was in 1974. Canadians thus typically express little enthusiasm about any of the national parties. This lack of fervour is very consistent with the high levels of flexibility that characterize their partisan attachments.

Conclusion

Although the 1993 election result differed dramatically from the results of earlier elections, it is important to recall that some of those earlier outcomes also seemed to be harbingers of great political change. Evidence presented in this chapter suggests that such large-scale changes

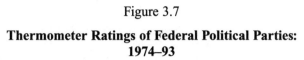

Figure 3.7

**Thermometer Ratings of Federal Political Parties:
1974–93**

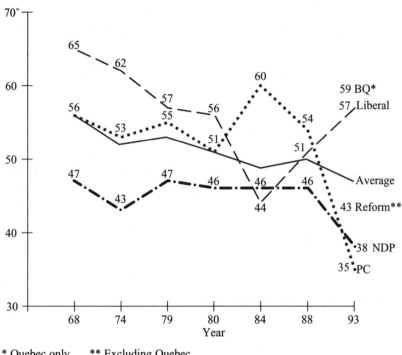

* Quebec only   ** Excluding Quebec

Source: 1968–80 – CNES; 1984–93 – PSC.

are always possible, given the volatility inherent in Canadians' partisan attachments, and their lack of strong positive feelings for the parties. High levels of individual-level partisan change are evident not just in the last decade, but in the 1960s and 1970s as well. Although partisan attachments have weakened in recent years and feelings about the parties have become more negative, these orientations do not constitute a sudden or sharp break with what has gone before. The lack of widespread affection for the parties, and the weakness, instability, and cross-level inconsistency of partisan attachments are long-standing features of Canadian politics. They have made it possible for parties to lose or gain large numbers of supporters over relatively brief periods of time, as short-term forces associated with salient issues and party leader images sway the attitudes and behaviour of many voters. The result is a party system through which the winds of change continually blow, sometimes with gale-like intensity.

Notes

1. For a discussion of the concept of party identification and its importance in the literature on voting behaviour, see R. Niemi and H. Weisberg, eds., *Controversies in Voting Behaviour*, 2nd ed. (Washington, D.C.: CQ Press, 1984), pp. 393-477. See also the several articles in *Political Behavior* 3 (September 1992). For studies of party identification in several different countries, see I. Budge, I. Crewe, and D. Farlie, eds., *Party Identification and Beyond* (London: Wiley, 1976).

2. See, for example, H.D. Clarke and M.C. Stewart, "Canada," in M. Franklin, T. Mackie, and H. Valen, eds., *Electoral Change: Responses to Evolving Social and Attitudinal Structures in Western Countries* (Cambridge: Cambridge University Press, 1992), Chapter 6. See also, H.D. Clarke, J. Jenson, L. LeDuc, and J.H. Pammett, *Political Choice in Canada* (Toronto: McGraw-Hill Ryerson, 1979; abridged, 1980), Chapter 4.

3. Flexibility of partisanship is not unique to Canada. See, for example, J. Thomassen, "Party Identification as a Cross-National Concept: Its Meaning in the Netherlands," in Budge et al., eds., *Party Identification and Beyond*, Chapter 4; L. LeDuc, "The Dynamic Properties of Party Identification: A Four Nation Comparison," *European Journal of Political Research* 9 (1981): 257-68; L. LeDuc, H.D. Clarke, J. Jenson, and J. Pammett, "Partisan Instability in Canada: Evidence From a New Panel Study," *American Political Science Review* 78 (1984): 470-83.

4. Clarke et al., *Political Choice in Canada*, Chapter 5. The sequence of questions used to measure partisanship in federal politics reads: "Generally speaking, in *federal* politics, do you usually think of yourself as a Liberal, Conservative, NDP, or what?...How strongly do you feel—very strongly, fairly strongly, or not very strongly?" Those not indicating any party identification are asked: "Do you generally think of yourself as being a little closer to one of the *federal* parties than to the others?" "If 'yes': Which party is that?" In 1993, the Bloc Québécois was added to the list of parties asked about in Quebec, and Reform was added in the rest of Canada. A parallel sequence of questions is used to measure partisanship in provincial politics.

5. Clarke et al., *Political Choice in Canada*. Chapter 10 discusses the construction of the typology of partisanship and political interest. The measure of political interest is a combination of expressed general interest in politics and interest in the most recent federal election.

6. P. Abramson, J. Aldrich, and D. Rohde, *Change and Continuity in the 1988 Elections* (Washington, D.C.: CQ Press, 1990), Chapter 8.

7. For this and other references to the earlier panel studies, see LeDuc et al., "Partisan Instability in Canada: Evidence From a New Panel Study," pp. 470-83, and Harold D. Clarke et al., *Absent Mandate*, 1st ed. (Toronto: Gage Educational Publishing Company, 1984), esp. pp. 63-75 and 152-58.

8. The dependent variables in these analyses are the percentage of very strong identifiers and the percentage of non-identifiers in a given year (1979-93). The independent variables include a constant, a linear trend term, and a dummy (0-1) variable designating each year as either an election year or a non-election year. See Harold D. Clarke and Allan Kornberg, "Evaluations and Evolution: Public Attitudes Toward Canada's Political Parties: 1965-91," *Canadian Journal of Political Science* 26 (1993): 287-312.

9. These figures are calculated counting the Bloc Québécois and the Parti Québécois as the same party. If the BQ and PQ are treated as separate parties, the percentages of fully and partially consistent partisans are 36% and 16%, respectively.

10. If the BQ and PQ are treated as different parties, the percentage of split identifiers for the country as a whole increases to 31%.

11. In 1988, the percentages of split identifiers by region were: Atlantic provinces, 10%; Quebec, 49%; Ontario, 12%; Prairies, 17%; British Columbia, 42%. Earlier surveys also reveal that split identifiers are present in every region. In 1974, for example, the percentages were: Atlantic provinces, 7%; Quebec, 23%; Ontario, 11%; Prairies, 23%; British Columbia, 35%.

12. See Clarke et al., *Political Choice in Canada* (Toronto: McGraw-Hill Ryerson, unabridged, 1979), pp. 301-8; H. Clarke and M. Stewart, "Partisan Inconsistency and Partisan Change in Federal States: The Case of Canada," *American Journal of Political Science* 31 (1987): 383-407; M. Martinez, "Partisan Reinforcement in Context and Cognition: Canadian Federal Partisanships," *American Journal of Political Science* 34 (1990): 822-45.

13. Across the 1974-79 panel, 34% maintained the same party identification at the same intensity; 29% maintained the same party identification but changed intensity; 20% moved to or from party identification and non-identification, and 17% changed their identification from one party to another. For the 1979-80 panel, where successive interviews were separated by only nine months, the comparable figures are 41%, 31%, 15%, and 13%, respectively.

14. If only the Liberals, Conservatives, and NDP are considered, the size of this negative trend is about −.43 points per year over the 1968-93 period. Including the nationwide thermometer scores for Reform and the BQ in the 1993 data strengthens the trend to −.52 points per year.

Leading
the Campaign

Campaigns matter. The extent to which the events of the campaign can determine the results of an election however has long been a matter of debate. In a world of strong party loyalties and enduring political issues, election campaigns would serve only to reinforce decisions already made by most voters. But we have seen that the Canadian political world is one in which party loyalties are weak and changeable, and in which the issue agenda can be altered rapidly. Brokerage parties will generally concentrate their energies on trying to find the right formula for victory. When their electoral prospects appear bleak, new issues, new tactics, or a new leader may seem attractive. But can an election be won or lost in the short period of time that is generally referred to as the campaign, when many people will make their actual voting decisions? Can a new leader or a new set of issue positions really overcome a party's past performance? In this chapter, we will examine the structure of Canadian election campaigns, the panaroma of images that they present to the voter, and the role that party leaders, electoral strategies, and the events of the campaign itself play in elections.

Campaigns: Long and Short

The concept of *the campaign,* as understood here, extends well beyond the formal 47-day period that commences with the call of an election. In parliamentary countries such as Canada, the initiative for calling an election normally rests with the government. Most governing parties begin to engage in the early steps of strategic campaign planning around the end of their third year in office, generally anticipating that an election will be called about a year hence. While there is no rule that prevents a governing party from serving its full five-year term in office, a party that does so gives up much of its strategic advantage and is rarely re-elected.[1] Early moves toward placing the governing party on an election footing are often evident in events such as a budget speech, a cabinet shuffle, or a party policy conference. Governing parties will generally try to ensure that all the "bad news" is well behind them as they begin to position themselves for an election. Opposition parties, anticipating and reacting to many of these activities, likewise begin to assume a state of election readiness as a government's term of office approaches its end.

The overall effect of these strategic manoeuvres is to lengthen considerably the period of time devoted to what can rightly be called campaigning. The period of a year or more in which a governing party devotes its attention toward improving its re-election prospects is sometimes referred to as the "long campaign."[2] While the events of the long campaign, which will ultimately affect the outcome of the election to follow, are less readily identifiable than those of the formal campaign period, they are often no less important. The election-related activities of the long campaign are often subtle, and blend easily into the day-to-day activities of government. The actions of parties and leaders, on the other hand, during the formal campaign period are direct, and are explicitly intended to engage the attention of the electorate and to influence their voting choice.

Naturally, attention tends to shift to the more directly observable activities of the formal campaign period once the election has been called. There is considerable evidence to suggest that the interest of the public is aroused in a variety of ways by the intensity of an election campaign. Only a small minority of voters report little or no interest in the events of a campaign (Figure 4.1). Most claim to be "very interested" or at least "fairly interested," a pattern that varies only slightly from one election to another. Through television and newspapers, the main vehicles by which the modern mass public acquires much of its political information, voters interpret the events of the campaign. Television has come to dominate this process. In 1988, about a third of the respondents said that they paid "little or no" attention to the newspapers, but only about one voter in six made such a statement regarding television (Table 4.1). The large audience attained by the televised debates in each of the last three elections attests to the potential of this medium. The messages that are transmitted to the public through debates, political advertising, commentary, and news programs are readily received by much of the electorate.

But what messages? It is not the media itself that initiates most of the information that forms the substance of an election campaign but rather the parties, their leaders, advisers, pollsters, and strategists. The people will ultimately decide, but their decision will be structured by the architects of

Figure 4.1

**Interest and Involvement in the Election Campaign:
1984–93**

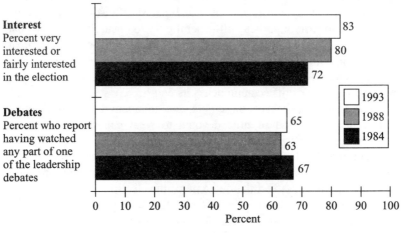

Interest
Percent very
interested or
fairly interested
in the election

83
80
72

1993
1988
1984

Debates
Percent who report
having watched
any part of one
of the leadership
debates

65
63
67

0   10   20   30   40   50   60   70   80   90   100
Percent

Source: 1984, 1988 – CNES; 1993 – PSC.

Table 4.1

Exposure to the Mass Media in Election Campaigns

Television		1984	1988
Watched political	Quite a bit, often	31%	57%
programs on television	Some, sometimes	38	27
during the campaign:	Seldom, never	31	16
Newspapers			
Read newspapers	Quite a bit, often	42%	38%
during the campaign:	Some, sometimes	31	31
	Seldom, never	27	31

Source: 1984, 1988 – CNES.

the campaign, who set the agenda and devise strategy. In a previous era, election campaigns were fought in each constituency by individual candidates, bound together only by their party affiliation and the basic elements of the party platform. Today, they are fought largely on television by the party leaders, relying on unseen strategists and advisers to guide them. In a sense then, the campaign is now more accessible to the public but also more remote. The images presented to the voter, of the party, the leader, and even the issues, are carefully designed to attract attention and support and to structure the voting decision. When a party succeeds in focussing the campaign on *its* agenda, it is often halfway down the road toward achieving its objectives.

Setting the Agenda

The struggle to control the issue focus of the campaign constitutes a major part of a party's electoral strategy. Given the centrality of the media, particularly television, in modern campaigns, it is sometimes argued that the media play a major role in setting the agenda.[3] But more accurately, it is the parties themselves and their professional strategists who attempt to promote their own issues through the media. Recent Canadian elections provide numerous examples of parties' successes and failures in the battle for the campaign agenda. In the 1979 election, for example, the Liberals enjoyed some degree of success in raising the salience of issues such as national unity and leadership, even though the opposition Conservatives tried to keep attention focussed on the economic record of the Trudeau government and on specific economic issues such as inflation.[4] In the 1988 election, the governing Conservatives attempted to de-emphasize the free trade issue, but that issue nevertheless came to dominate much of the campaign. Later however, they did enjoy some success in shifting attention to the leadership qualities of John Turner, and ultimately went on to win that election in spite of the unpopularity of the FTA with a large part of the electorate, as seen in Chapter 2.

The period leading up to the November 1988 election provides an example that is fairly typical with respect to a number of decisions taken by the government in anticipation of an election. Formal planning of the campaign began with the party conference in February, about seven months before the election call.[5] Provincial meetings and organizational planning followed, and various campaign themes were tested through polling and focus groups. Over the spring and summer, various federal projects were announced by the prime minister or members of the Cabinet. Slowly, the Conservatives' standing in the polls began to rise. By fall, the governing party was well positioned to fight a strong campaign. It had succeeded in structuring a large part of the agenda through the vehicle of the long campaign, even though it could not have fully anticipated the dramatic events that would follow once the formal campaign was under way. The theme chosen by the party for its campaign—"Managing Change"—was designed to portray the government's record in a positive light while at the same time keeping the focus of attention away from specific elements of its economic restructuring activities. Later in the campaign, the strong negative attacks on the leadership qualities of John Turner would serve much the same purpose.

The 1993 campaign, and the sequence of events leading up to it, is illustrative of the structure of a campaign that might be anticipated when a governing party is *not* firmly in control of the electoral agenda. The Conservatives' continued low standing in the polls and Mulroney's personal unpopularity appeared to doom the Tories' ambitions for a third term of office. The continuing grip of the recession plagued the economy. Preoccupation with constitutional issues in the aftermath of the failure of the Meech Lake Accord also disrupted what might have been a more normal election timetable. The referendum, which finally sealed the fate of the Mulroney constitutional initiatives, took place in October 1992, almost exactly four years after the 1988 election. Mulroney announced his intention to resign in February 1993, and the convention to choose his successor was scheduled for June.

The Conservatives thus drifted into the fifth year of their term without a clear election strategy except for the vague plans for party renewal that might come with a change in leadership. Kim Campbell's victory at the convention however put in place what was perhaps the only strategy that seemed to offer any hope of success to a party carrying so much baggage, namely a campaign focussing on the personal attributes of a new leader. Recognizing this fact, Campbell began her campaign almost immediately upon her assumption of the party leadership. Following a summer consisting primarily of pre-campaign electioneering ("the barbecue circuit" as it was dubbed in the press), the Conservatives recovered to what seemed to be a competitive position, about four points behind the Liberals according to most polls. Deprived of the strategic opportunities that a genuine "long campaign" might have afforded, Campbell sought to maximize the high visibility that came with the office of prime minister, even though the time available to her before the election had to be called was very short. This unusual "long campaign" appeared to have given Campbell and her party at least a fighting chance.

Whether the seemingly dramatic improvement in the Conservatives' re-election prospects, which took place following Mulroney's resignation and Campbell's selection as leader, was illusion or reality may never be known. The 1993 election provides a compelling example of the strategic battle for the agenda that was waged between the parties over the course of that campaign. The Conservatives, saddled with the legacy of nine years in power and the unpopularity of Brian Mulroney and many of his policies, centred their campaign around Kim Campbell and the desirability of a "new style of politics." The Liberals countered with their "Red Book" strategy, which kept the focus of attention on policy questions, particularly those associated with economic performance. Thus, while the Conservatives sought as much as possible to focus the campaign around personalities, the Liberals were ultimately successful in shifting attention away from the leader and back toward the record of the party in power. The other parties meanwhile enjoyed mixed success in trying to identify *both* Liberals and Conservatives with the failed policies of the past.

The 1993 campaign bears some similarity to that of 1984, in which a change of leadership prior to the election likewise appeared to offer some hope to a governing party plagued by its past.[6] But that hope quickly vanished in the first few weeks of the formal campaign. The theme introduced in the Conservatives' first television advertising foray of the 1993 campaign ("It's Time") seemed a particularly vacuous choice for a party with a long record in office. Probably, it was meant by Tory strategists to convey the sense of a new beginning under Kim Campbell, while shifting attention away from the economic restructuring and constitutional policies and from the Tories' performance in office. But it reminded many observers of an equally empty and ill-starred slogan chosen by a Liberal government ("The Land Is Strong") in the disastrous campaign of 1972. And Jean Chrétien was quick to grasp the tactical potential. "It's time," he told reporters in an initial response to the Conservative theme, "to throw them out!"

Canadian elections are not "presidential" contests, important as the party leaders have become to modern campaigns. While changing its leader can give a party a new look, and some of the components of a new image, it will not transform voters' perceptions of the party overnight. Over time, the images of all of Canada's political parties are subject to very substantial change, given the relatively weak linkages to factors such as ideology or social cleavages. Nevertheless, it would have been unlikely that Kim Campbell could have, in a few months, completely transformed the image of the Conservative Party away from the style, performance, policies, and issues so readily associated with its nine years in power under Brian Mulroney.

Image Politics

While the images of parties and their leaders are linked together in various ways, they are not identical. Voters form images of the parties based partly on the perceptions of leaders and partly on other, often policy- or performance-related factors. Voters who had been hostile toward Mulroney for instance may have disliked certain of his personal qualities, or may have disapproved of policies associated with him such as the Free Trade Agreement or the GST.[7] Likewise, voters form impressions of the leaders that are partly linked to partisan images and partly independent of these. Leaders who have enjoyed a long presence on the national political stage, such as Trudeau or Mulroney, become progressively more closely identified with their parties in the minds of many voters. Trudeau's successors gradually placed their own stamp on the Liberal Party, but many of the associations with Trudeau's personality, style, and policies remained.

Similarly, Brian Mulroney's retirement from public life did not immediately remove from the image of his party all of the factors associated with his period of leadership. From the perspective of Conservative campaign strategists in 1993, distancing Campbell and the party from Mulroney became a major preoccupation. But given the obvious linkages between party and leader images, such a task was nearly impossible in the time available. Campbell had been prime minister for less than two months at the time of the election call, while Mulroney had held the position for more than nine years.

By their very nature, the personal images of party leaders tend to contain both changeable and stable elements. Most new political leaders do not enter public life with highly developed public images. Neither Pierre Trudeau nor Brian Mulroney was a well-known figure at the time that he assumed the party leadership.[8] The traits that would later come to dominate the personal images of both men were visible only in embryonic form during their first few years in office. Voters quite early recognized Trudeau's intelligence and leadership skills and Mulroney's confidence and self-assurance. But later, Trudeau came to be seen by many voters as "arrogant," and Mulroney as a man who "could not be trusted." Some of these traits, as perceived by the public, were as much a function of Trudeau and Mulroney's actions in office as of particular personal qualities. Having relentlessly attacked John Turner during the 1984 campaign over the issue of patronage appointments, Mulroney dispensed them freely as prime minister. He engaged in dubious tactics such as "packing" the Senate in order to force through the unpopular GST. Had Mulroney chosen to stay on and fight the 1993 election, it is unlikely that even the most sophisticated advertising campaign could have measurably changed the unfavourable public image that clung to him at the end of his second term in office.

If the task of an established party leader is to change or refine a well-defined image, the challenge of a new leader is somewhat different. Many of the components of leader images described above have been developed in multiple election campaigns or through activities in government. Leaders of smaller parties, or those chosen as leaders when their parties are in opposition, do not have the same opportunities to establish highly visible public images. The day-to-day activities of Parliament do not command the levels of public attention found in the intensity of an election campaign. Before he became prime minister in 1979, Joe Clark had led his party for three years, but was still an unknown quantity to many voters. Similarly, Audrey McLaughlin's leadership of the NDP for the three years prior to the 1993 election campaign provided her with few opportunities to establish her credentials with the public. It is really only through the campaign itself that the leaders of parties that have not been in power can begin to command the attention needed to firmly establish themselves with the voters.

Figure 4.2

Thermometer Ratings of Party Leaders:
1974–93

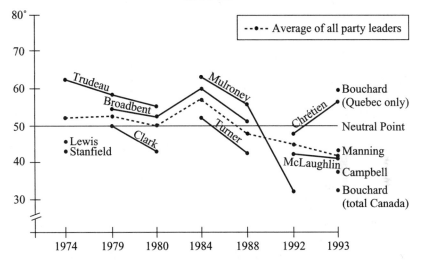

Source: 1974–80 – CNES; 1984, 1988, 1993 – PSC; 1992 – CRS.

The thermometer scale measures of feeling toward various party leaders, which have been included in surveys since 1968, provide a convenient summary of the feelings of the electorate toward individual leaders, and also permit comparisons among leaders and across time (Figure 4.2). It is evident that there has been a steady erosion of public support for political leaders, both as individuals and collectively. This pattern is perhaps most evident in the case of the two longest serving prime ministers over the past two decades, Pierre Trudeau and Brian Mulroney. At the time of his first election in 1984, Mulroney was well regarded by the public; his rating of 63 on the thermometer scale was second only to that of Pierre Trudeau at the peak of his popularity in 1968. Within four years, Mulroney's rating had dropped to barely neutral on the scale, and by the time of the referendum in 1992 he had recorded the lowest rating of any political leader in recent Canadian history, eclipsing the low point registered by John Turner in 1988.[9] Almost all party leaders of the past two decades have declined in public esteem from the benchmark established in their first election campaign.[10] This general pattern of decline is evident in the average ratings given all political leaders over the past two decades (Figure 4.2), as well as in the cases of individual leaders who have fought more than one election campaign. Leaders such as Robert Stanfield, Joe Clark, John Turner, or Ed Broadbent all finished their political careers with a lower rating on the thermometer scale than that which they had enjoyed in their first election campaign. Even other new political leaders such as Audrey McLaughlin or Preston Manning have not received high ratings on this overall summary measure of public affect. Clearly, the Canadian public in recent years has been disillusioned with its political leaders, regardless of party or issue considerations.

In a number of studies, respondents have also been asked to comment on qualities that they liked or disliked about individual political leaders. Ratings of leaders on particular attributes or "traits" have also been employed in some studies to measure particular components of a leader's public image.[11] Together, these measures provide a more comprehensive picture of the public's perceptions of political leadership.[12] Personality rather than issue characteristics tend to predominate. Leaders are perceived as being "honest," "capable," "sincere," "intelligent," "arrogant," "slick," or "indecisive." Particular attributes associated with Trudeau, for example, such as "intelligence" and "arrogance" became more firmly established over time, as did "untrustworthy" or "phony" in the case of Brian Mulroney. The public considered Joe Clark more "inexperienced" *after* his brief term as prime minister than before it began. Once in place, such images do not change easily, because they are associated with the person rather than with a particular set of circumstances or issues.

There are nevertheless particular traits that, while falling within the general category of personality characteristics, *do* seem more prone to be driven by events. Some of these may be related to the particular style or theme of a campaign, while others may be connected with performance, either in office or as a party leader. The "concern for ordinary people" often associated with Ed Broadbent, for example, reflected the NDP campaign themes of 1984 and 1988 as much as it did the characteristics of the man himself. The fact that the two seemed to complement each other was at least in part a function of the party's deliberate strategy in those two campaigns. Similarly, the perception that Turner "couldn't control his party" was at least partially related to performance. These were less personality traits than persistent images of the leaders conveyed to the public by the daily news. While these are often developed and reinforced over a substantial period of time, they can also be influenced by campaign events, particularly those with wide exposure to the public such as televised debates.

An examination of the 1993 campaign provides an indication of the success or failure of the parties' and leaders' strategies in attempting to structure a positive image. As a new party leader and relatively unknown national political figure, Kim Campbell faced the challenge of establishing a positive image with the electorate in a very short period of time. That she ultimately failed in this task is evident from the low thermometer score rating shown in Figure 4.2. While improving somewhat on the extremely low ratings accorded Brian Mulroney in the final years of his term, Campbell received a thermometer rating lower than that of any other major party leader in recent years, including John Turner or Joe Clark in their losing election campaigns. She was rated only slightly above her party, which itself had reached new depths of unpopularity (see Figure 3.7, p. 67). Campbell found herself on the defensive almost from the very beginning of the campaign. Her early stumbles such as the remark that unemployment would remain at high levels through the year 2000 (10 September) or the later comment that an election was not the time to discuss social programs (23 September) left her clarifying and explaining her positions during the early campaign period.[13] Anxious to avoid too close an identification with the Mulroney years, the Conservative campaign lacked any clear policy focus. Following the release of the Liberals' Red Book, the Conservatives found that they had no equivalent reference document. Again and again, Campbell returned to the theme of deficit reduction, an unconvincing issue for a party that had been in power for nine years. That Campbell's difficulty was at least partly a function of her poor campaign performance is evident from her low performance rating (Figure 4.3). But the fact that she found herself at the head of a party which itself had become so unpopular with much of the electorate indicates clearly that the failure of the Conservative campaign was not hers alone.

The challenge faced by Jean Chrétien and the Liberals at the beginning of the formal campaign period was very different than that of Campbell and the Conservatives. Although he was also leading his party in a national campaign for the first time, Chrétien was, unlike any of the other four party leaders, a well-known and well-established political figure. But this was not necessarily an advantage. Dubbed "yesterday's man" by his detractors, and highly distrusted by Quebec francophones, Chrétien's leadership of the party was widely regarded as more of a liability than an asset.[14] This difficulty was reflected in the Liberal campaign strategy.[15] The Liberals' release of their Red Book at the beginning of the campaign quickly made it their main focus, thereby taking the emphasis off the leader and reinforcing the principal Liberal campaign themes of "jobs" and "the economy." But as the campaign developed, it became clear that the leader also had to play a more active role. As one Liberal strategist discovered, policy statements that did not come directly from the leader tended to receive less attention in the media. Giving a solid performance throughout the campaign, Chrétien proved up to the task. He managed to raise his thermometer score to a respectable level, something that few political leaders over the last 20 years have been able to accomplish. That he did so largely through a strong performance in the campaign is evident from the rating given him on "performance" (Figure 4.3). His overall thermometer rating by the end of the campaign was about equal to that of his party, and both were generally positive.

Figure 4.3

Ratings of Party Leaders on Performance, and Honesty and Ethics: 1993 and 1988

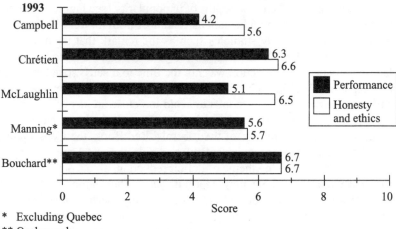

* Excluding Quebec
** Quebec only

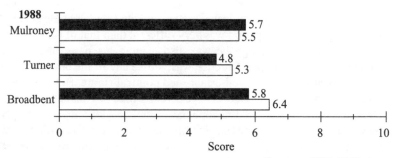

Source: 1988, 1993 – PSC.

The leader debates, which took place at the midpoint of the eight-week campaign, undoubtedly helped to shape public attitudes toward the party leaders. Increasingly, debates have become a centrepiece of the formal campaign, even though their effects on the actual outcome of elections are somewhat uncertain.[16] Since 1984, debates have become so firmly established as major campaign events that it is now doubtful that any parties or leaders could avoid participating in them, even if they wished to do so. Debates have also become a major component of a party's strategy, providing opportunities to highlight or adjust the party's chosen issues and themes at a critical stage of the campaign. In part, the potential of debates to affect the course of a campaign is a function of not only the large audiences that such events generally attain, but also of the emphasis accorded to them by the parties themselves and of the expectations raised by the media in their coverage of these types of "mega" campaign events.

The debates that took place in both the 1984 and 1988 election campaigns proved to be dramatic events, in each case altering significantly the public's perception of some of the party leaders at the midpoint of the campaign. In 1988, Turner's strong performance in the debates was associated with a turnaround of more then 10 points in the public opinion polls in the days immediately following the debates.[17] It also had the effect of refocussing the campaign more clearly around the free trade issue, a quite deliberate strategy on the part of Turner and the Liberals.[18] Through the medium of the debates, the Liberals were able to highlight the Conservatives' handling of economic restructuring and to increase the salience of the free trade issue, both of which the Conservatives would have preferred to downplay in the campaign. While the Tories were ultimately able to adjust their strategy by moving to attack John Turner and leaving much of the campaigning in support of the FTA to non-party groups, the debates nevertheless demonstrated the potential power of such events to rearrange both the public's perception of the party leaders and the issue agenda.

From the very beginning of the 1993 campaign, it was clear that the Conservatives needed the debates to establish a positive image for Kim Campbell and to attempt to exploit perceived weaknesses in Chrétien's leadership. But the Liberals would also have to use the debates to quell nagging doubts about Chrétien's suitability as a potential prime minister. For the NDP, Reform, and Bloc Québécois leaders, the debates afforded equal time with Campbell and Chrétien, something that no other segment of the campaign really does, given the vast differences in budgets, advertising, and media coverage. For these leaders, participation in the debates provided the opportunity to reach a mass audience and posed few political risks. The 1993 debates differed from those of the two previous elections in that five parties rather than three participated in them. Unlike the debates of 1984 or 1988, however, the 1993 debates proved to be relatively insignificant.[19] Polls taken immediately before and after the debates showed little change in the parties' shares of the vote.[20] The debates however did signal the failure of the Conservatives' leader-centred strategy in that Campbell did not achieve the dramatic breakthrough that many felt would have been needed to ignite her campaign. Few saw her as the winner (Table 4.2, part A). While attitudes toward Chrétien appeared to become somewhat more positive after the debates, the overall Liberal share of the vote varied relatively little over the course of the campaign according to most polls (see Figure 4.4C).

Table 4.2

Perceptions of Party Leaders in the Televised Debates: 1984, 1988, 1993

A. Leader perceived as having given the best performance in the debates†

	1984	1988		1993
Turner	4%	58%	Chrétien	32%
Mulroney	38	20	Campbell	7
Broadbent	33	7	McLaughlin	8
Don't know, None	25	15	Manning	22
			Bouchard	11
			Don't know, None	20

B. Thermometer ratings of leaders by exposure to debates

		Watched debates	Did not watch
1984	Turner	51*	49
	Mulroney	64*	60
	Broadbent	59*	55
1988	Turner	48*	45
	Mulroney	54	52
	Broadbent	52	50
1993	Chrétien	58*	55
	Campbell	39	38
	McLaughlin	44*	40
	Manning	44	43
	Bouchard	33	32

* differences significant, p ≤ .01
† debate watchers only

Source: 1984, 1988 – CNES; 1993 – PSC, INS.

Figure 4.4

Parties' Monthly Gallup Poll Standings in Election Years

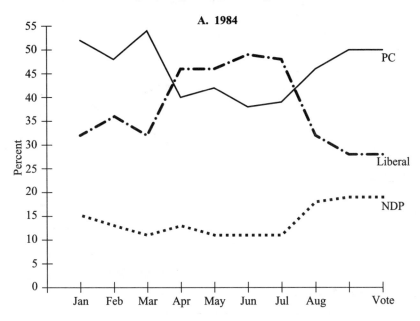

A. 1984

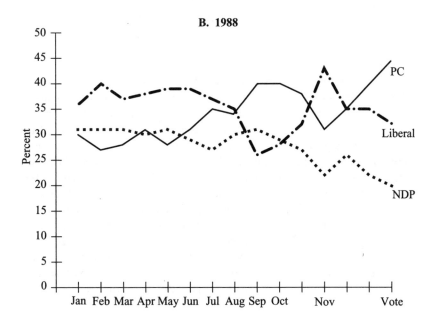

B. 1988

Figure 4.4 (CONTINUED)

Parties' Monthly Gallup Poll Standings in Election Years

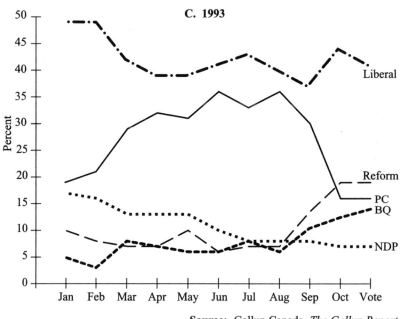

Source: Gallup Canada, *The Gallup Report*

From Election to Election

The formal campaign represents only a fragment of the much larger and more complex process that culminates in an election. Governments in parliamentary democracies such as Canada typically follow a four- or five-year cycle that commences with their assumption of power. Some of the actions that they will take during their first few years in office may represent positions and policies that have not even been discussed over the course of the election campaign that brought them to power. They often return quickly to economic restructuring or constitutional questions once the election is out of the way. Since the last election, the new Liberal government has initiated a high-profile review of social programs, and has shifted its focus to deficit reduction, the policy area most stressed by its Conservative and Reform opponents during the campaign. Moving agressively in both of these areas during their first two years in office is in line with the most familiar elements of the policy/election cycle. As noted earlier, the Mulroney government introduced the GST during the first session of Parliament after the 1988 election, even though the proposed tax had not been part of the party's policy agenda as discussed during the campaign. And the Trudeau government, following the 1974 election, implemented the very policy (wage and price controls) that the Liberals had attacked during the campaign.

Canadian parties rarely feel constrained in office by the positions that they took in an election campaign. Their larger and more complex projects do not generally form a substantial portion of the rhetoric of a campaign, although fragments of these will often surface in at least some parts of the campaign discourse. Rarely (perhaps never) will a party wish to place on the electoral agenda a multifaceted package of issues emanating from long-term projects like economic restructuring or constitutional renewal. Rather, some elements of these are more likely to be repackaged for the electorate as a need for "change" or a desire for "national unity." Or, party slogans such as "managing change" or the attributes (positive or negative) of the party leaders may provide convenient and attractive substitutes.

The first year or so in office is, in a strategic sense, the ideal time for a governing party to renege on its election promises, alter its policy agenda, or push through its most unpopular programs. Trudeau's revival of the constitutional project immediately following the 1980 election, or the Mulroney government's more aggressive stance on economic restructuring after 1988, both serve as examples of instances in which a newly elected government realizes that its period of greatest policy freedom to pursue its real objectives would come in the first two years *after* an election. It is not surprising then that the popularity of a new government often declines fairly soon after an election. Within 14 months of their victory in the 1980 election, the Liberals had again fallen behind the Conservatives in the polls, in spite of the fact that the party at the time was still led by Joe Clark, whose unpopular and short-lived government had so recently suffered a crushing defeat. A similar fate befell the Mulroney government following the 1984 election. The Tories had achieved a huge landslide victory in that election, yet found themselves trailing the Turner-led Liberals in the polls barely a year later. The Conservatives' slide in popularity following the 1988 election was even more abrupt.[21] The Chrétien government, although it likewise utilized the period of post-election policy freedom to pursue objectives quite different than those discussed during the election campaign, did not pay an immediate political price for this course of action.[22] While it may eventually do so, the fragmented nature of the parliamentary opposition and the prime minister's continued personal popularity may have given the Liberals a more extended honeymoon period than has typically been accorded a new governing party.

A governing party that holds a solid majority of the seats in Parliament can risk temporary unpopularity in order to further its policy objectives. But by the end of its third year in office, a government's attention will inevitably begin to turn toward the electoral agenda. If possible, projects that might constitute an electoral liability are shelved, even if only temporarily. Others are rushed to completion in an effort to provide a maximum amount of time for opposition to dissipate before the election. Suddenly, the economic outlook is made to look brighter. More popular policies such as tax cuts or public works projects begin to appear in budgets. And leaders begin to polish their images, now finding time for television appearances, party functions, and regional tours. Speculation about possible election dates becomes a staple of political commentary, even though the prime minister will invariably deny that any thought is being given to such matters! The reason why such a cycle is played out again and again in politics is that every government seeks to set the agenda in such a way as to maximize its chances of re-election. In parliamentary systems, one of the most valuable tools possessed by prime ministers and their advisers is the prerogative of calling an election. But the political advantage associated with this simple function extends far beyond the mere power to set the election date. Rather it involves the enormous strategic advantage of a governing party being able to fight the election on its own terms, to structure the agenda in such a way as to give itself every possible advantage.

There are occasions however when the electoral timetable plays itself out somewhat differently. The Mulroney government's attention was diverted by the failure of the Meech Lake proposals, the negotiation of the Charlottetown agreement, and the October 1992 referendum, which followed these events. Further, its ability to prepare the ground for an election was affected by the severity of the recession and by Mulroney's deep unpopularity with the public. Another type of constraint sometimes occurs when a governing party commands only a minority of the seats in Parliament. In such circumstances, the party in power may be more risk averse, or may find its ability to arrange the electoral agenda to suit its own purposes severely limited. The Clark government, defeated in a non-confidence vote just before Christmas in 1979, found itself having to fight an election for which it was thoroughly unprepared, at a time not of its own choosing, and over policies such as the imposition of an 18-cent gasoline tax that were never intended to be part of an electoral agenda. This inability to time the election and to structure the agenda were among the factors that contributed to the government's defeat in the election that followed. A governing party may also find that the policy agenda is not quite so easily managed as it had hoped. The Conservatives expected to have the passage of the Free Trade Agreement completed well in advance of the 1988 election. But the debate over the FTA in the Senate dragged out the timetable, forcing the issue onto the electoral agenda in a way that was not entirely consistent with the government's plans. While the 1988 election was not exactly the "referendum" on free trade that the Liberals claimed to want, neither was the campaign the one that had initially been scripted by the Conservatives and their strategists.

Probably, there is no election campaign that follows a party's plan exactly. But a party that senses itself ahead in the race will generally try to avoid deviating significantly from its prepared strategy. The 1993 Liberal campaign, for example, stuck closely to the Red Book, taking few risks and seizing every opportunity to reinforce the party's basic themes. The Conservatives, in contrast, became increasingly more desperate over the course of the campaign as it became clear that their leader-centred strategy was failing. Following the debates, Conservative strategists introduced, and then quickly withdrew, a set of tasteless and poorly conceived "attack ads" on Jean Chrétien. They cobbled together a "Blue Book" of policy initiatives (pulled mainly from the last budget) in an attempt to counter the Liberal Red Book. And Campbell found herself stretched to the limit by the frenzied pace of a campaign that depended so heavily on her alone. The NDP likewise was forced to revise its strategy more than once during the campaign, as its fortunes sagged and it found itself fighting for mere survival in the final weeks.

Each of the last three federal elections has seen substantial movement in the public opinion polls during the campaign, providing a rough test of the success or failure of particular strategies or the influence of particular events. In the case of the 1988 election, it is clear that Turner's performance in the debates triggered an abrupt surge in Liberal support, but also that the apparent shift in his party's fortunes proved to be short lived. Equally dramatic swings have sometimes been triggered by events that occur at the beginning of a campaign, or sometimes even before the start of the formal campaign period. In 1993, for example, it is evident that a large positive shift in Conservative support was initiated by Mulroney's resignation in February and not by the selection of Campbell or by later events associated with the campaign (Figure 4.4c). But the decline in Tory support in the early campaign period was equally dramatic, as virtually all of their improvement in the polls evaporated during the first three weeks. As Tory support crumbled, the fortunes of the Bloc Québécois and Reform rose, with a substantial portion of the gains made by these parties coming during the second half of the formal campaign period.

Only about a third of Canadian voters might be said to have their minds made up regarding their voting decision before the formal campaign gets under way. The proportion who claim to have "already decided" at that stage in fact varies little from one election to another.[23] Public opinion polls generally confirm this tendency of voters to reserve judgment, invariably

Figure 4.5

Reported Time of Vote Decision: 1988, 1993

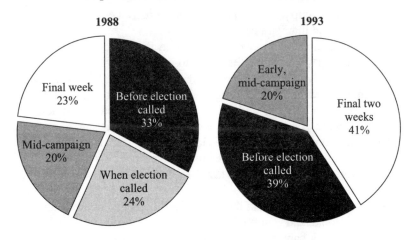

Source: 1988 – CPS; 1993 – CNES.

showing substantial numbers of "undecideds" during the course of a campaign.[24] Some voters however will be able to come to a decision quickly once the campaign gets under way. In 1988, for example, about a quarter of the electorate reported making its decision "when the election was called" (Figure 4.5). This tendency to decide quickly may be particularly noticeable in elections where significant pre-campaign events have been instrumental in setting the election agenda. The parliamentary debate on the Free Trade Agreement in 1988, for example, or the defeat of the Clark budget in 1980, are illustrative of significant events that occurred just before the beginning of the formal campaign and that in many ways set the stage for the election that followed. But even allowing that some voters will decide early, surveys consistently show that there are many who will not reach a final voting decision until much later. For some voters, significant events such as the leader debates may be of importance. Others, however, may wait until the final days before coming to a firm decision. Studies of the last five federal elections have all found at least 20% of all voters reporting that they did not make their final decision until the last week, including many on election day itself.[25] In 1993, 41% reported making their final decision in the last two weeks of the campaign (Figure 4.5). If many politicians tend to feel that an election is "not over until it's over," they would find ample evidence to support this view in surveys of the electorate taken over the course of a campaign.

Conclusion

If we think of the period of a year or so before an election as constituting "the campaign," then it is evident from the movement of the polls over each of the last three elections that the "long" and "short" campaign periods are both important. It is entirely possible that a party can lose an election before the formal campaign even begins, because some forces such as economic conditions may be beyond the control of party strategists. But it is also evident that the shorter and more intense campaign that ensues once the election is finally called provides plenty of room for fortunes to change. Parties rarely give up hope, even when the polls show them behind at the beginning. But by the time election day arrives, the trend is often clear. Final poll forecasts made a few days before the vote are generally accurate, and the television networks can frequently project results quickly on the basis of exit polls or small samplings of returns.[26] This does not imply that the result was pre-ordained, but rather that the effects of the campaign, long and short, have already done their work. For the party leaders, the end game is more often than not a critical juncture in their careers. Party leaders may not survive an electoral defeat and gain the opportunity to fight another campaign. John Turner did so in 1984, and led his party to a second defeat in 1988. But Kim Campbell resigned almost immediately after the 1993 election, and Audrey McLaughlin indicated her intention to resign as leader of the NDP about a year later. The cycle of government, campaigns, and elections is often a cycle of leaders' careers as well.

Notes

1. The defeat of the Trudeau government in the 1979 federal election is one example. Having planned the election for the fall of 1978, the government then changed its mind, delaying the election until the following spring. John Turner's defeat in 1984 is another. Having succeeded Trudeau too late in the election timetable to have much flexibility, Turner called an election immediately and was soundly defeated. There are numerous other examples of a similar nature in provincial elections and in other parliamentary countries. A rare exception to this pattern was the victory of John Major in the 1992 British election, following his succession of Margaret Thatcher as party leader.

2. For a more detailed development of the concept of the *long campaign*, and a discussion of its unfolding in the 1987 British general election, see William L. Miller, Harold D. Clarke, Martin Harrop, Lawrence LeDuc, and Paul F. Whiteley, *How Voters Change: The 1987 British Election Campaign in Perspective* (Oxford: Oxford University Press, 1990), pp. 59-82.

3. See, for example, Richard Joslyn, *Mass Media and Elections* (Reading, MA: Addison-Wesley, 1984), esp. pp. 164-75. On the role of the media in the 1988 federal election campaign, see Richard Johnston et al., *Letting the People Decide* (Montreal: McGill-Queen's University Press, 1992), pp. 112-140.

4. Harold D. Clarke, Jane Jenson, Lawrence LeDuc, and Jon H. Pammett, *Absent Mandate*, 1st ed. (Toronto: Gage Educational Publishing Company, 1984), pp. 79-89.

5. For a discussion of Conservative strategy in the 1988 campaign, see Robert Krause, "The Progressive Conservative Campaign: Mission Accomplished," in Alan Frizzell, Jon H. Pammett, and Anthony Westell, eds., *The Canadian General Election of 1988* (Ottawa: Carleton University Press, 1989), pp. 15-25. For accounts of the Liberal and NDP campaign strategies, see Stephen Clarkson, "The Liberals: Disoriented in Defeat," and Alan Whitehorn, "The NDP Election Campaign: Dashed Hopes," in the same volume.

6. The strategy of changing leaders in the hope of improving the chances of electoral success has been tried again and again by political parties with dubious results. For a systematic investigation of the efficacy of this strategy, see David Stewart and R.K. Carty, "Does Changing the Party Leader Provide an Electoral Boost?" *Canadian Journal of Political Science* 26 (1993): 313-30.

7. See Johnston et al., *Letting the People Decide*, pp. 169-84. See also Steven Brown et al., "In the Eye of the Beholder: Leader Images in Canada," *Canadian Journal of Political Science* 21 (1988): 729-56.

8. A more detailed discussion of the perceived leadership attributes of Trudeau and Mulroney, together with similar profiles of the public images of Joe Clark, Ed Broadbent, and John Turner, may be found in Harold D. Clarke, Jane Jenson, Lawrence LeDuc, and Jon H. Pammett, *Absent Mandate*, 2nd ed. (Toronto: Gage Educational Publishing Company, 1991), pp. 92-101.

9. And his rating on the scale dropped even lower following his resignation. Voters sampled at the time of the 1993 election rated Mulroney at a mean of 24° on the thermometer scale. [1993 PSC].

10. Except apparently Jean Chrétien, whose thermometer score rose eight points between the time of the 1992 referendum and the 1993 election, and who has continued to enjoy a high degree of personal popularity ever since the election according to most polls. It remains to be seen however whether Chrétien can sustain this position through a second election campaign, which would present a more satisfactory comparison with the data shown in Figure 4.2.

11. Brown, "In the Eye of the Beholder," pp. 745-52; and Johnston et al., *Letting the People Decide*, pp. 175-85, tap a detailed list of leader "traits," including attributes such as "intelligence," "compassion," "vision," "trust," "competence," and "moral character."

12. The data discussed here are reported in greater detail in Clarke et al., *Absent Mandate*, 2nd ed., pp. 92-101. For comparable information on leaders in the 1974 election, see H.D. Clarke, J. Jenson, L. LeDuc, and J.H. Pammett, *Political Choice in Canada* (Toronto: McGraw-Hill Ryerson, 1979; abridged, 1980), Chapter 7.

13. For a discussion of Conservative strategy in the 1993 campaign, see Peter Woolstencroft, "Doing Politics Differently: The Conservative Party and the Campaign of 1993," in Alan Frizzell, Jon H. Pammett, and Anthony Westell, eds., *The Canadian General Election of 1993* (Ottawa: Carleton University Press, 1994), pp. 9-26.

14. At the time of the 1992 referendum, Chrétien's mean thermometer rating was a mildly negative 48° [CRS]. Prior to the election call in September, the percentage of respondents in one poll who felt that Chrétien would make the "best prime minister" was 19%, compared to 39% for Kim Campbell (*The Globe & Mail*, 16 October 1993). By election day, both of these figures had improved significantly.

15. For a discussion of Liberal campaign strategy, see Stephen Clarkson, "Yesterday's Man and His Blue Grits: Backward Into the Future," in Frizzell et al., *The Canadian General Election of 1993*, pp. 27-39.

16. See, among other sources, Cathy Widdis Barr, "The Importance and Potential of Televised Leaders Debates," and Robert Bernier and Denis Monière, "The Organization of Televised Leaders Debates in the United States, Europe, Australia and Canada," both in Frederick Fletcher, ed., *Media, Elections, and Democracy* (Toronto: Dundurn Press, 1991); Lawrence LeDuc, "Party Strategies and the Use of Televised Campaign Debates," *European Journal of Political Research* 18 (1990): 121-41; and David J. Lanoue, "Debates That Mattered: Voters' Reaction to the 1984 Canadian Leadership Debates," *Canadian Journal of Political Science* 24 (1991): 51-65.

17. *The Gallup Report*, 7 November 1988. See also Johnston et al., *Letting the People Decide*, pp. 169-74.

18. Clarkson, "The Liberals: Disoriented in Defeat," in Frizzell et al., *The Canadian General Election of 1988*, pp. 36-7.

19. For a more detailed account of the 1993 debates, see Lawrence LeDuc, "The Leaders' Debates: Critical Event or Non-Event?" in Frizzell et al., eds., *The Canadian General Election of 1993*, pp. 127-42.

20. An Angus Reid poll taken just after the debates placed the Liberals at 37% of the vote, the same level at which polls by the Reid organization and others had placed them in the two weeks preceding the debates. The Conservatives' vote percentage showed somewhat greater fluctuation across this period although, unlike 1988, this does not appear to be connected in any very specific way to the debates.

21. Nine months after the 1988 election, the Conservatives had dropped to 27% support in a national poll, well behind the Liberals at 43%. *The Gallup Report*, 17 August 1989.

22. Nearly a year after the election, the Liberals stood at 60% in the Gallup Poll, far ahead of their nearest rivals. Approval of Chrétien's performance as prime minister was also very high at 62%. *The Gallup Report*, 10 September 1994.

23. Thirty-two percent in 1984, for example. Or 38% in 1979. Clarke et al., *Absent Mandate*, 2nd ed., p. 110.

24. A Gallup poll in 1993, for example, taken late in the campaign, found 28% "undecided." *The Gallup Report*, 22 October 1993.

25. In 1993, almost 14% reported making their decision on the day of the election, while in 1988 the comparable figure was 10% [1993 and 1988 CNES].

26. The final Angus Reid poll in 1993, for example (October 22), placed the Liberals at 43%; Conservatives, 17%; BQ, 14%; Reform, 17%; and NDP, 7%. Gallup's final estimates, published on the same date, were similar, and both of these polls varied only slightly from the actual vote totals (Liberals, 41%; Conservatives, 16%; BQ, 14%; Reform, 19%; NDP, 7%).

5

From Old Choices
to New Ones

Large-scale projects for restructuring the economy and revamping the constitution have done much to define the content of the national political agenda over the past two decades. The political choices these projects present are very important, but debates concerning them are conspicuously absent from election campaigns. Although national elections focus heavily on issues, and parties strive to forge positive linkages between salient campaign issues and themselves in the public mind, or, conversely, negative ones vis-à-vis their competitors, connections with the larger economic and constitutional projects prominently featured in political discourse in other contexts are not explicitly established. Rather, election issues have ad hoc and free-floating qualities; they vary markedly from one election to the next, and they typically are presented as discrete "national problems" for which parties claim to have solutions. This aspect of parties' electioneering strategies is often combined with a heavy emphasis on party leaders; leaders are presented as the individuals who, if their party gains power, will rapidly solve the country's problems as currently defined. National election campaigns thus are characterized by the interplay of a highly changeable mix of short-term issues and party leader images. These short-term forces operate in a political environment in which many voters' partisan attachments are weak and changeable. As documented in Chapter 3, surveys conducted since the late 1960s regularly show that from approximately three-fifths to three-quarters of the electorate are flexible partisans. Moreover, a majority of these people have moderate or high levels of political interest, and many of them pay attention to news about election campaigns in the mass media. When called upon to cast their ballots, many voters thereby are predisposed to react to the issues and leader images that dominate federal elections.

Societal Cleavages and Electoral Choice

How, in fact, do Canadians make up their minds when they go to the polls? Evidence from national surveys shows that many voters respond to the highly volatile short-term forces that define the substance of successive election campaigns. In contrast, long-term factors such as voters' socio-demographic characteristics are only weakly related to their behaviour in the voting booth. One such characteristic is social class. Although social class divisions constitute one of the major fault lines in party systems in many Western countries, Canada is an exception. Surveys conducted since the mid-1960s show that relationships typically are quite weak between indicators of social class such as education, income, and occupation, on the one hand, and voting behaviour, on the other.[1]

These relationships are not constant, however. In 1988, the dominance of the free trade issue, and the associated perception that the Free Trade Agreement might have particularly negative effects on working people strengthened the correlation between social class and voting behaviour. Thus, as Table 5.1 shows, the governing Conservatives, the proponents of the FTA, received 59% of the vote of persons with family incomes over $70,000 per year, but only 41% of the vote of those earning less than $20,000 per year. In contrast, the NDP received considerably more support (26%) from the latter group than from the former one (10%). However, in 1993, Conservative and NDP voting fell dramatically in all income categories and, although the New Democrats continued to receive more support from persons with lower incomes, differences in Tory voting among those in various income categories virtually evaporated. Indicative of the more general weakness of the relationship between social class and vote, support for other parties was largely unrelated to income in both 1988 and 1993 but levels of support for these parties by persons in different class groupings were likewise not constant. Rather, Liberal and Reform voting surged in all income categories between 1988 and 1993.

Over the past quarter century, other socio-demographic characteristics also have tended to have quite modest relationships with voting behaviour. However, some of these factors have shown increasing potential to structure political debate and, thereby, to affect electoral choice. An example is gender. As we have seen in Chapter 2, recent elections have witnessed differences in the issue concerns of men and women, and the two groups have tended to favour different parties on the election issues defined as most important. There have been differences in their voting behaviour as well. In both 1988 and 1993, the Liberals were more strongly supported by women than by men and, in the former year, the Tories received proportionally more support from men than women (Table 5.1). In 1993, the gender differential in Conservative voting disappeared, but it resurfaced in voting for the Reform Party and Bloc Québécois, with both of these parties being more heavily favoured by men than women.

94

Table 5.1

Voting Behaviour by Gender, Income, and Region: 1993, 1988

A. 1993 Vote

	Liberal	PC	NDP	Reform	BQ	Other
Gender						
Men	36%	14	8	23	17	2
Women	48%	13	11	15	12	2
Income						
<$20,000 per year	43%	14	13	14	15	2
$20,000-39,999	39%	14	11	15	19	2
$40,000-59,999	44%	11	9	23	12	2
$60,000-69,999	47%	10	9	18	14	2
$70,000 or more	41%	15	5	22	15	3
Region						
Atlantic	61%	22	10	6	0	1
Quebec	34%	8	1	0	56	2
Ontario	55%	15	9	18	0	2
Prairies	31%	14	10	43	0	1
British Columbia	23%	13	23	37	0	4

B. 1988 Vote

	Liberal	PC	NDP	Reform	Other
Gender					
Men	25%	51	19	2	3
Women	32%	43	21	2	2
Income					
<$20,000 per year	29%	41	26	2	2
$20,000-39,999	29%	43	24	2	2
$40,000-59,999	24%	54	18	2	2
$60,000-69,999	29%	48	18	1	5
$70,000 or more	26%	59	10	1	4
Region					
Atlantic	45%	41	12	0	2
Quebec	20%	61	18	0	2
Ontario	37%	41	19	0	3
Prairies	21%	50	20	8	1
British Columbia	20%	38	35	4	4

Source: 1988, 1993 – PSC.

95

Differences in the voting patterns of linguistic and regional groups also are readily apparent in recent elections. As Table 5.1 shows, such differences were very much in evidence in 1993, with Reform support being heavily concentrated in the West, and the Bloc appeal in Quebec being effectively limited to francophone residents of that province. Like many voters elsewhere in the country, Quebeckers and Westerners abandoned the Conservatives in droves in 1993 and, by choosing different alternatives, they produced large regional differences in party support. Regional variations in voting behaviour were apparent in 1988 too. However, in that election, the Conservatives received especially strong support in Quebec and the Prairies, and the incidence of Liberal voting in parts of the latter region was much lower than the result five years later.

These changes in regional voting patterns between 1988 and 1993 are impressive, but they are not novel. Rather, they exemplify a more general volatility in support for various parties in different regions that long has characterized the Canadian electorate. For example, after giving the Liberals strong backing in the early post-World War II period, many Quebeckers rallied to the Conservatives in 1958 and to the Créditistes in the following two elections. In the Trudeau era, Quebec again became a Liberal bastion, and the party received strong support from both francophones and anglophones. In the 1984 and 1988 elections, however, the Conservatives swept the province. Quebec's electoral volatility is not unique. Support for the Conservatives eroded markedly between 1988 and 1993 in all parts of Canada, just as it had surged across much of the country between 1980 and 1984. Similarly, the Liberal vote fell precipitously in several regions across this earlier pair of elections, and it increased sharply in every region in 1993. Such large-scale over-time changes indicate that voting behaviour is quite changeable throughout the country, and the presence of regional differences in parties' vote shares in a specific election should not be interpreted as indicating that regional cleavages are long-term forces anchoring support for particular parties.

Nor should the strength of regional effects on voting behaviour in a given election be exaggerated. The tendency to emphasize these effects is understandable because, in terms of electing candidates to Parliament, Canada's single-member plurality electoral system favours parties with regionally concentrated bases of support. At the individual level, however, relationships between region and voting behaviour are less impressive. The point may be illustrated by multiple regression analyses that attempt to explain voting for each of the parties in terms of region, language, and several other socio-demographic variables (age, education, gender, income).[2] These analyses show that only small percentages of the vote for any of the parties can be accounted for by these characteristics. In 1993, for example, the explanatory power (measured on a 0-100% scale) of all of

Figure 5.1

**Variance Explained in 1988 and 1993 Vote by Socio-
Demographic Characteristics and Short-Term Forces**

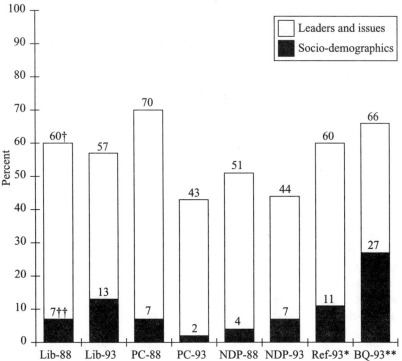

*   excluding Quebec
**   Quebec only
†   Total variance explained
††   Variance explained by socio-demographics

Source: 1988, 1993 – PSC.

these variables is only 13% for Liberal voting, and merely 2% and 7%, for
Conservative and NDP voting, respectively (Figure 5.1). These variables also
fail to account for much of the support for the new parties; they explain
11% and 27% of the variance in Reform and BQ voting, respectively. The
1988 analyses are very similar; they account for 7% of the variance in
Liberal and Conservative voting, and 4% of that in NDP voting. These
results resemble those for earlier elections; long-term forces associated with
socio-demographic variables always leave much of the variance in voting
behaviour unexplained.

Making Choices

The finding that voting patterns are not strongly or consistently associated with socio-demographic variables does not mean that Canadians' electoral choices are inexplicable. On the contrary, they are heavily influenced by short-term forces operating in the political arena at particular times. Pre-eminent in this regard are voters' perceptions of which party is closest to them on the most important election issue and their feelings about the party leaders. These perceptions and feelings can change markedly over time, and they have important effects on electoral choice.

The impact of issues and leaders is illustrated by regression analyses of voting behaviour in 1988 and 1993 that include issue and leader variables[3] along with the socio-demographic ones discussed above. In both years, the percentage of each party's vote that can be explained increases sharply when issue and leader variables are considered. Controlling for the effects of the socio-demographic characteristics, the issue and leader variables account for an average additional 42% of the variance in voting behaviour in 1993, and for an average additional 54% in 1988 (Figure 5.1). Issue perceptions and feelings about the party leaders also had strong effects on Reform and Bloc Québécois voting in 1993. Even though support for Reform tended to concentrate in parts of the West, the impact of the issue and leader variables vastly exceeds those associated with region or other socio-demographic characteristics. When the issue and leader variables are included in the Reform analysis, its explanatory power increases by more than fivefold, from 11% to 60% (Figure 5.1). Similarly, in Quebec, BQ voting was effectively confined to the francophone community but, nevertheless, issue and leader perceptions more than doubled the variance explained, increasing it from 27% to 66%. Support for Reform and the BQ in 1993 was affected by the same sorts of issue and leader forces that long have done much to determine voting for other parties.

Given the characteristics of partisanship documented in Chapter 3, one would not anticipate that these issue and leader effects would be distributed equally across the electorate. Rather, they should be concentrated among persons with flexible partisan ties. Some of these flexible partisans will react primarily to the issues stressed by the parties and the mass media in a particular election campaign, whereas others will be affected more strongly by perceptions of party leaders. Voters with durable partisan ties, in contrast, should be more resistant to the impact of short-term forces, and thus less likely to switch their votes across successive elections.

A statistical technique, the analysis of commonalities, is useful for summarizing the impact of several different factors acting on voting choice. This technique measures the unique effects of specific factors, as well as the total effect of all of them.[4] Figure 5.2 depicts the explanatory power of short-term forces (party leader images and issue perceptions) as

Figure 5.2

Effects of Long-Term and Short-Term Forces on Conservative Voting in 1988 and Liberal Voting in 1993 by Partisan-Political Interest Types

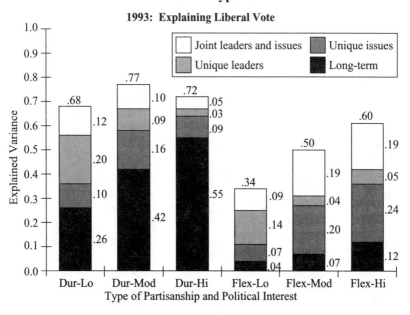

1993: **Explaining Liberal Vote**

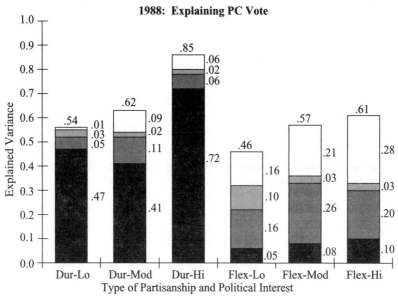

1988: **Explaining PC Vote**

Source: 1988 – CPS; 1993 – PSC.

compared to long-term forces, on Conservative voting in 1988 and Liberal voting in 1993 for various groups of partisans. In both cases, the impact of short-term forces (that is, the unique and joint effects of party leader images and issue perceptions) is much stronger for flexible than for durable partisans. Indeed, the short-term issue and leader forces together account for a large majority of the explained variance in voting behaviour for the three groups of flexible partisans.

In sharp contrast, in both years long-term forces have stronger effects on the voting behaviour of durable partisans. Similar analyses of voting in several earlier elections tell the same story. In every instance, leader images and issue perceptions account for much of the voting behaviour of flexible partisans, and long-term forces predominate among durable partisans. Clearly, there are significant differences in the kinds of factors that influence the electoral choices of the two types. Persons in the flexible group are strongly influenced by factors associated with particular election campaigns, whereas those in the durable group respond more strongly to long-term party loyalties.

Figure 5.2 also illustrates that the impact of short-term forces on flexible partisans differs according to levels of political interest. In most elections, the influence of issues is relatively greater among flexible partisans with high levels of interest, whereas feelings about party leaders have relatively stronger effects on the flexible low-interest group. Among flexible low-interest partisans in 1993, unique issue effects on Liberal voting (.07) are only half as large as those for leaders (.14) (Figure 5.2). In contrast, among high-interest flexible partisans, the unique explanatory power of issues (.24) is nearly five times as great as that of leaders (.05). Similar differences in the impact of issues and leader images on the voting behaviour of these groups also are apparent in 1988, as well as in earlier elections.

It is also evident that the relative strength of issue and party leader effects differs over time. Voters, regardless of type of partisanship or level of political interest, are not influenced by short-term factors to exactly the same extent or in exactly the same ways in every election. In several cases, including 1979, 1980, 1988, and 1993, issues appear to be more important. For example, in 1988, issue effects on PC voting were larger than those of leaders among all three categories of flexible partisans. In 1993, this was true for two of three groups (flexible moderate- and high-interest partisans). In other elections such as 1984 or 1968, leaders were relatively more important. Although one can expect that short-term forces will exert powerful effects in an electorate with large numbers of flexible partisans, it is difficult to forecast exactly which of these forces will be most important in any particular election.

The performance of the parties and their leaders on the hustings account for some of these differences. In 1993, Kim Campbell's mishandling of questions regarding Conservative economic and social policies generated substantial adverse publicity, and internecine bickering between Campbell and other prominent Conservative candidates contributed to an impression that the Tory campaign was in serious disarray. Similarly, in 1984, widely publicized gaffes committed by Liberal leader John Turner, coupled with his generally poor campaign performance, severely eroded his credibility and magnified the impact of short-term feelings about him and other party leaders.

Campaign strategies and tactics are influential as well. The emphasis accorded to leaders varies. In 1993, the Conservatives made Kim Campbell the centrepiece of their campaign, whereas the Liberals focussed more heavily on issues. Similarly, the Liberals gave far less emphasis to Pierre Trudeau in their 1980 campaign than they had in the 1979 contest only nine months earlier. In both 1979 and 1974 the Liberals had highlighted their leader, stressing the "competence edge" Mr. Trudeau enjoyed over his Conservative counterparts. Both of these elections, in turn, saw a different emphasis on the leaders than had occurred during the Trudeaumania spring of 1968.

The way in which issues are treated varies too. The Liberals' decision to "go for broke" in opposing free trade in 1988 did much to make this election a single-issue contest. In contrast, although the Liberals also emphasized the economy in 1993, the issues selected and the way in which they were presented were markedly different than in 1988. By focussing on unemployment as a national problem and claiming that they would solve it, the Liberals' 1993 campaign resembled that of the Conservatives in 1984. But there were differences too. In 1984, the Tories largely confined themselves to stressing the need for "jobs, jobs, jobs," whereas in 1993 the Liberals coupled the emphasis on unemployment with assurances that they had a plan to jump-start the sputtering economy.

Issues and Leaders

Issue and party leader effects are short-term forces that vary considerably over time. For example, free trade, the dominant issue in the 1988 campaign, was not even on the issue agenda in 1984, and by 1993, its salience had sharply receded. Similarly, unemployment, a major concern in 1984, disappeared from the agenda in 1988, only to reappear as a leading issue in 1993. Nor do the images of the party leaders remain the same. Between 1984 and 1988 overall levels of public support for Conservative leader Brian Mulroney declined sharply, and many voters became increasingly negative about him and the other party leaders. The replacement of party leaders is a major source of change as well. In 1993, three of the parties had new leaders. Two of these, Kim Campbell and Audrey McLaughlin, were less popular than their predecessors. In contrast, although Jean Chrétien did not generate widespread enthusiasm in 1993, voters were more positively disposed toward him than they had been toward John Turner in either 1984 or 1988 (Figure 4.2, p. 77).

The effects of feelings about issues, leaders, and parties on electoral choice are often closely intertwined. Some voters may rationalize their choice in issue terms when, in fact, they actually decided on the basis of their reactions to the leaders' personalities. Similarly, leaders' pronouncements concerning salient campaign issues are widely publicized, and voters' attitudes toward the leaders may be shaped by perceptions of how they will handle these issues. In some cases, references to issues or leaders mask the effects of long-standing party loyalties. The analyses presented in Figure 5.2 hint at these complexities by showing that although issues and leaders each have unique effects on voting, they also have joint effects.

Voters' own reports of their reasoning in making their choices also illustrate the interplay of issues, leader images, and feelings about parties. In a number of surveys, respondents have been asked to rank the importance of party leaders, local candidates, and the parties as a whole as factors in their voting decisions.[5] Figure 5.3 shows that the percentages giving priority to each of the three factors were relatively constant in the 1974, 1979, and 1980 surveys, with large percentages citing "parties as a whole" and "party leaders" as most important. The picture changes appreciably thereafter. In 1984, and especially in 1988 and 1993, the importance of parties increased, reaching 57% in 1993. In contrast, the percentages citing leaders declined; in 1988 and 1993, only one voter in five ranked leaders as most important, whereas the average for the four elections between 1974 and 1984 had been slightly over one in three. The percentages citing local candidates is less variable over time, ranging from a minimum of 20% (1980) to a maximum of 27% (1974, 1988). Although a sizable minority of people in every election survey refer to local candidates when explaining their voting decisions, the influence of local candidates invariably recedes when other factors are controlled. Local candidate effects may vary over time and from one locality to another, but their overall impact is always marginal.[6] This is true for durable and flexible partisans alike. In general, public reactions to local candidates do little to explain either individual voting behaviour or broader processes of electoral stability and change.

When respondents are asked a follow-up question about why they selected parties, leaders, or local candidates as most important for their vote, the percentage mentioning issues is always substantial, but it was considerably greater in 1988 and 1993 than in previous elections. In the earlier contests, slightly over 50% of those citing leaders, and about 40% of those mentioning parties or local candidates, specified that issue concerns affected their choice of the key factor prompting their vote. In 1988, in contrast, over 70% of those designating leaders, and nearly 60% of those

Figure 5.3

Most Important Factor in Vote Decision: 1974–93

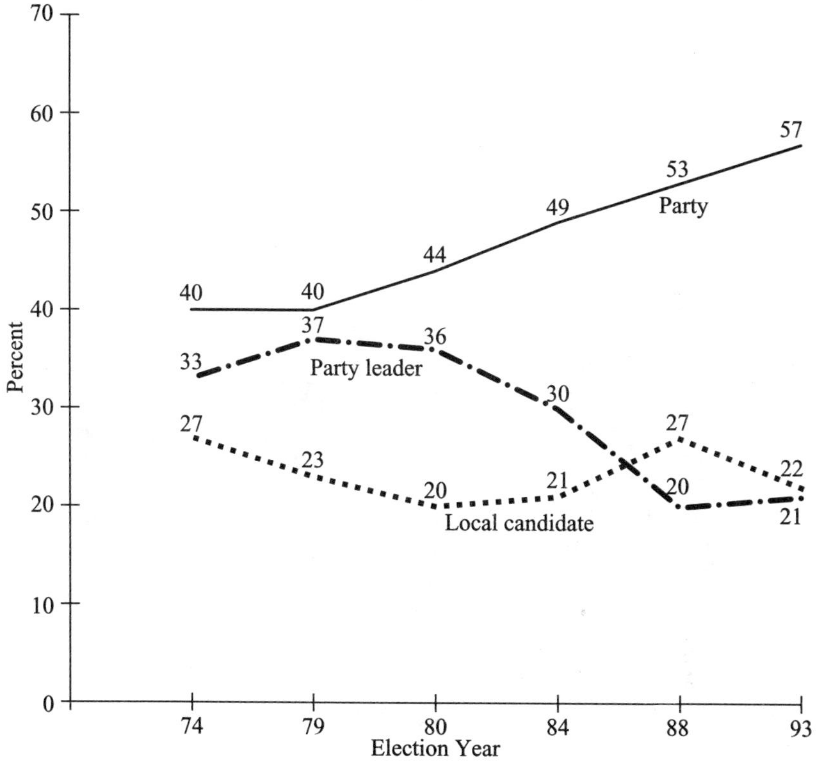

Source: 1974–84 – CNES; 1988 – CPS; 1993 – INS.

referring to parties or local candidates said there was an issue basis for their choice (Figure 5.4). In 1993, issue responses receded somewhat, but still remained well above the pre-1988 figures. Data from the 1974-84 surveys[7] indicate that the issues voters have in mind when they answer these questions are not an assortment of private hobbyhorses with little or no public salience; rather they are the issues featured in specific election campaigns.

Issues, of course, are not the only factors cited as underlying the choice of party, leader, or candidate as the most important element in the vote decision. Even in 1988, when the free trade issue dominated campaign rhetoric, well over one-third of all those surveyed referred to a non-issue component—leaders' and candidates' "personal qualities," and parties' "general approach to government." The meaning of these non-issue responses varies. For some people, especially durable partisans, "party"

Figure 5.4

**Issue Basis for Selecting Party, Party Leader, or Local Candidate
as Most Important Factor in Vote Decision:
1984, 1988, 1993**

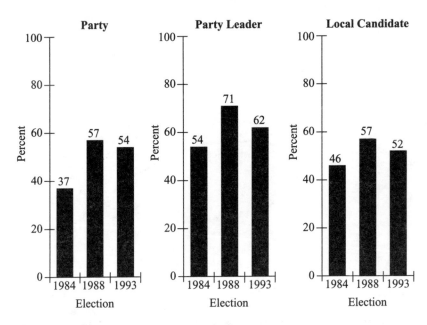

Source: 1984 – CNES; 1988 – CPS; 1993 – INS.

may refer to a long-standing commitment, a loyalty that resists corrosion by the events and conditions associated with an election campaign. For others, as shown above, a party response is a shorthand way to refer to an issue associated (positively or negatively) with certain parties at a given time. Similarly, party leader and local candidate responses may signal a variety of short- or long-term reactions to the personalities of specific politicians.

The reasons voters give for their decisions change from one election to another. It would be a mistake to assume that the electorate is easily classified according to susceptibility to party, leader, candidate, or issue factors, with some voters being highly issue-oriented and others attuned only to candidates' or leaders' personal traits. Although flexible partisans with high levels of political interest generally are more sensitive to issues, there is substantial variation over time in the ordering that all types of voters accord to party, leader, and candidate factors. The extent of this change may be seen in the responses of persons participating in the 1988-93 PSC panel survey. Their answers to the question asking about the relative significance of parties, leaders, and candidates in their voting decision show that nearly 50% identified a different factor as most important. Similarly, in the 1974-79-80 CNES three-wave panel, more than two-thirds changed the most important reason for their decision at least once. The varying emphasis placed on leaders and issues and the changing mix of issues in different elections increase the likelihood that voters—especially those highly attuned to short-term forces—will shift their views of what is most important. It is not the passage of time alone that accounts for this high level of change, but the differing contexts of successive election campaigns.

Loyalty, Voice, Exit?

Between 1988 and 1993, changes in voting behaviour were endemic. As Figure 5.5 shows, fully 51% of the survey respondents reported that they switched their vote from one party to another between these elections, and a further 6% said they switched to non-voting. Although the amount of switching between 1988 and 1993 was high, such changes in voting are not unusual. Rather, earlier surveys reveal that from 19% (1974, 1980) to 30% (1988) of those voting for a particular party in one election switched their vote in the following one. When the effects of abstention are added, from 28% (1980) to 37% (1984) abandoned the party they had voted for in a previous election. Overall levels of vote switching were somewhat higher in 1984 and 1988 than previously, but differences between these two contests and earlier ones are matters of degree. Moreover, this behaviour is not strongly associated with the length of time between elections; although the 1980 election occurred less than a year after the 1979 one, and the 1974 and 1979 elections were nearly five years apart, levels of switching and abstention were quite similar in all three cases. In any given election, large numbers of voters do not put a premium on loyalty. If, for whatever reason, they are dissatisfied with their previous choice, they either move on to another party, or refuse to back any party, and exit, at least temporarily, from the active electorate.

In 1993, an unusually large percentage of voters chose to voice their unhappiness with the political status quo by switching their votes. Many of them used their ballots to pass harsh judgment on a governing party that they had previously supported, and that party suffered a devastating defeat. More generally, however, the volume of vote switching is not strongly related to election outcomes. Like the 1993 election, those in 1979, 1980, and 1984 brought about the defeat of governments, whereas the 1974 and 1988 contests produced victories for an incumbent party. On average, levels of vote switching were no higher in the former than in the latter. There is, then, reason to doubt that the large incidence of vote switching in 1993 represents a "sea change" in the dynamics of Canadian voting behaviour. Rather, these tendencies were readily apparent in earlier elections. The

Figure 5.5

Vote Switching and Abstention:
1984, 1988, 1993

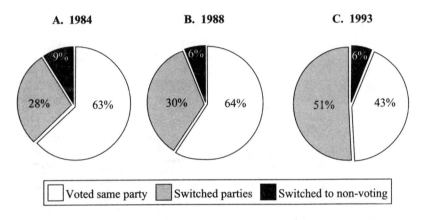

| A. 1984 | B. 1988 | C. 1993 |

Voted same party   Switched parties   Switched to non-voting

Source: 1984 – CNES; 1988 – CPS; 1993 – PSC.

consistently high levels of instability in voting behaviour across the 1974-88 period suggest that a large volume of change in party support is the norm. Each ensuing election campaign and the advent of a new set of short-term forces prompt large numbers of people to switch their votes. These forces and the volatile behaviour they engender are the rule, not the exception, in Canadian elections.

The impact of issue perceptions and party leader images varies across different segments of the electorate, being much greater for flexible than for durable partisans. The mix of issue concerns and leader images also varies across elections. One would expect, therefore, that switching and abstention would be concentrated among persons with flexible partisan attachments. This is, in fact, the case. Although vote switching was very widespread in 1993, it was a considerably more frequent practice among flexible than durable partisans (see Figure 5.6). For the three flexible partisan groups, an average of fully 68% reported either switching their votes between 1988 and 1993 or moving to non-voting in the latter year. The comparable figure for the three durable partisan groups is 42%. The same patterns obtained for the 1984-88 and 1980-84 election pairs; in both cases the percentages of flexible and durable partisans changing their votes or abstaining after voting in the previous election were 49% and 17%, respectively. These differences between flexible and durable partisans are not confined to the post-1980 period; they occurred in the 1970s as well.

Figure 5.6

Vote Switching and Abstention: 1984–93 by
Partisan-Political Interest Types

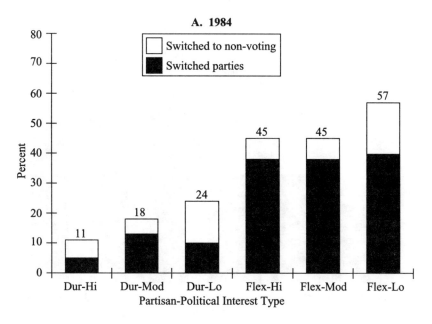

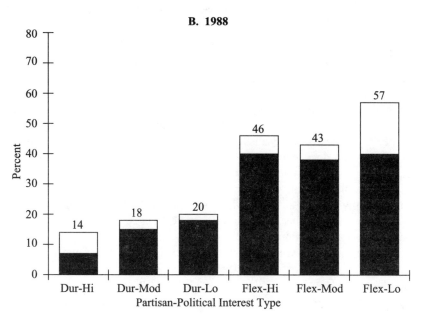

Figure 5.6 (CONTINUED)

Vote Switching and Abstention: 1984–93 by
Partisan-Political Interest Types

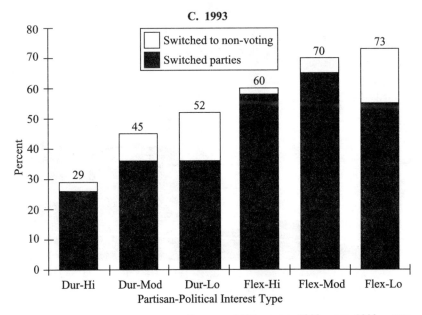

C. 1993

Source: 1984 – CNES; 1988 – CPS; 1993 – PSC.

The nature of partisanship rather than level of political interest per se tends to govern the incidence of switching and abstention.[8] For the 1988-93 election pair, as well as for the 1984-88 and 1980-84 ones, *all* groups of flexible partisans have higher (typically much higher) rates of switching and abstention than do any of the durable partisan groups (see Figure 5.6). Given that they constitute a large proportion of the electorate, the greater propensity of flexible partisans to switch their votes or to abstain means that their behaviour does much to account for the ongoing volatility in Canadian elections. Moreover, switching away from governing parties is concentrated in the flexible partisan groups, and helps to explain the defeat of these parties. Fully 87% of all those who voted for the governing Conservatives in 1988 but for another party in 1993 were flexible partisans. Similarly, flexible partisans comprised 91% of those who supported the governing Liberals in 1980 but voted for another party in 1984. The importance of flexible partisans in explaining the defeat of governing parties does not simply stem from their numbers alone. In 1993, these voters were much more likely to desert the Conservatives than to move in other directions. In that election, twice as many flexible partisans switched away from the Conservatives as compared to all other types of switches. The comparable ratio in this regard for durable partisans was 1.5 to 1. In 1984, the comparable ratios of flexible and durable partisans abandoning the then governing Liberals were 3.2 to 1 and 2 to 1, respectively. These patterns for the two most recent elections where a governing party was defeated are similar to those of 1979 and 1980, also elections that witnessed the rejection of governing parties. In those years, flexibles were generally one and one-half to two times as likely as durables to abandon the governing party as to engage in other types of switching. In every Canadian election of recent years that has seen the defeat of a government, flexible partisans have been the key agents of change.

Changing Choices

Why do some Canadians mark their ballots differently from one election to the next? A useful place to begin to answer this question is with voters' own explanations. When people participating in the election surveys are asked open-ended questions about their reasons for voting as they did, their answers are cast in terms of issue considerations, as well as evaluations of party leaders, local candidates, and party performance in general. The issues cited by switchers, and their references to leaders, local candidates, and parties resemble those that characterize the electorate more generally. In 1993, for example, a plurality of all voters (41%) referred to issue or policy concerns. The percentages of switchers and those who stayed with their 1988 party doing so were 46% and 35%, respectively. Similarly, party leaders and local candidates were cited less frequently by both groups—9% of the switchers and 16% of the stayers cited leaders, and 7% and 11%, respectively, mentioned local candidates. General references to parties were made by 16% of the switchers and 27% of the stayers, and 14% of the former and 8% of the latter simply said it was "time for a change." Switchers thus are not "a breed apart," but rather are in most respects typical voters. The reasons switchers give for their actions are not different in kind from those offered by persons who stick with a party.

Persons who switch also are more likely to report that they make their decisions late in the campaign, and that they consider alternatives before finally deciding how to vote.[9] This suggests that switchers often make their choices after considerable deliberation and in reaction to the stimuli generated by a particular election campaign. Changing perceptions and evaluations of issues and party leaders—the key short-term forces influencing the electoral choices of flexible partisans—are especially important in this regard.

Regarding issues, the crucial factor is not which ones voters believe are significant, but rather their changing perceptions of which party is closest to them. When salient issues are *positional*, that is, when they are debated in "pro/con" or "for/against" terms, and parties take opposing stands on them, links between the issues and the parties are readily made, and voters can easily establish which party is closest to their personal position. If the party later changes its position on such an issue, voters who had previously supported it may be inclined to move to another party, particularly if that party has adopted a position closer to their own. Free trade is an example of the type of issue that might cause voters to change parties. However, as shown in Chapter 2, issues in Canadian elections are more likely to be *valenced*, that is, parties and public alike agree that a particular condition such as high levels of unemployment constitutes a pressing problem requiring governmental action. In such circumstances, debate focusses on which party has the best solution to the problem or, more frequently, which party or party leader can most competently deal with it. In some cases, such as in the 1993 or 1984 elections, one party may succeed in convincing voters that it has "what's needed" and, as a result, benefits handsomely from party/issue links and the vote switching that results. In others, no party may be able to make a persuasive case, and party/issue links are either not established or are made in such a fashion that no party has a *net* advantage on the issue.

Changing perceptions of party leaders and changing feelings about them also enhance the likelihood of vote switching or abstention. Although public affection for a particular leader may decline between successive elections, similar decreases in affection for other leaders may occur concurrently. As shown in Chapter 4, there is, in fact, considerable evidence that such parallel downward trends have characterized public feelings about several party leaders over the past two decades. Between 1984 and 1988, for example, feelings about Prime Minister Mulroney became more negative, whereas feelings about John Turner, already at a low ebb in 1984, receded even further. This enabled Mulroney to retain an edge over his Liberal rival. Even though he was relatively more popular than his counterparts, feelings about the then NDP leader, Ed Broadbent, followed a similar downward course. More generally, large numbers of voters change their leader preferences over time. Between 1984 and 1988, for example, only 40% ranked the three national party leaders in the same order of preference. Other surveys suggest similar amounts of individual level volatility in leader preferences.

The conventional view that variations in feelings about party leaders can prompt vote switches is well founded. Controlling for changing perceptions of which party is closest on the most important issue and for the flexibility of partisan attachments, changing party-leader preferences increased the likelihood of vote switching. This does not mean, of course, that such tendencies will necessarily work in favour of a party that has decided to go with a new leader; voters' feelings about new leaders may likewise be either negative or positive in relation to those for the leader who was replaced.[10] Moreover, changing feelings about the leaders frequently will occur in a context where other forces acting on the vote are shifting as well. Flexibility of partisanship combines with mutable feelings about issues and leaders to generate the high levels of volatility in party support that long has characterized the Canadian electorate.

Issues vs. Leaders: Voting for Change in 1993

Like several other recent elections, the 1993 contest resulted in the defeat of an incumbent party. The swing away from the governing Conservatives was massive throughout the country, and the day after the balloting, the erstwhile majority party found that it held merely two seats in Parliament. Only a few months earlier, the Conservatives had launched their bid for a third consecutive victory by replacing their decidedly unpopular leader, Brian Mulroney, with Kim Campbell. By fighting the election with a new leader, the Tories hoped this would provide the spark needed to bolster their flagging popularity. Once the campaign was underway, however, Campbell failed to strike a responsive chord with the electorate, and in the wake of the Conservatives' disastrous defeat, many inside and outside of the party claimed that her poor performance was a key factor in the rout. While this argument has prima facie plausibility, it is not correct.

Leader effects are not the only short-term force at work; issue perceptions are highly significant, and the relative importance of leaders and issues varies with the circumstances of particular election campaigns. What do the survey data tell us about the 1993 case and, more specifically, how likely is it that the Tories could have won again, or at least avoided a crushing defeat, if their new leader had proved to be more popular, with so many issues working so strongly against them?

To answer these questions, we employ data from a 1990-93 panel survey and estimate the effects of issues and leaders on voting for each of the five competing parties, controlling for prior (1990) federal and provincial party identifications, and several socio-demographic characteristics.[11] As expected, feelings about the party leaders and issue perceptions affected voting for all five parties. For every party, including the Conservatives, more positive feelings about the leader of that party were associated with an increased probability of voting for it (Figure 5.7). Also, in most cases, increasingly positive feelings about the leaders of *other* parties lessened the probability of voting for the party in question. Issues were important as well; voters' perceptions that a party was closest to them on the issue that they considered most important significantly enhanced the likelihood that they would support that party. As in earlier elections, both leader images and issue perceptions had influenced voting for the Conservatives and other parties in 1993.

Figure 5.7

Probit Analysis: Predictors of Voting in 1993 Federal Election

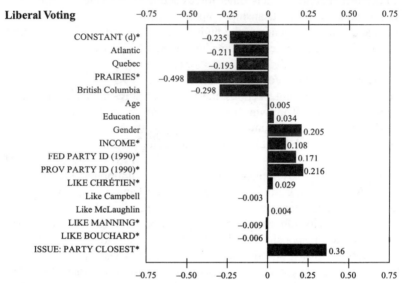

Liberal Voting

Estimated R^2 = .78; percentage correctly classified = 87.5; PRE: lambda = .70
* significant predictors in upper case, p < .05
(d) coefficient divided by 10

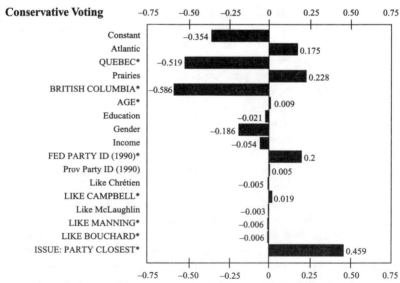

Conservative Voting

Estimated R^2 = .61; percentage correctly classified = 92.7; PRE: lambda = .59
* significant predictors in upper case, p < .05

Figure 5.7 (CONTINUED)

Probit Analysis: Predictors of Voting in 1993 Federal Election

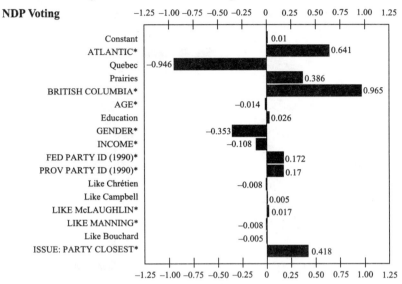

NDP Voting

Estimated R^2 = .68; percentage correctly classified = 94.9; PRE: lambda = .49
* significant predictors in upper case, p < .05

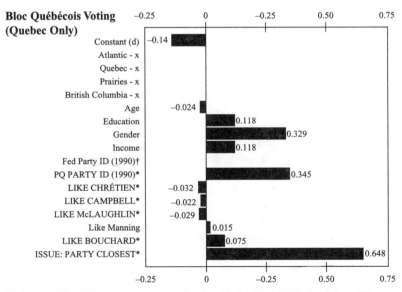

Bloc Québécois Voting (Quebec Only)

Estimated R^2 = .95; percentage correctly classified = 92.6; PRE: lambda = .87
* significant predictors in upper case, p < .05
† not available
x - variable not included in model
(d) coefficient divided by 10

Figure 5.7 (CONTINUED)

Probit Analysis: Predictors of Voting in 1993 Federal Election

Reform Voting (All Provinces Except Quebec)

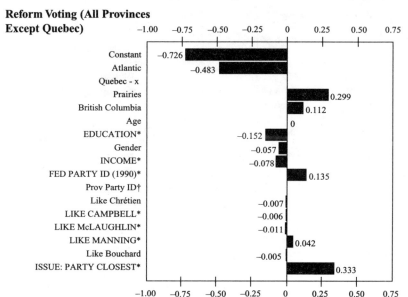

Estimated $R^2 = .77$; percentage correctly classified = 91.3; PRE: lambda = .67
* significant predictors in upper case, $p < .05$
† not available
x - variable not included in model

Source: 1993 – PSC.

The estimated leader and issue effects on Conservative voting enable us to answer the "what if" question about the impact of Campbell's (un)popularity posed above. To determine the extent to which feelings about her affected the probability that a voter would cast a Conservative ballot, we consider experimental scenarios[12] in which her popularity was artificially increased to the level obtained by her predecessor, Brian Mulroney, in 1988 (51 points on the thermometer scale), and then to that of her Liberal rival, Jean Chrétien, in 1993 (56 points). We even consider the possibility that Campbell might have been able to generate an unusually high level of popularity, setting her thermometer score equal to that obtained by Pierre Trudeau in 1968 (68 points).

The effects of these hypothetical Campbell thermometer scores on the probability of voting Conservative are considered in combination with four alternative possibilities concerning the links between the Conservatives and a voter's perception of the most important election issue. As a baseline, we first consider the real average score that the Tories received on the party-issue variable (Scenario A). As seen in Chapter 2 (p. 47), in 1993 an overwhelming majority of voters selected a party other than the Conservatives on the issue they

114

believed was most important and, thus, the Tories' actual average issue score was negative. We then hypothesize issue neutrality (Scenario B); voters did not favour the Conservatives or any other party on the issue they thought was most important; or did not think *any* issue was important. Next, we assume a weakly positive Conservative issue link (Scenario C); voters favoured the Tories on the most important issue, but considered this to be a relatively unimportant factor in their vote decision. Finally, we consider a strongly positive Conservative issue link (Scenario D); voters preferred the Tories on the most important issue, and held this to be a very important factor in their vote decision.

The results of these "what if" scenarios show that, *by themselves*, even very large increases in Campbell's popularity would have done little to bolster Conservative fortunes in 1993. Given the actual distribution of preferences for the parties on the issues, if Campbell had an average thermometer score equal to that of her rival, Jean Chrétien, the probability of a Tory vote in 1993 would have increased only marginally—from 12% to 17% (Table 5.2). Indeed, even if she had provoked a very atypically enthusiastic response like that accorded Pierre Trudeau in 1968, she would have increased the probability that a voter would opt for the Conservatives to a still dismal 23%. The failure of their new leader to generate a high level of personal popularity clearly was not the key to the Conservative defeat in 1993.

What did matter a great deal was how the voters assessed the parties on the issues. As Table 5.2 shows, for each alternative assumption about Campbell's popularity, the likelihood of a Conservative vote increased handsomely if her party was preferred, on the issue considered most important. For example, using Campbell's actual thermometer score (39 points), the probability of a Conservative vote increases from 12% (Scenario A) to fully 79% as party-issue preferences move from their actual 1993 average value to a situation where voters had a Tory preference on an issue they considered very important to their vote (Scenario D). Indeed, even if the issue was not deemed to be a very significant factor (Scenario C), the probability of a Conservative ballot increases nearly fourfold (to 45%). Of course, the Conservatives' problem in 1993 was that there were so few voters who favoured them on the issues. Well before the 1993 campaign officially began, the Tories had been "tried and found wanting" on the issues of concern to a large majority of the electorate. In particular, many voters had concluded that the Conservatives bore responsibility for the high levels of unemployment, mounting national deficit, and threats to cherished social programs that had accompanied the protracted recession plaguing the country. Moreover, during the campaign the Conservatives were unable to convince the electorate that, if returned to office, they would restore national prosperity or, at a minimum, they had as good a chance of doing so as did any of the opposition parties. Given this highly negative issue context, the Tories' brokerage politics gambit of playing the "leader card" in the run-up to the election was a loser. In 1993, issues trumped leaders.

Table 5.2

**Probabilities of Voting Conservative in 1993 by Alternative
Assumptions about Leader Popularity and Party-Issue Preferences**

Assumptions about Campbell's Popularity

If Campbell had been as popular as:

	Actual Popularity (39)*	Mulroney in 1988 (51)	Chrétien in 1993 (56)	Trudeau in 1968 (68)
Assumptions About Party-Issue Preference				
A. Actual party-issue preference in 1993	12	14	17	23
B. Neutral among parties or no important issue	28	35	39	48
C. Favour PCs and issue not very important	45	54	58	66
D. Favour PCs and issue very important	79	84	87	91

* scores on 100-point thermometer scale
Note: Numbers in table are probabilities of voting Conservative in 1993 given alternative assumptions about leader popularity and party-issue preferences.

Source: 1993 − PSC.

Conclusion

High levels of instability in voting behaviour can be understood in terms of how short-term forces at work in an election interact with voters' partisan characteristics. Changing perceptions of parties' issue positions and issue competence are often crucial. The key factor is not which issues voters believe are especially significant, but rather their beliefs about which party is *closest* to them on these issues. The images of the party leaders also are influential. Sometimes a change in the impact of leader images stems from replacing a party leader, but the images of the same leaders can also change

116

over time. Always present, leader effects do not necessarily offset other forces, particularly when these are running strongly against a party. An excellent example is provided by the case of Kim Campbell. Even if she had been greeted with much greater enthusiasm, personal popularity would not have offset the negative issue evaluations that bedevilled the Conservatives in 1993.

Processes of electoral change in Canada are complex, and oftentimes swift. Many Canadians are flexible partisans who do not have enduring party loyalties. It is these flexible partisans who illustrate the predominant public reaction to the economic agenda of recent elections. Recognizing that the Liberals, Conservatives, and even the NDP share the commitment to neoconservatism, despite the rhetoric of the moment, Canadians invest little emotional energy in establishing solid and lasting ties to any of the parties. Rather they are treated as interchangeable, and voters choose those that seem most credible at the moment that a decision has to be made. This moment is often late in an election campaign, when the leaders and pundits have had their say and the time for quiet reflection on past performance and future prospects has arrived.

A brokerage party system produces a highly volatile issue agenda and abrupt changes in party leader images. Since large segments of the electorate are sensitive to these short-term forces, the possibility of substantial swings in party support from one election to the next is always present. This chapter has examined the choices made by individual voters. How these choices come together to produce a collective decision that confers, or fails to confer a mandate on a governing party is the topic of Chapter 6. Chapter 7 examines the behaviour of Canadian voters in another context of political choice, the October 1992 national referendum on the constitution.

Notes

1. On the persistent weakness of the relationship between measures of social class and Canadian voting behaviour, see Harold D. Clarke and Marianne C. Stewart, "Canada," in M. Franklin, T. Mackie, and H. Valen, eds., *Electoral Change: Responses to Evolving Social and Attitudinal Structures in Western Countries* (Cambridge: Cambridge University Press, 1992). See also H.D. Clarke et al., *Political Choice in Canada* (Toronto: McGraw-Hill Ryerson, 1979; abridged, 1980), Chapter 4.

2. These variables are measured: age—in years; annual family income—nine categories ranging from $10,000 per year or less = 1 to $80,000 per year or more; education—elementary school or less = 1, some secondary school = 2, completed secondary school or technical school, community college = 3, some university = 4, completed university (B.A., B.Sc. or more) = 5; region/ethnicity—a set of dummy (0-1) variables—Atlantic provinces, Quebec-francophone, Quebec-anglophone, the Prairies, British Columbia (Ontario is the reference category).

3. The party leader variables are scores on the 100-point thermometer scales for the five party leaders (Bouchard, Campbell, Chrétien, Manning, and McLaughlin). The issue variable differs according to which party's vote is being analysed. For example, in the Liberal case, voters selecting the Liberals as closest on the most important election issue are scored 1, those selecting another party, −1, and those selecting no party or saying there was no important issue, 0. These scores are weighted by multiplying them by a variable assessing the perceived importance of the issue in the vote decision. This latter variable is scored: "very important" = 3, "fairly important" = 2, "not very important" or "don't know" = 1. The resulting index ranges from +3 to −3. Similar issue variables are constructed for analysing voting for the other parties.

4. For a more detailed discussion of the method employed here, as well as comparable analyses of voting in the 1968 and 1974 federal elections, see Clarke et al., *Political Choice in Canada* (unabridged, 1979), pp. 343-55. Analyses of voting in the 1979, 1980, and 1984 elections may be found in H.D. Clarke et al., *Absent Mandate*, 1st ed. (Toronto: Gage Educational Publishing, 1984), pp. 131-35; and H.D. Clarke et al., *Absent Mandate*, 2nd ed. (Toronto: Gage Educational Publishing Company, 1991), pp. 110-13.

5. The survey question was: "In deciding how to vote in the recent election, which was the most important to you—the party leaders, the candidates here in this constituency, or the parties taken as a whole?"

6. For analyses regarding the weakness of local candidate effects, see *Political Choice in Canada* (unabridged, 1979), pp. 343-48, and *Absent Mandate*, 1st ed., pp. 131-35. See also John Wilson, "The Myth of Candidate Partisanship," *Journal of Canadian Studies* 3 (1968): 21-31; Robert Cunningham, "The Impact of the Local Candidate in Canadian Federal Elections," *Canadian Journal of Political Science* 4 (1971): 287-310; and William P. Irvine, "Does the Candidate Make a Difference?" *Canadian Journal of Political Science* 15 (1982): 755-82.

7. Data on the specific issues of concern to voters mentioning an issue basis for their selection of parties, party leaders, or local candidates as the most important factor in their vote decision are not available for 1988 or 1993.

8. For analyses documenting that, net of other factors, levels of political interest do not affect the likelihood of switching or abstention, see Clarke et al., *Absent Mandate*, 2nd ed., pp. 122-23.

9. In 1988, for example, 41% of those switching their votes from the previous election indicated that they made up their minds during the last two weeks of the campaign, whereas 25% of those not switching made their voting decision this late [CPS]. Similar distinctions in the time of vote decision for switchers and non-switchers are found in data from earlier elections.

10. See D.K. Stewart and R.K. Carty, "Does Changing the Party Leader Provide an Electoral Boost? A Study of Canadian Provincial Parties: 1960-1992," *Canadian Journal of Political Science* 26 (1993): 313-30.

11.   Probit analyses are used to estimate the effects of the various predictor variables in these vote models. See, for example, R.S. Pindyck and D.L. Rubinfeld, *Econometric Models and Economic Forecasts*, 3rd ed. (London: McGraw-Hill, 1991), Chapter 10. The socio-demographic variables in the analyses are described in note 2 above; the issue and party leader variables are described in note 3. The measures of federal and provincial party identification used depend on which party's vote is being analysed. For example, in the Liberal analysis, the measures are scored: very strong Liberal = +3, fairly strong Liberal = +2, not very strong or leaning Liberal = +1, non-identifier = 0, not very strong or leaning other party identifier = –1, fairly strong other party identifier = –2, very strong other party identifier = –3. Similar party identification variables are constructed for analysing voting for the other parties.

12.   Except for region and gender, other variables in the vote models are fixed at their mean values. Region is set to Ontario, and gender, to female. The decision to examine the behaviour of a hypothetical female voter in Ontario is, of course, only one of many different possibilities. However, the choice is not consequential; other region and gender combinations also show that party-issue linkages, and not feelings about the Conservative leader, were the key factor in understanding the Tories' electoral misfortunes in 1993.

Promise, Performance, Mandate?

In Chapter 5, we addressed the question: "How do voters decide?" Just as important, however, are the more complex questions: "What decides elections?" and "What do elections decide?" The former calls for an aggregation of the reasons for individual decision making, in order to find the overall patterns of stability and change within them. The latter question is more speculative. It requires an interpretation of the meaning of an election result in terms of its policy consequences. In a democracy, even though elected representatives make the key decisions, there is expected to be a close connection between the policy directions favoured by the citizenry and the actions of government. In theory, elections are supposed to provide that linkage by signalling voters' policy preferences. Do elections give politicians a mandate to enact particular policies?

Politicians often act as if they do. In 1993, the victorious Liberals claimed a popular mandate, not just to govern, but to implement various pledges contained in their campaign manifesto, the Red Book. They moved quickly to cancel a contract to purchase helicopters for the armed forces, and also to abrogate an agreement entered into by the previous government, which would have privatized part of Pearson International Airport in Toronto. They started allocating money under their Infrastructure Program. Other parties also acted as if the 1993 election result had given them mandates. The Reform Party took as its parliamentary mission the task of prodding the government to cut the budget. The Bloc Québécois asserted that the people of Quebec had supported their calls for independence, whereas Jean Chrétien said "I don't have any mandate to negotiate separation."[1] Similar interpretations of the meaning of the balloting can be culled from post-mortems of nearly every federal or provincial election. The Progressive Conservative government interpreted its 1988 victory as giving it a mandate to proceed with its plan for free trade with the United States, and the opposition reacted by dropping their delaying tactics, which had been holding up passage of the FTA legislation. The notion that election results confer mandates also is widely accepted by the general public, causing people to become agitated when elected governments ignore their campaign promises. In 1984, the Conservatives pledged that keeping social programs safe from attack in government efforts to cut the budget deficit was a "sacred trust." When they then attempted to de-index pensions and change the unemployment insurance rules, the public expressed outrage at this seeming betrayal. Similarly, during the 1974 election, the Conservatives committed themselves to imposing a 90-day wage and price freeze, which led many observers to view the subsequent Liberal victory as a direct repudiation of an incomes-policy approach to combatting inflation. When the Trudeau government adopted a wage-and-price control program less than a year later, a common reaction was that this betrayed the will of the voters. The Liberals' review of social policy after the 1993 election has been criticized on the grounds that the Red Book published during the campaign made no mention of this impending reassessment.[2] Regardless of the circumstances under which an election is called, all election campaigns give considerable attention to issue questions (see Chapter 2). In the process, the belief is encouraged that the election will produce a clear verdict and will have direct policy consequences.

We have seen earlier that elements of the economic restructuring project appear in election campaigns under various circumstances, often disguised or piecemeal, but at times in a form suitable for a clear public judgment to be rendered. Free trade, and the speed of deficit reduction are two recent examples. The norms of participatory democracy would seem to suggest that such opportunities to pass judgment, while imperfect, are very important, both because of the magnitude of the economic project being undertaken and because elections and referendums are currently the only political institutions in which the participation of the entire citizenry is expected and solicited. They should be examined for indications that the public has accepted or rejected the specific policies that implement the vast elite projects in the economic or constitutional spheres that have driven Canadian politics over the past quarter century.

A more elitist school of democratic thought does not accept this premise, but rather believes that the role of the public is limited to selecting the representatives who will govern them for periods of time. "Fortunately," says Donald Forbes in an examination of an earlier edition of *Absent Mandate*, "the Canadian system of government is *representative* democracy, not direct democracy along Athenian lines, and not the Swiss system of constitutional legislation by referenda."[3] This view of democracy holds that the election results in terms of seats won are all that matters; the reasons for the public decision are many and are not relevant to an interpretation of the meaning of the outcome. Thus, the important thing about the 1988 federal election was that the Conservatives won it, regardless of whether or not the country wished the Free Trade Agreement to determine their economic future. Elections should not be probed too deeply for evidence of the presence or absence of policy mandates given or denied to those in government by the electorate.

That we disagree with this position is obvious. Despite the numerous difficulties that voters encounter in making clear their wishes in various policy areas, there is considerable evidence that they wish to do so, and are in fact frustrated at the obstacles that stand in the way. We do not embrace the "realist" view of elections as cattle markets, where voters are only engaged in selecting the choicest sides of beef. Rather, we believe that an examination of the difficulties of achieving policy mandate connections between electors and elected may allow us to better understand the growing public cynicism about politics.

However, the elite theorists ask an important question. Is it reasonable to interpret elections in policy terms in the first place? A mandate that does not exist in any meaningful sense can hardly be betrayed and need not be fulfilled. Just what was it about the voting in 1988 that might have given the Conservatives a go-ahead on free trade? And where should we look for 1993 mandates in the party competition over who could best reduce the unemployment rate and cut the budget deficit? This chapter examines the validity of policy-related interpretations of elections. It also assesses the extent to which governments can be considered to have received mandates for their proposals in an election, or conversely, whether a party's electoral loss demonstrates conclusively that its policies lack public support.

One Election or Many?

The considerable degree of instability evident in individual voting behaviour in Canada is not always translated into wide swings in election results. Between most pairs of elections, the overall national vote for each party varies within a fairly narrow range. However, elections occasionally produce large turnovers of parliamentary seats, such as the landslides of 1958 and 1984, and the shake up of the party system in 1993. Part of the explanation for the unpredictable nature of the national results lies in the regional nature of Canadian politics.

Support for parties in the various regions of the country may change abruptly. Nowhere is this more apparent than in Quebec over the last decade. Previously a bastion of Liberal support in federal politics, Quebec shifted massively to the Conservatives in 1984 and maintained this stance in 1988.

However, the electoral situation in 1993 in Quebec was completely different; the collapse of the Conservatives was accompanied by the dramatic rise of a new party, the Bloc Québécois, which captured 49% of the province's vote. Quebec is not an exception; voting change in the other regions of the country also has been substantial. In successive elections since 1979, the Liberal vote in the Atlantic provinces went down 8%, then up 9%, then down almost 12%, up 10%, and finally up another 12%. The swings in the Ontario vote have often been of similar magnitude, and were actually greater in 1993 because of the Reform Party's strong showing in the province. Changes in the vote in Ontario take on particular importance given the number of parliamentary seats at stake in that province. The Liberal sweep of 98 of Ontario's 99 seats in the 1993 election was by itself nearly enough to secure the result. And even though the West has been a stronghold for the Conservatives ever since the Diefenbaker era, that party has suffered gains and losses from one election to the next, culminating in the defection of much of its vote in the West to the Reform Party in 1993.

In some elections, like 1984 and 1993, the victorious party increased its vote in all parts of the country, albeit at different rates. In others, however, a party takes the reins of power with only some regions delivering a positive verdict on its performance. When the Conservatives formed the government in 1979, for example, they had increased their percentage of the vote in only six of the ten provinces. Although the Liberals declined precipitously in the West in that election, the party actually managed to improve its showing in Quebec. The 1980 election saw the same type of regional variation in the results. The broad improvement in Liberal fortunes that occurred in Quebec, Ontario, and the Atlantic provinces did not extend to the West, where the party's meagre representation was reduced even further. In 1988, results showed substantial Liberal gains from the PCs in the Atlantic region, while the NDP and smaller parties took votes from the PCs in the West. The 1993 election saw different parties in different regions benefitting from the collapse of the Conservative vote.

Such regional variation presents one of the first obstacles to the ability of any party to achieve a true mandate in an election. When one part of the country renders a positive verdict on an incumbent government, or an incoming government, and another does not, the implications for policy can be difficult to ascertain. At times, these regional disparities can directly affect the governability of the country. Representation of the West in the federal Cabinet was a serious problem for several Liberal governments during the Trudeau years. A shortage of francophone talent from Quebec for government ministries affected the Conservatives in 1979, and the Liberals in 1993. Feelings of exclusion from the corridors of power engendered by these disparate regional voting patterns helps to create an atmosphere in which political discontent thrives.

Sources of Electoral Change

The changes that take place from one election to another stem from two sources—conversion and replacement. *Conversion* refers to the transfer of voting support from one party to another. *Replacement*, in contrast, refers to the fact that the electorate does not remain exactly the same from one election to the next. Replacement generally takes place over a substantial period of time as new generations of voters enter the electorate and older ones exit. Occasionally, however, changes in electoral laws, patterns of immigration and emigration, or sharp changes in voting turnout may significantly alter the composition of an electorate more quickly.

As the baby boom generation began to enter the electorate in the late 1960s, the age profile of Canadian voters became for a time progressively younger. Relatively high postwar birth rates, along with the lowering of the voting age to 18 years, combined to add significant numbers of new voters to the lists. This infusion of young people into the electorate peaked in 1979, when 2.3 million new voters joined the rolls, amounting to 15% of all those eligible to vote. More recently, this trend has slackened due to a lowering of birth rates and the ageing of the boom generation. The proportion of new voters entering the electorate dropped to about 8% in 1988 and 1993. Although in more modest proportions, more new voters still enter the electorate in each election than leave it through death or emigration. While not all newly eligible voters go to the polls, any significant differences between their behaviour and that of persons voting in previous elections can clearly affect the results.

Another type of replacement that can exert an impact on election outcomes stems from the behaviour of *transient* voters, that is, those who do not vote in every election. While turnout in Canadian federal elections fluctuates, it generally does so within a fairly narrow range.[4] When turnout does decrease, there is usually some readily identifiable cause. In 1980 and 1993, turnout dipped to 69.3% and 69.6%, respectively, from its normal average of 75%. In both of these cases a voting list was used that was a year out of date rather than compiled at the time of the election call.[5] In every election, a number of individuals who did not vote the preceding time re-enter the active electorate, while others who had previously cast a ballot choose to drop out. Together, these transient voters represent a replacement factor as large as that of the cadre of newly eligible voters.

The relative balance of conversion and replacement effects in four elections may be seen in Figure 6.1. In all of these elections, both types of effects were substantial. Of those participating in the 1979 contest, 20% were persons who switched their votes, while 55% voted for the same party as in the previous election. The remainder (25%) represents other changes in the voting population, divided about equally between new voters and

124

Figure 6.1

Sources of Change in Four Federal Elections

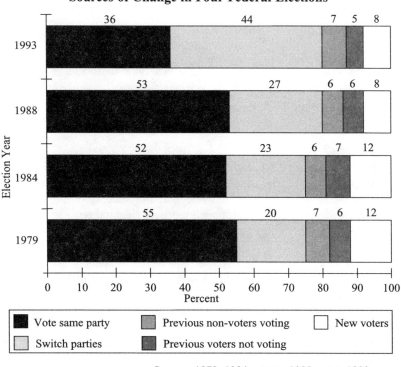

Source: 1979, 1984 – CNES; 1988 – CPS; 1993 – PSC.

transient voters moving into or out of the electorate. The replacement effect was of similar magnitude in 1984, and since the amount of vote switching was higher for the 1980-84 pair of elections than it was for the 1974-79 pair, the impact of conversion in 1984 nearly equalled that of replacement. By 1988, the infusion of new voters had slowed to 8%, and the total replacement effect was reduced to 20% of the electorate, a level that was maintained in 1993. Conversion effects increased in importance in 1988, and the dramatic increase in vote switching in 1993 further accentuated these effects.

Population trends, assuming they continue in the current direction, will reduce the importance of the net replacement effect in future Canadian elections. Nevertheless, the existence of any new group of voters participating in each instance hinders the interpretation of a given election as having produced a mandate for or against certain policies, in the sense that voters are seen as delivering retrospective judgments on incumbent governments. The electorate that voted to oust the Liberals from power in

125

1979 was quite a different electorate from the one that had entrusted them with office five years previously. The electorate that sustained the Conservatives on the government benches in 1988 was also a different group from that which had given them a landslide victory in 1984. And the voters who took chances on two new parties in 1993 were not all the same ones who had sustained the old party system in 1988. Too many changes over time occur in the composition of the electorate to allow us to think in terms of a fixed complement of voters rendering periodic judgments, retrospective or otherwise, on the policies and performance of a government.

Who Gains?

Vote switchers, new voters, and transient voters, as we have identified them in the previous section, have been differentially important in recent elections. A strong case can be made that the success of the Trudeau Liberals during the 1970s was founded more on electoral replacement than conversion. For example, when that party went from being a minority government in 1972 to a majority in 1974, it did so despite the fact that patterns of vote switching between the two elections actually favoured the Conservatives by a slight margin.[6] However, new voters in 1974 heavily favoured the Liberals, as did transient voters. The 1979 election produced a minority Conservative government, but here again new voters favoured the Liberals. The Liberals' strength among new voters was not enough to save this election for that party, but it may have limited the scope of the Conservative victory and set the stage for the fall of the Clark government only seven months later. The size of the complement of new voters in 1979 alone was enough to assure that any differences in support for one of the parties would be felt in the result.[7]

The 1980 election represented the last hurrah for the Liberal Party prior to its comeback in 1993. In 1980, the behaviour of switchers (that is, the conversion effect) favoured the Liberals. It also worked to the benefit of the NDP, as that party gained 30% of the vote among people who switched their votes between 1979 and 1980. Transient voters in 1980 were not nearly as favourable to the Liberals as were switchers, although the party enjoyed a slight advantage among this group. More important, perhaps, was the effect of 1979 Conservatives who chose not to vote in 1980. Such a "stay-at-home" effect has periodically appeared in Canadian elections, to hurt an incumbent government seeking re-election. The government's supporters are discontented, but cannot bring themselves to support the opposition.

The Conservative landslide victory in 1984 was produced by four distinct elements. First, the switching pattern was virtually unidirectional; while the total amount of vote switching from 1980 to 1984 was only slightly higher than normal, it was mostly toward the Conservatives. In fact,

Table 6.1

Electoral Turnover: 1984–88

1988 Vote

1984 Vote	Liberal	PC	NDP	Other	Not Voting
Liberal	12.6	4.3	1.7	0.6	1.8
PC	7.3	30.5	3.9	2.3	2.9
NDP	1.8	1.4	9.2	0.2	0.5
Other	0.2	0.9	0.3	0.4	0.2
Not voting	1.9	2.0	1.0	0.4	3.5
Not eligible	2.1	3.0	1.2	0.2	1.6

100%

Note: Entire table adds to 100%; individual rows or columns do not.

Source: CPS; behaviour of newly eligible voters calculated from other surveys.

almost as much of the total electorate switched to the Conservatives from a 1980 Liberal vote as stayed with the Liberals (13.4% versus 15%.) These Liberal-Conservative switches were countered by a move on the part of only 1% of the electorate in the opposite direction. A similar switching imbalance favouring the Conservatives was that by 1980 NDP voters. The Liberal debacle was complete when over five times as many people changed from a Liberal vote to the NDP as did the opposite.

Three other factors helped to produce the 1984 result. A large number of 1980 Liberals cast no ballot at all in 1984. Next, the Conservatives showed an edge in capturing the votes of 1980 non-voters who moved into the active electorate in 1984. Substantially more of these transient voters supported the PCs in 1984 than voted for all the other parties combined. Finally, for the first time since the election of Diefenbaker, new voters favoured the Tories. The Conservative margin among this category of voter was not as high, however, as with switchers or transients; the party won only a plurality of the new voters, not a majority. Still, for the first time in years, the Conservative party in 1984 had gained more than its rivals from the processes of electoral replacement. The way in which it had fashioned its victory gave its strategists hope that the building blocks for future successes were firmly in place.

The pattern of electoral turnover from 1984 to 1988 is shown in Table 6.1.[8] When the net results of various switching patterns are computed, the changes favour the opposition parties. From their overall majority of the

Table 6.2

Electoral Turnover: 1988–93

1993 Vote

1988 Vote	Liberal	PC	NDP	Reform	BQ	Other	Not Voting
Liberal	18.1	1.3	0.7	2.1	1.5	0.3	1.8
PC	9.4	7.8	1.2	8.5	4.9	0.4	3.6
NDP	4.2	1.3	4.1	2.2	0.9	0.7	2.1
Reform	–	0.1	–	0.9	–	–	–
Other	–	0.1	0.1	0.2	0.5	0.3	0.1
Not voting	1.9	0.5	–	1.4	0.5	0.1	5.1
Not eligible	3.5	0.6	0.3	1.1	0.9	0.1	4.2
							$\overline{100\%}$

Note: Entire table adds to 100%; individual rows or columns do not.

Source: 1993 – PSC, INS.

popular vote in 1984, the Conservatives lost votes through conversion to the Liberals, the NDP, and smaller parties. As in previous elections, an incumbent government lost some of its previous support in 1988. In the case of the 1988 Conservatives, however, the votes were being lost from such a massive total that those remaining were more than enough to give the party victory with a reduced majority of parliamentary seats.

In addition, the process of replacement helped the Conservatives offset the losses they suffered through vote switching, just as it had sustained the Liberals in previous decades. The Tories won a very slight plurality of transient voters who moved into the electorate from a 1984 abstention. But those who behaved in the opposite manner, deciding *not* to cast a ballot in 1988, were slightly more likely to have been 1984 Conservatives (2.9% of the electorate, as compared to a combined total of 2.5% for all the other parties). For a second time, newly eligible voters favoured the Conservatives. Thus, the PC government sustained itself in power in 1988 by limiting its losses through conversion and gaining marginally from the replacement process.

Table 6.2 shows that the Liberal victory in the 1993 election was produced by a combination of factors. Retention of past supporters was a major key to the party's success. Added to this was a flow of votes to the Liberals through conversion from other parties. For example, 9.4% of the electorate was composed of PC voters who switched to the Liberals, while only 1.3% went the other way. There was a similar imbalance in the NDP-

Liberal switching pattern. There was a massive amount of vote switching between 1988 and 1993 (Figure 6.1, p. 125). In fact, if we consider only those people who voted in both elections, the proportion of switchers rises to over half. Much of this behaviour involved people abandoning the Conservatives and the NDP. Fewer Conservatives stayed with their party from 1988 to 1993 than switched to the Liberals or Reform.[9] A further substantial percentage changed from the Tories to the Bloc Québécois. The NDP lost slightly more of their 1988 voters to the Liberals than they retained for themselves, and lost a further substantial group to Reform. Overall, the proportion of people changing their behaviour between 1988 and 1993 was probably the largest between any pair of federal elections in modern Canadian history.

Replacement also contributed to the Liberal victory in 1993. Table 6.2 shows that 1988 Conservative and NDP voters who decided not to vote in 1993 were more numerous than Liberal voters who did the same. Of the three major parties who contested both elections, only the Liberals achieved an approximate equivalence between 1988 voters who decided not to vote this time, and previous non-voters deciding to vote for the party. Finally, the Liberals gained substantially from the influx of new voters in 1993; more of them went to the Liberals than to all the other parties combined.

While these statistics indicate the relative importance of conversion and replacement in explaining election outcomes, they do not tell the whole story. To address the "why" rather than the "who" of elections, we need to look at the reasons behind voting choices. Part of this question has been addressed in the preceding chapter. We know that much of the total change that takes place in any given election is accounted for by flexible partisans, and that issues and leaders are both important in explaining individual voting behaviour. But the extent to which these factors explain election outcomes remains to be determined. An examination of the last four federal elections enables us to see how these factors shaped their results.

The 1980 Election

The Conservative minority government formed in 1979 did not last long.[10] The extent of the Tories' decisive defeat in 1980 could be traced both to the fact that the party lost ground nearly everywhere (it lost seats or votes in every province except Newfoundland), and to its inability to mobilize all the voters who had brought it to power nine months earlier. The decline in voting turnout that took place in 1980 worked strongly against the PCs. The proportion of the electorate moving from the Conservatives in 1979 to non-voting in 1980 was nearly as large as the percentage switching from Conservative to Liberal. Disillusionment with the short-lived Clark government was thereby manifested in two ways by many of its previous supporters: either they voted for the opposition or they did not vote at all.

The explanations for the 1980 Tory defeat were largely rooted in the circumstances of the election of the previous year. The Conservatives believed that they had won a clear mandate in the 1979 contest, and that they should govern as if they had a majority. Yet, in attempting to deliver on its campaign promises, the Clark government displayed a sense of uncertainty and hesitation that left it open to charges of policy flip-flops. The plan to move the Canadian embassy in Israel to Jerusalem was abandoned, but only after much public agonizing and considerable pressure from abroad. The proposal to allow the deduction of mortgage interest from income taxes turned out to set lower limits than many had expected. Promises to cut taxes were postponed. In short, the Clark government sought both to fulfil a dubious policy mandate and to hedge its bets at the same time.

The issues on which the 1980 election was fought were quite different from those of 1979. In part, this was because the election came about through the defeat of the government budget, thereby making it and the economic policies that it sought to implement the focal point of the campaign. The budget had announced an 18-cent increase in federal taxes on gasoline. Though energy conservation was one rationale for this tax, the underlying effect was to implement a move to world pricing for energy. A companion move was the announced intention to privatize Petro-Canada, the government-run oil company that had been assembled at considerable cost during the years of the energy crisis in the early 1970s. The decision to bring in these policies represented attempts to decrease the role of government and to increase the reliance on market forces, positions supported by influential members of the Conservative caucus.[11] But as already noted, these policies were not intended to be the centrepiece of an election campaign. In spite of their minority status in the House of Commons, the Tories did not seem to realize that their government was vulnerable. Rather, these components of the economic restructuring project were to be introduced at the beginning of the government's term in office, and were expected to be accepted as the status quo by the time the next election would be called. And, when that election did take place, the Conservatives expected to face a Liberal Party led by Donald Macdonald, a man as committed to neoconservative economics as Michael Wilson or Sinclair Stevens.

It was commonly believed that the Crosbie budget, and particularly its provision of a hefty gasoline tax, were responsible for the Tories' electoral defeat. The evidence suggests otherwise. While the budget itself was not especially popular with the public, it was not as unpopular as some of its critics believed. In fact, opinion concerning the budget was nearly evenly divided. In 1980, 53% of those expressing an opinion on the budget were favourably disposed to it, while 47% were unfavourable. This division of opinion was reflected in the voting patterns among the 13% of the 1980

Table 6.3

Effects of Party Leaders: 1980–93 Elections

A. 1980 Election

Voting pattern	1980 Vote		
	Liberal	PC	NDP
Switch to	1.9	0.6	0.9
Remain	9.0	1.7	1.0
Enter/re-enter	0.4	0.1	—
	11.3	2.4	1.9

B. 1984 Election

Voting pattern	1984 Vote		
	Liberal	PC	NDP
Switch to	0.4	4.0	0.3
Remain	1.7	3.3	0.7
Enter/re-enter	0.5	2.1	0.2
	2.6	9.4	1.2

C. 1988 Election

Voting pattern	1988 Vote		
	Liberal	PC	NDP
Switch to	0.2	0.5	0.8
Remain	0.6	1.8	0.5
Enter/re-enter	—	0.2	—
	0.8	2.5	1.3

D. 1993 Election

Voting pattern	1993 Vote				
	Liberal	PC	NDP	Reform	BQ
Switch to	1.7	0.3	0.1	0.6	1.4
Remain	1.7	0.3	0.1	–	–
Enter/re-enter	0.4	0.1	—	—	—
	3.8	0.7	0.2	0.6	1.4

Note: Respondents mentioning leader personality as most important factor in voting decision; percentages of total electorate.

Source: 1980, 1984 – CNES; 1988 – CPS; 1993 – INS.

Table 6.4

Effects of Issues in the 1980 Election

Most Important Issue Mentioned

All economic issues

Voting pattern	1980 Vote		
	Liberal	**PC**	**NDP**
Switch to	2.4	2.2	2.3
Remain	9.5	10.4	4.7
Enter/re-enter	0.6	0.9	0.2
	12.5	13.5	7.2
Issue voters only	7.3	9.4	4.3

The Crosbie budget

Voting pattern	1980 Vote		
	Liberal	**PC**	**NDP**
Switch to	1.2	0.8	0.7
Remain	3.8	4.4	1.5
Enter/re-enter	0.4	0.6	0.1
	5.4	5.8	2.3
Issue voters only	2.1	2.3	1.0

Oil and gas prices, the 18-cent tax

Voting pattern	1980 Vote		
	Liberal	**PC**	**NDP**
Switch to	1.2	1.1	0.8
Remain	5.0	5.7	1.4
Enter/re-enter	0.4	0.5	–
	6.6	7.3	2.2
Issue voters only	2.4	2.9	1.3

Note: Voters only; percentages of total electorate.

Source: 1980 – CNES.

electorate who defined the budget as *the* most important election issue. Table 6.4 shows that, within this group, votes for the two major parties divided as evenly as did opinion on the budget, with the Conservatives actually doing slightly better overall than the Liberals.[12] Among switchers alone, there was a slight Liberal advantage, but it was not large enough to affect the result. No party gained a clear advantage on the resource issues in the 1980 election, although substantial numbers of voters did name them as the most important issue in the election.

As we examine each subsequent election to see whether the voters conferred a policy mandate on the victors, it is useful to go one step further than just noting which issues were named as the most important. It is useful to know, as well, whether this issue was particularly important to the voter. After all, as we have seen earlier, people may make their voting decisions for a variety of leader, candidate, and party reasons, only some of which have to do with the issues that the politicians embrace. Using the series of questions in which voters were queried as to whether there were issue reasons behind their choice of leader, candidate, or party as the most important factor in their voting decision, we identify in Table 6.4 and subsequent tables, a group of *issue voters*. These issue voters are the subgroup of the electorate who have the real potential to give a government a policy mandate, since they are the ones who report making their decisions on this basis. Table 6.4 indicates that in the 1980 election, there were only small differences in the parties chosen by issue voters concerned with economic issues in general, and the budget and resource issues in particular.

The leadership factor presents an entirely different picture (Table 6.3A). Leadership was not any more salient to the 1980 electorate than it had been previously, but the Liberals enjoyed a much greater advantage in this area than they had even in earlier elections during the Trudeau period. Joe Clark's popularity had reached a very low ebb by the time of 1980 election, while Trudeau's, although lower than in 1974 or 1979, was nevertheless greater than that of his rivals (see Chapter 4, p. 77). The net effect of this Liberal advantage may be seen in Table 6.3A. Among those naming leader personality as the most important factor in their voting decision and switching parties between 1979 and 1980, the Liberal advantage was about 3 to 1. It was more than 5 to 1 among those remaining with the same party in the two elections. Overall, the percentage of voters who named leadership most important *and* who cast a Liberal ballot was 11.3% of all voters, while the parallel PC group accounted for only 2.4%. An effect of this magnitude would have been extremely difficult for the Conservatives to overcome, even had one or more issues worked more clearly in their favour. Although the issue preference for the Tories had been sufficient in 1979 to overcome the Liberal advantage on the leadership factor, no such offsetting process was at work in 1980.

In spite of its seemingly decisive outcome, the 1980 election failed to deliver a clear mandate for any particular set of policies from either Liberals or Conservatives. While the Tory budget, and issues associated with it (such as the 18-cent tax) were the focus of the campaign, public opinion on these questions remained divided throughout. The same was true of the more general economic issues, which rarely yield any clear policy mandate. The Liberals talked of the need for a new industrial strategy, the regulation of oil prices, and the goal of greater Canadian ownership of the oil industry, but did not spell out in detail what was to become their National Energy Program, the focus of so much controversy once the party achieved office. In 1980, only on the question of "leadership" did there appear to be a decisive choice on the part of the electorate—a clear rejection of Clark in favour of Trudeau. But such a choice delivers a mandate, not for new policies, but only for different leaders. Within little more than a year, the Trudeau Liberals were once again riding low in the polls.

The 1984 Election

Restored to the government benches in the winter of 1980, the Trudeau Liberals embarked on an ambitious program of action on both the economic and constitutional fronts. Though some observers claim to see the Liberal program as fulfilling promises made during the 1980 campaign,[13] the National Energy Program went far beyond the campaign rhetoric about sharing the nation's energy resources to create a true Canadian community and creating "blended" or "made in Canada" oil prices.[14] In an attempt to counter the privatizing impulses of the Tories, the Liberals announced a nationalizing and interventionist economic thrust that was dubbed by Donald Smiley the "Third National Policy."[15] The National Energy Program was designed to assert the authority of the federal government over the provinces through control of oil prices and provide an enhanced role for Petro-Canada in oil exploration and development.[16]

Several factors combined to blunt the Trudeau initiative and reassert the basic direction of the market-driven economic strategy that the Conservatives had started to implement. Faced with an irate Alberta government and a hostile Reagan administration in the United States, the Trudeau government backtracked and compromised in an effort to escape criticism for the deteriorating economic conditions of the early 1980s. Unemployment, which had been moving upwards throughout the previous decade, took another leap, reaching double digits for the first time since the Great Depression (see Figure 1.1, p. 5). In 1982, the gross national product actually declined for the first time since the 1930s. The Canadian dollar slipped in value against the U.S. dollar, a development welcomed by exporters. Consumers, however, suffered a drop in purchasing power. Interest rates were pushed to record levels of over 20%, stopping most new investment and home buying, and threatening mortgagees with the loss of their homes. The budget deficits of the federal government and most of the provincial governments also rose, leaving little room for new fiscal initiatives to alleviate the situation. The only bright spot was a reduced inflation rate, which had declined to 6% by 1983. However, the fact that it took a recession to bring it down meant that economic problems still held centre stage.

Adding to its economic woes, the country had also gone through an unprecedented period of constitutional upheaval. The Quebec referendum was held in May 1980, but that momentous event provided no rest from proposals for change in the framework of government. Prime Minister Trudeau seized the occasion of his unexpected return to office to advance his long-standing plan to patriate the Canadian constitution from its nominal control by Great Britain. As the country had come to expect, there was no consultation of the general public on this plan, either in the 1980 election or subsequently. Trudeau was prepared for the federal government to act unilaterally if necessary in carrying out its constitutional plan. In the end, it was accomplished through a prolonged negotiation with the provincial governments, in which discussion focussed on the main stumbling block to patriation, the establishment of an amending formula that affirmed the rights of the provinces without allowing each one a veto over any change.[17] Agreement was finally achieved on such a formula, together with one of Trudeau's main projects—the addition to the Canadian constitution of a Charter of Rights and Freedoms, which provided a list of "entrenched" rights for citizens. The agreement, however, was achieved only with the nine provinces other than Quebec, which had refused to sign the accord or participate further in the constitutional reform process. There was controversy about the Charter as well, both over its contents and the "notwithstanding clause," a provision that provinces could exempt some of their laws from it if they wished. Thus, the acclaim the Liberals might have expected for "bringing home the constitution" was tempered by the limited nature of the accomplishment, and by criticism that interested groups throughout the country had had to struggle to make their voices heard.

Embattled on all issue fronts, the Liberals retreated to their old ally, the leadership factor, in designing their 1984 campaign strategy.[18] The party accepted Trudeau's resignation and chose a new leader. But the ghost of Trudeau's leadership continued to haunt his successor, John Turner. Trudeau exacted a promise from Turner to make a series of prominent patronage appointments of colleagues and party officials loyal to the former prime minister. This promise generated negative reactions by the press and public, and was exploited by Conservative leader Brian Mulroney in the television debates of the 1984 campaign (see Chapter 4). Turner proved to be much less popular than his predecessor, and Table 6.3B shows that the leadership factor worked strongly in the Conservatives' favour in 1984.

Table 6.5

Effects of Issues in the 1984 Election

Most Important Issue Mentioned

All economic issues

Voting pattern	1984 Vote		
	Liberal	**PC**	**NDP**
Switch to	1.3	11.0	2.3
Remain	10.1	18.0	6.5
Enter/re-enter	_3.4_	_7.0_	_1.6_
	14.8	36.0	10.4
Issue voters only	4.5	12.4	4.6

Unemployment

Voting pattern	1984 Vote		
	Liberal	**PC**	**NDP**
Switch to	0.7	6.6	1.7
Remain	6.2	9.8	4.7
Enter/re-enter	_2.4_	_4.0_	_1.1_
	9.3	20.4	7.5
Issue voters only	3.3	6.9	3.2

Social issues

Voting pattern	1984 Vote		
	Liberal	**PC**	**NDP**
Switch to	0.1	1.9	0.8
Remain	1.7	2.1	1.2
Enter/re-enter	_0.6_	_0.7_	_0.5_
	2.4	4.7	2.5
Issue voters only	0.5	1.2	0.3

Note: Voters only; percentages of total electorate.

Source: 1984 – CNES.

The 1984 landslide reduced the Liberal vote from 44% to 28%, and their seat total to only 40. All of the issues discussed during the 1984 election show a substantial tilt toward the Conservatives (Table 6.5). The various elements of the nation's economic malaise were discussed in 1984 primarily in terms of unemployment, though attention was also given to economic stimulus and to reduction of government spending. The last items were indications that the Conservative Party was interested in using its electoral victory to embark on various components of the economic restructuring project, as yet undetermined. However, none of their policies relating to this project were raised with the voters for their approval during the 1984 campaign. The issues of 1984 were defined in problem-type terms, and the Tory message was that they would get the economy moving again, and would work to create "jobs, jobs, jobs."

The nature of the "mandate" conferred by the 1984 election was therefore very general. Table 6.5 shows that "issue voters" comprised only about one-third of those identifying either economic issues generally, or unemployment specifically, as the most important issues. Among these people, the Conservatives had between a 3 to 1 and 2 to 1 edge. Certainly one could say the first Mulroney government received a mandate to reduce unemployment and to stimulate economic growth. However, the Conservatives did not seek any particular *policy* mandate to do so, and specifically did not propose the free trade program that they were shortly to adopt. Social programs (a "sacred trust"), they said, would not be threatened by a Conservative government. Despite the landslide win, the Mulroney government was soon no higher in the polls than previous administrations had been. And the FTA, the focus of the Conservatives' first term in office, was not among the factors that had produced its electoral victory.

The 1988 Election

The question of whether the 1988 election produced a mandate for the Conservatives to enact the Free Trade Agreement has engendered considerable discussion.[19] All of the necessary elements seemed to be present. To an exceptional degree, the parties were divided on a specific program rather than a general problem. Even though the Conservatives had not intended to place free trade before the public prior to its implementation, this happened inadvertently as a result of the constellation of events between 1984 and 1988. A series of delays and cliffhanging negotiations produced a massive document, which finally was submitted to Parliament in 1988, but which had not been passed by the Senate before the election was called. The political parties divided clearly on the issue, and the Conservatives won a hard-fought election.

Table 6.6 presents several dimensions of the potential impact of the free trade issue on the 1988 result. The voting patterns of those who named

Table 6.6

Effects of the Free Trade Issue in the 1988 Election

	1988 Vote			
A. Free trade most important issue				
Voting pattern	**Liberal**	**PC**	**NDP**	**Other**
Switch to	8.1	5.5	5.0	2.2
Remain	8.1	24.4	7.6	–
Enter/re-enter	1.9	2.4	1.1	0.4
	18.1	32.3	13.7	2.6
B. Free trade most important issue; issues most important factor in vote decision	16.9	21.5	10.2	1.7
C. Free trade most important issue; issues most important factor in vote decision; free trade opinion affected vote	12.4	15.8	7.0	1.3
D. Free trade most important issue; issues most important factor in vote decision; free trade opinion affected vote; voted for party with same free trade views	9.8	15.6	6.5	

Note: New voters in 1988 not included; voters in election only; percentages of the total electorate.

Source: 1988 – CPS.

free trade as the most important election issue are shown in panel A. Switching patterns based on free trade clearly went against the Conservatives. Indeed, switching to the NDP on this issue was almost as great as switching to the Tories, despite the fact that most observers clearly felt that the NDP decisively lost the election. Similarly, transient voters who believed that free trade was the most important issue split almost evenly between the Liberals and the Conservatives. This initial tabulation clearly shows, however, the large number of voters who stayed with the Conservatives between 1984 and 1988 and named free trade as the most important issue in the campaign. This group was crucial to the PC victory, but how much did their free trade views really contribute to their vote choices?

Because the free trade question was so dominant in the campaign, it was cited by an overwhelming proportion of the voters when asked about the most important issue. In the succeeding panels of Table 6.6, we can see more clearly how many voters were truly influenced by free trade when they cast their ballots. Panel B identifies the "issue voters," in the same manner as we have done in Tables 6.4 and 6.5, those survey respondents who said they had an issue basis for their choice of party, leader, or candidate as the most important factor in their vote decision. The most considerable drop between panels A and B involves Conservative voters, indicating that a higher proportion of those supporting that party were not really casting a "free trade vote." Rather, they were simply identifying the issue as important in the election and voting PC for other reasons.

Where, then, are the "real" free trade voters? A further question in the 1988 survey asked respondents how much their opinion on free trade affected their vote, offering the options "a great deal," "some," or "not much." By excluding those who said "not much" from the calculations (20% of the voters), what remains is the group of voters displayed in Table 6.6C. Reductions can be seen in that proportion of the electorate voting for each of the parties, with the result that 36.5% of the 1984-88 panel met the requisite conditions to this point.

One more qualification is in order before identifying the appropriate group who might have produced a free trade mandate in 1988. Since the three major parties were closely identified with certain positions on the Free Trade Agreement, panel D of Table 6.6 excludes those who voted for a party with free trade views opposite to their own. If issue-motivated voters chose to vote for a party with views that did not fit their own on the most important issue, there must have been some very powerful reasons for them to do so. This group can hardly, however, be said to be giving their vote choice a mandate on the free trade issue. Here the drop is most conspicuous among Liberal voters, indicating that some of them favoured the policy. When push came to shove, there were a number of pro-free-trade voters who felt unable to support the PCs for other reasons.

Just under a third of the 1984-88 panel, then, fulfilled the following conditions: (1) they voted; (2) they identified free trade as the most important issue in the election; (3) they specified that issues were the major reason for their voting decision; (4) they stated that their opinion on free trade affected their vote at least somewhat; and (5) they voted for a party having the same position on free trade as they did. This pool of 1988 voters split almost evenly, with 15.6% voting Conservative and 16.3% voting for either the Liberals or the NDP, both of which opposed the Agreement. The existence of such evenly balanced minorities of the total electorate is one indicator that no clear policy mandate for the Free Trade Agreement emerged from the 1988 election.

The 1993 Election

After nine years of Conservative government, the country was ready to render an overall verdict on their stewardship. The result, in which the Tories were not only thrown out of office but also came very close to being shut out of Parliament altogether, was clear and decisive. However, any possible policy mandate for the victorious Liberals was quite general, resembling somewhat that which resulted from the 1984 election. The major issue, as we have seen in Chapter 2, was once again unemployment. Although the general problem of unemployment was bemoaned by all parties during the campaign, there was little willingness to discuss job losses as one result of the implementation of the economic restructuring project. Free trade, the most dramatic change in the country's economic policy, was only mentioned by 2% as the most important issue in the 1993 campaign (see Table 2.1, p. 29).

A substantial portion of "issue voters" cited unemployment or job creation as the most important issue in the election (Table 6.7). The proportion who did so, and who voted Liberal was 11.8%, whereas the total of issue voters voting for the other four parties was 10.4%. However, the fact that this non-Liberal vote was spread among several other parties, and the fact that the Liberals succeeded in establishing their policy on job creation as a specific distinct policy position during the campaign, argues for the importance of the unemployment issue to the Liberal victory. It is also reasonable to consider that the Liberal "infrastructure" plan to create short-term jobs received a mandate in the 1993 election. It was a salient issue to the public, and being a heavily discussed part of the Liberal Red Book, it was clearly identified with that party. While we cannot measure the component of the unemployment-related voting in Table 6.7 that was specifically connected to the jobs plan, it seems reasonable to conclude that at least some of it was.

The other important issue of a specific nature for issue voters was deficit reduction. Voting on this issue looks quite different than that motivated by concern for unemployment. Although a plurality of voters concerned with deficit reduction chose the Reform Party, it was by such a small margin that it cannot really be said that Canadian voters endorsed Reform's views, or indeed any party's views, on the right way to accomplish deficit reduction. The concept of a mandate makes most sense when applied to the winner of an election, who is in a position to put specific campaign ideas into practice. The first panel of Table 6.7 indicates that when all economic issues are considered together, the public's verdict was much

Table 6.7
Effects of Issues in the 1993 Election

Most Important Issue Mentioned

All economic issues

			1993 Vote		
Voting pattern	**Liberal**	**PC**	**NDP**	**Reform**	**BQ**
Switch to	9.2	2.1	1.2	10.1	5.2
Remain	13.7	6.0	2.7	0.7	–
Enter/re-enter	2.5	0.7	–	1.6	0.7
	25.4	8.8	3.9	12.4	5.9
Issue voters only	17.1	6.0	2.6	8.4	4.0

Unemployment

Voting pattern	**Liberal**	**PC**	**NDP**	**Reform**	**BQ**
Switch to	6.4	1.1	0.8	3.9	3.3
Remain	9.3	2.4	2.4	0.1	–
Enter/re-enter	1.5	0.3	0.1	1.1	0.2
	17.2	3.8	3.3	5.1	3.5
Issue voters only	11.8	2.4	2.0	3.5	2.5

The deficit

Voting pattern	**Liberal**	**PC**	**NDP**	**Reform**	**BQ**
Switch to	1.0	0.8	0.3	4.0	1.0
Remain	2.2	2.9	0.1	0.6	–
Enter/re-enter	0.6	0.2	–	0.5	0.3
	3.8	3.9	0.4	5.1	1.3
Issue voters only	3.1	2.7	0.4	3.9	0.4

All other issues

Voting pattern	**Liberal**	**PC**	**NDP**	**Reform**	**BQ**
Switch to	2.7	0.2	0.7	2.1	1.6
Remain	2.8	0.9	0.8	0.1	–
Enter/re-enter	0.9	0.1	0.1	0.6	0.1
	6.4	1.2	1.6	2.8	1.7
Issue voters only	3.5	0.5	0.9	1.6	1.1

Note: Voters only; percentages of total electorate.

Source: 1993 – INS.

more mixed than when unemployment is considered on its own. Among issue voters, more people were favourable to other parties than to the Liberals (21.0% versus 17.1%), and furthermore this category includes a number of people who simply expressed general views on the need for economic improvement rather than specific ideas about policy.

Regarding leader effects (Table 6.3D), we find a major difference between the two most recent elections and those prior to 1988. Both the 1988 and 1993 elections witnessed what might be called "the demise of leadership" as an issue, and a sharply reduced impact of leaders on voting decisions. This table, it will be recalled, looks at the voting behaviour of those who identified leaders as the most important factor in their voting decisions, and then specified that it was the personalities of the leaders rather than the issues they stood for that was of greatest importance. Explanations for the outcomes of elections of the Trudeau era rested heavily on Trudeau's personal appeal, and Mulroney's personality likewise captured voters in 1984. By 1988, however, Mulroney's personal appeal had virtually disappeared, and very few voters were looking at this aspect of the election campaign. Despite the presence of *four* new leaders in 1993 (the only holdover being Preston Manning) leader personality was barely present in the voting calculus in that year. The Conservatives built their campaign around Kim Campbell as a fresh new leader, but by election day few voters found her appealing. Audrey McLaughlin of the NDP appears to have barely registered on the public consciousness. And Jean Chrétien, despite being universally praised for the conduct of the Liberal campaign, attracted few voters on the basis of personal appeal alone.

The Liberal mandate in 1993 was a very constrained one. It was limited to a general public approval of its pledge to reduce unemployment, a mandate that any winning party could have easily claimed. Joining this was public support for the Liberals' announced plan to organize a $6 billion plan to create jobs, a specific but very limited policy to make a start on the reduction of unemployment. No party received clear public instructions to make deep cuts to social programs to reduce the deficit, despite the fact that the new Liberal government immediately instituted a review of all social programs designed to pave the way for such cuts. The election did not feature an extensive debate on the ratification of NAFTA, which would solidify the neoconservative economic restructuring project for the foreseeable future. Though the Liberals, mirroring public opinion (see Figure 3.3, p. 61) expressed reservations about NAFTA and pledged to renegotiate the draft treaty, they quickly ratified it with virtually no meaningful changes shortly after taking office.

Conclusion

One conclusion that can be drawn from the analyses presented in this chapter is that it is extremely difficult for any government to obtain a true policy mandate. The free trade issue in 1988, jobs in 1993 and 1984, the gasoline tax in 1980, and other examples, were commonly given post-election interpretations, both inside and outside of government, which suggested that Canadians had endorsed a particular position on these issues. We have seen that such mandates seldom exist. Either the issues were not as important to the outcome of the election as were generally thought, were phrased so generally as to defy a specific policy referent, or showed no clear trend of opinion. In the case of the Liberal jobs plan in 1993, where we have identified a likely mandate, the policy was a minor part of a much larger agenda dominated by deference to the demands of global market forces.

A part of political mythology is that elections are called to resolve policy differences. When the smoke of battle has cleared, it is expected that an incoming government will have been given a mandate to implement specific policies. But cases in which this actually happens are extremely rare. More often, elections turn on only the most general of issues (such as "the economy," "jobs," "getting spending under control,") or on a multiplicity of smaller issues that together provide only the fuzziest of electoral mandates. "Leadership," when important during campaigns, provides a mandate not for a set of policies but only for a set of actors. The mandate given a political leader in an election is a potentially fleeting one, lacking any real substance.

Elections, then, are not referendums on public policy, even though they are sometimes interpreted as such. Expectations built on such interpretations invariably are frustrated. Governments may ignore their own campaign promises, as the Conservatives seemed to do in attacking social programs in 1985 and the Liberals appear to be doing following their 1993 victory. At other times, new governments may attempt to implement a largely non-existent mandate, as the Conservatives did during their brief term of office in 1979, or as the Liberals did after their return to power in 1980. Elections can focus the attention of the public and politicians on important societal problems and reflect or even generate issue conflicts. However, their ability to produce policy mandates is doubtful. Given the prevalence of brokerage politics in the Canadian political system, absent mandates are likely to be the rule, not the exception. Elections decide who shall govern, but rarely the substance of public policy.

Notes

1. *The Ottawa Citizen*, 24 June 1994, p. A3.

2. Mark Kennedy, "The surprise social policy agenda," *The Ottawa Citizen*, 14 October 1994, p. A3.

3. H.D. Forbes, "Absent Mandate '88?: Parties and Voters in Canada," in Hugh G. Thornburn, ed., *Party Politics in Canada*, 6th ed. (Toronto: Prentice-Hall, 1991), p. 266. Emphasis in original. This article was written before the constitutional referendum of 1992.

4. A comprehensive analysis of voting turnout in Canada is presented in articles by Munroe Eagles, Jon H. Pammett, and Jerome H. Black in Herman Bakvis, ed., *Voter Turnout in Canada*, vol. 15 of the Research Studies of the Royal Commission on Electoral Reform and Party Financing (Toronto: Dundurn Press, 1991).

5. The basis for the 1993 voters list was that compiled at the time of the 1992 constitutional referendum. While opportunities were presented for revision of that list, there is speculation that the list was not sufficiently purged of those incorrectly registered because of relocation. To some extent, then, the 1993 turnout was actually higher than it appears. The same phenomenon was likely to have occurred in 1980 when, because of the relatively short time span since the previous election, no new enumeration was undertaken.

6. H.D. Clarke et al., *Political Choice in Canada* (Toronto: McGraw-Hill Ryerson, 1979), p. 361.

7. H.D. Clarke et al., *Absent Mandate*, 2nd ed. (Toronto: Gage Educational Publishing Company, 1991), p. 132.

8. Comparable tables presenting the voting turnover for previous pairs of elections can be found in *Absent Mandate*, 2nd ed.

9. Jon H. Pammett, "Tracking the Votes," in Alan Frizzell, Jon H. Pammett, and Anthony Westell, eds., *The Canadian General Election of 1993* (Ottawa: Carleton University Press, 1993), p. 146.

10. For an account of the 1979 election, and that of 1974 which preceded it, see *Absent Mandate*, 1st ed. (Toronto: Gage Educational Publishing Company, 1984.)

11. For a detailed account of the policy ramifications of the 1980 election see William P. Irvine, "Epilogue: The 1980 Election," in Howard R. Penniman, ed., *Canada at the Polls, 1979 and 1980* (Washington, D.C.: American Enterprise Institute, 1981), pp. 337-398.

12. Table 6.4, and subsequent tables in the same format, are designed to show the proportion of the total pool of voters who cited particular issues as most important in the election, and who cast votes in particular directions. We are able to identify by this method the conversion effects of issues (by looking at the number of vote switchers who thought they were important) and the replacement effects (those who entered or re-entered the electorate), as well as those who remained with the same party as in the previous election.

13. Stephen Clarkson, *Canada and the Reagan Challenge* (Ottawa: Canadian Institute for Economic Policy, 1982), p. 3.

14. Irvine, "Epilogue," p. 366.

15. Donald Smiley, *The Federal Condition in Canada* (Toronto: McGraw-Hill, 1987), pp. 178–184.

16. For a detailed analysis of the NEP, see G. Bruce Doern and Glen Toner, *The NEP and the Politics of Energy: the Development and Implementation of the National Energy Program* (Toronto: Methuen, 1984).

17. For an account of the changes, see Keith Banting and Richard Simeon, eds., *And No One Cheered: Federalism, Democracy and the Constitution Act* (Toronto: Methuen, 1983).

18. For accounts of the 1984 election see Alan Frizzell and Anthony Westell, *The Canadian General Election of 1984* (Ottawa: Carleton University Press, 1985), and Howard Penniman, ed., *Canada at the Polls, 1984* (Durham, N.C.: Duke University Press, 1988).

19. The 1988 election is analysed in Alan Frizzell, Jon H. Pammett, and Anthony Westell, *The Canadian General Election of 1988* (Ottawa: Carleton University Press, 1989).

7

Consulting the People: The October 1992 Referendum

Although referendums have rarely been employed in Canada to resolve important political issues, the concept of the referendum is often discussed by scholars, politicians, and members of the public.[1] There are a number of reasons why referendums have not been used more frequently in Canada. The very questions that would appear to be the most logical to put to a referendum are often those for which it has proven to be extremely difficult to build nationwide public support. Neither the constitution nor economic restructuring, the two main projects that have been at the top of the national political agenda in Canada over the past three decades, would be likely to win approval if put to a national vote. The Free Trade Agreement, for example, over which much of the 1988 election campaign was fought, almost certainly would have been defeated had it been put directly to a vote of the people (see Chapters 2 and 6). Thus the political elites who have pursued these projects over such a long period of time, often with little in the way of a popular mandate, are generally disinclined to seek any type of direct vote on them. Although it is appealing to talk about "letting the people decide," political parties and their leaders rarely have had much interest in doing so.

The few referendums that *have* taken place in Canada have occurred in highly unusual circumstances. Perhaps the most famous, the conscription plebiscite of 1942, left a legacy of division and discord that later caused the concept of a referendum to be viewed with suspicion. In Canada, as in other countries whose political institutions evolved from British parliamentary traditions, referendums tend to be held only when public pressure for consultation on a fundamental political question makes one unavoidable.[2]

The same has generally been true at the provincial level as well. Newfoundlanders were asked to vote on confederation with Canada in a 1949 referendum, and Quebec voters were consulted about the Lévesque government's "sovereignty-association" proposal in 1980. But in spite of these precedents and the implicit democratic appeal of a direct popular vote, referendums remain a rarity in our political life.

The constitutional impasse that the country faced after the failure of the Meech Lake Accord made more compelling the idea of involving the people directly in some way in a new constitutional procedure.[3] However, the process of consultations that eventually led to the Charlottetown Accord is illustrative of the tensions between elite negotiations and democratic participation that have characterized the constitutional project throughout its long history.[4] The Citizens' Forum on Canada's Future (the Spicer Commission) employed a number of innovative devices including group discussions, a toll-free "idea line," and six "electronic town hall meetings" in attempting to broaden public involvement in the constitutional process. Its report,[5] which documented the public's anger at the country's political leadership, preceded by only two months the federal government's own constitutional proposals set out in the document *Shaping Canada's Future Together.*[6] In Parliament, a Special Joint Committee on a Renewed Canada (the Beaudoin-Dobbie Committee), which reported in February 1992, also conducted extensive public hearings as part of its proceedings.[7] Similar types of consultative processes were undertaken in every province and territory throughout the long and complicated "constitutional odyssey."[8] Six constitutional conferences that were held in early 1992 brought together ex officio delegates with representatives of interest groups and "selected" public participants, some recruited through newspaper advertisements. The subsequent round of meetings (March-June 1992) chaired by Constitutional Affairs Minister Joe Clark comprised accredited delegates of many different groups, including representatives of four national Aboriginal associations. As the long-running constitutional drama in which Canadian politicians participated between June 1990 and the signing of the Charlottetown Accord in August 1992 approached a conclusion, it was not obvious that the country was headed toward a referendum. The government might have tried to claim that the public had already been consulted extensively throughout the entire process.

What then explains the decision to put the Charlottetown Accord to a referendum?[9] The decision to do so was taken quickly, and with little real discussion or debate. A general feeling had developed that any agreement would have to be put to a referendum in order to legitimate it. The decision to move quickly was essentially strategic, taken in the belief that time was more likely to be on the side of the Accord's potential opponents. Thus, what was sought in the October referendum was not more public participation in the constitutional process but rather public endorsement of the Charlottetown Accord as negotiated by the elites. The architects of the Accord hoped to structure the agenda in such a way as to minimize the basis for opposition, control the public debate, and thereby increase the probability of a YES vote. A quick and clean referendum campaign seemed to offer this hope, much in the same way that an election called immediately after a leadership convention sometimes seems to offer the best chance to a governing party, which is otherwise at risk of losing. But since these types of electoral strategies fail at least as often as they succeed, the failure of this approach in the case of the Charlottetown Accord should perhaps not be all that surprising.

But why have a referendum at all? There was nothing in the constitutional process or even in Canadian political tradition that required a vote of the people in order to implement the provisions of the Charlottetown Accord. The agreement might, like the Meech Lake Accord, have simply been put to Parliament and the provincial legislatures for debate and ratification. However, the Charlottetown Accord represents a circumstance where the politicians were unable to structure the agenda. Rather, like an unpopular governing party in the waning days of its term of office, the Conservatives and their provincial counterparts had effectively lost control of the constitutional agenda. Quebec had already committed itself by law to hold a referendum, either on "sovereignty" or on a federal constitutional proposal, no later than 26 October 1992. Alberta and British Columbia had likewise made commitments to hold referendums on any new constitutional proposal. The prospect of separate referendums in Quebec and in other provinces, held at different times and following different electoral rules boxed in the authors of the agreement. A quick federal vote, held on the same day as the already scheduled Quebec referendum (which was then only two months away) became the only plausible strategy. It was, however, a decision taken from a position of weakness rather than strength.

Given the limited experience in Canada with referendums, it is perhaps not surprising that the public was somewhat ambivalent regarding this sudden new political development. The Canadian people were not to be asked whether they wanted to embark on a journey of constitutional reform, or to choose among competing visions of a "renewed federalism." Rather, their role was only to approve the document once all of the other stages in the process had been completed. By more than 2 to 1, people agreed with the proposition that the referendum would "give ordinary people a chance to help decide Canada's future" (Figure 7.1A). However, almost half (49%) believed that such matters were better decided by governments than by a referendum. Similarly, 46% felt that, like the infamous conscription plebiscite, the referendum might actually do more to divide the country than to unite it. Solid majorities agreed that the referendum "would not settle any

Figure 7.1

Attitudes Toward the Referendum: Process and Consequences

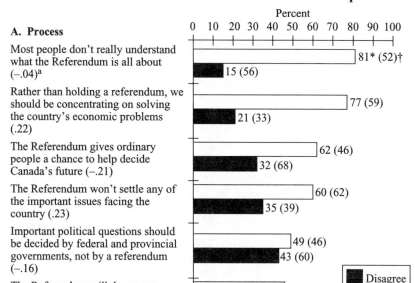

A. Process

Most people don't really understand what the Referendum is all about $(-.04)^a$

Rather than holding a referendum, we should be concentrating on solving the country's economic problems (.22)

The Referendum gives ordinary people a chance to help decide Canada's future (−.21)

The Referendum won't settle any of the important issues facing the country (.23)

Important political questions should be decided by federal and provincial governments, not by a referendum (−.16)

The Referendum will do more to divide the country than bring it together (.07)

* Percent with no opinion computed in percentages, but not shown in figure.
[a] Pearson correlation with NO vote shown in parentheses.
† Percentage of group voting NO.

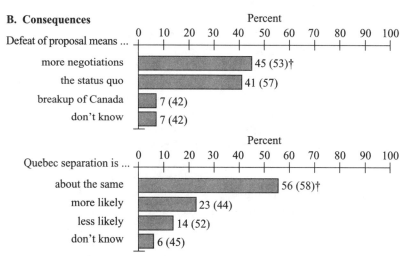

B. Consequences

Defeat of proposal means ...
more negotiations — 45 (53)†
the status quo — 41 (57)
breakup of Canada — 7 (42)
don't know — 7 (42)

Quebec separation is ...
about the same — 56 (58)†
more likely — 23 (44)
less likely — 14 (52)
don't know — 6 (45)

† Percentage of group voting NO.

Source: CRS.

of the important issues facing the country" (60%), that it would be preferable to "concentrate on solving the country's economic problems" (77%), or feared that people "didn't understand what the Referendum was all about" (81%). While Canadians were interested in the vote and took it seriously, only a few believed that it would finally and decisively resolve the long-standing constitutional impasse or that a possible NO vote might have dangerous consequences (Figure 7.1B). People tended to believe that this was just another move in the continuing constitutional chess game rather than the possible end of the game itself.

The Charlottetown Accord

In one form or another, the constitutional project has been central to the national political agenda in Canada throughout the postwar period. The Royal Commission on Bilingualism and Biculturalism explored it in the late 1960s. The Victoria Charter of 1971, the Canada Act of 1982, and the Meech Lake Accord in 1987, all represented pieces of an ongoing and multifaceted attempt to accomplish the process of constitutional renewal without tearing the country apart. Throughout this process, the members of the Canadian public have mainly been interested bystanders. To some, the Meech Lake Accord seemed to finally represent the "renewed federalism" that Pierre Trudeau had promised as an alternative to the "sovereignty" program of the PQ in the 1980 Quebec referendum campaign.[10] The Meech Lake provisions for recognition of Quebec as a "distinct society" and an effective provincial veto over constitutional change were, however, very different from Trudeau's vision. When the Meech Lake Accord expired in June 1990 as a result of the failure of Manitoba and Newfoundland to ratify the agreement, an entirely new round of constitution making was set in motion, leading to the Charlottetown Accord two years later.

The Charlottetown Accord was more comprehensive than previous constitutional proposals. From Meech Lake, it incorporated concepts such as recognition of Quebec's "distinct society." It proposed to create a new Senate in which all provinces would be equally represented. This provision was a variation of the "triple E" (elected, effective, equal) Senate that had become the principal objective of many Westerners throughout the post-Meech constitutional negotiations. In exchange, it guaranteed to Quebec in perpetuity a minimum of 25% of the representatives in an enlarged House of Commons. The Accord also proposed new arrangements for Aboriginal self-government, recognizing this as an "inherent right." It set out new divisions of federal and provincial powers in areas such as culture, labour, and resource policy, by granting greater power to provincial governments. It proposed to give all provinces a veto over fundamental constitutional changes such as those dealing with matters of representation or federal institutions.

Figure 7.2

Attitudes Toward the Specific Provisions of the Charlottetown Accord

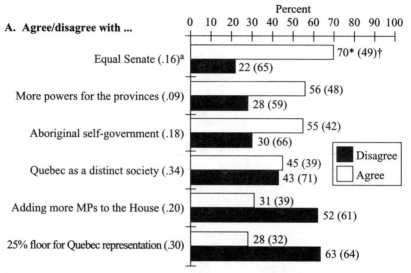

A. Agree/disagree with ...

	Agree	Disagree
Equal Senate (.16)[a]	70* (49)†	22 (65)
More powers for the provinces (.09)	56 (48)	28 (59)
Aboriginal self-government (.18)	55 (42)	30 (66)
Quebec as a distinct society (.34)	45 (39)	43 (71)
Adding more MPs to the House (.20)	31 (39)	52 (61)
25% floor for Quebec representation (.30)	28 (32)	63 (64)

* Percent with no opinion computed in percentages, but not shown in figure.
[a] Pearson correlation between "disagree" and NO vote shown in parentheses.
† Percentage of group voting NO.

B. Percent Voting NO: By Extent of Disagreement with Accord Provisions

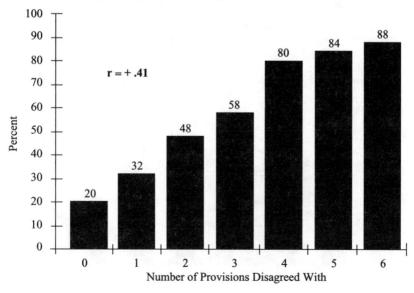

$r = +.41$

Number of Provisions Disagreed With: 0=20, 1=32, 2=48, 3=58, 4=80, 5=84, 6=88

Source: CRS.

Figure 7.3

Perceptions of Group Benefits of the Charlottetown Accord

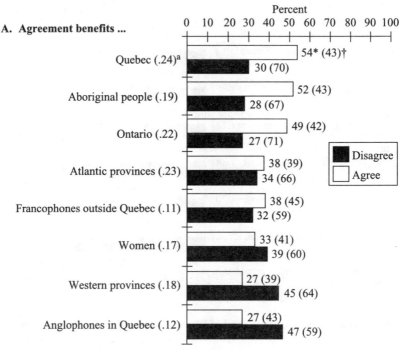

A. Agreement benefits ...

* Percent with no opinion computed in percentages, but not shown in figure.
[a] Pearson correlation between "disagree" and NO vote shown in parentheses.
† Percentage of group voting NO.

B. Percent Voting NO: By Number of Groups Perceived as Benefitting from Accord

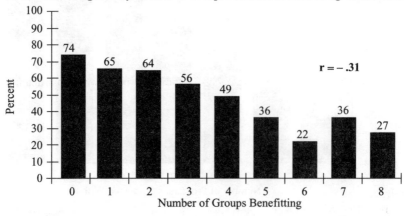

Source: CRS.

These specific provisions of the agreement met with varying degrees of public approval (Figure 7.2). The plan to reform the Senate found some favour, although a plurality of Canadians would probably have preferred to abolish the Senate entirely.[11] However, nearly three-quarters of those surveyed supported the concept of an equal Senate, including many who ultimately voted NO in the referendum. Two other parts of the agreement were also reasonably popular. Fifty-six percent supported the idea of "giving more powers to the provinces" and 55% approved of the plan to establish Aboriginal self-government.

Three elements of the Charlottetown proposal engendered higher levels of disapproval among the public. The first of these was recognition of Quebec as a "distinct society," a holdover (though in somewhat revised form) of the provision that had earlier contributed to the failure of the Meech Lake Accord. However, opposition to legal recognition of Quebec as a distinct society was not in itself a majority position in the electorate. Respondents were nearly evenly split on this issue—45% agreeing with it and 43% disapproving (Figure 7.2A). Two other elements of the agreement were more unpopular than the distinct society provision. The proposal to offer Quebec a guaranteed 25% of the membership of the House of Commons produced substantial opposition. Nearly two-thirds of all respondents expressed disagreement with this provision. Likewise, the plan to add more members of Parliament in order to compensate Ontario, Quebec, and B.C. for giving up seats in the Senate was not well received. A majority of the respondents (52%) opposed this item.

As is shown in Figure 7.2, disagreement with any one of the specific provisions of the agreement was related to voting NO but was not in itself decisive. Those items correlating most strongly with the vote were the distinct society provision and the 25% guarantee—the two items dealing specifically with Quebec.[12] Of those who disagreed with just one of the six major provisions, only 32% voted NO. As the number of disagreements increased however, the likelihood of a NO vote rose considerably (Figure 7.2B). Among those who disagreed with three or more items in the agreement, solid majorities voted NO.

Of course, the Charlottetown Accord was also a product of brokerage politics, not merely an exercise in constitution writing. It was constructed to appeal to the regions and provinces of Canada as well as to a number of specific interests such as Aboriginal peoples, women's groups, and linguistic minorities. Figure 7.3 shows the perceived success or failure of the agreement in satisfying these various groups and regions. On the surface, the politicians seemed to have done reasonably well in addressing the concerns of a number of different groups. Closer examination however reveals that the situation was more complicated. Consider, for example, the perception that Quebec had most of its concerns satisfied by the

Charlottetown Agreement. In Quebec itself, 56% agreed that Quebec's concerns were answered, but more than a third of these respondents still voted NO in the referendum. In the Western provinces, the belief that Quebec might be satisfied with the deal had quite different consequences. Over half (51%) of Westerners concluded that the deal did meet Quebec's concerns, and those who felt that way were also more likely to vote YES than those who believed that it had not. But in fact, a strong majority of Westerners in *both* of these groups voted NO. An important part of the Western feeling that the Charlottetown deal might satisfy Quebec also implied a suspicion that it did *not* favour the West. Only 27% of those surveyed thought that the concerns of Westerners had been adequately addressed by the Accord. Thus, the process of regional brokering, while designed to give all areas of the country some benefits, ended up aggravating regional resentments in tandem with mutual accommodation.[13] Ultimately, it was in the Western provinces that the agreement would be most resoundingly defeated in the referendum.

As was shown earlier with respect to negative opinions on the substantive components of the agreement, there was also a cumulative effect in believing that different regional and group interests were not adequately dealt with by the Charlottetown Accord. Believing that a few groups or regions did not have most of their concerns answered was not in itself an overwhelming deterrent to a YES vote (Figure 7.3B). However, the perception that more groups were dissatisfied made a YES vote on the agreement progressively less likely. Nevertheless, the perceived success or failure of the brokering process was not always definitive. Even among those who felt that *none* of the regions or groups had their concerns satisfied, 26% would still nevertheless vote YES.

Like an election, the referendum of October 1992 presented the voter with a set of issues, some of which, such as the distinct society clause, had been debated quite extensively before, and others that were entirely new to the Charlottetown agreement. And, also as in an election, these issues would have to be resolved by the electorate in a single vote—YES or NO—on the entire package.

The Campaign

The vote was to be a simple YES or NO on "the agreement of August 28th." It would be held on October 26, less than two months after the agreement had been signed at Charlottetown. Because the decision to hold a referendum had been taken so quickly, little thought was given by the first ministers to matters of organization, strategy, or even the wording of the question. As a result, the campaign got off to a very slow start. For a short time, it seemed that a real contest might take place only in Quebec, where organized opposition was already in place. The Parti Québécois almost immediately announced its intention to campaign for a NO vote, and the

Allaire Report, adopted in 1991 by the Liberal Party in Quebec, also produced an organized group of potential opponents of the agreement. There was little initial opposition elsewhere in the country. All ten provincial premiers representing three different political parties supported the agreement. The three leaders of the main federal parties announced that they would campaign actively for a YES vote. Leaders of the Aboriginal groups that had been involved in various phases of the constitutional negotiations indicated that they would support it. Some early polls seemed to suggest national approval ratings as high as 70%. Prime Minister Mulroney claimed that only "enemies of Canada" would oppose the agreement, a comment that he would later regret.

The first sour note in this chorus of self-congratulation appeared when the government was unable to produce a legal text of the agreement. The speed with which the decision to hold a referendum had been taken and the feverish pace of the final round of negotiations had left more than a few loose ends unresolved. The delays in producing the legal text allowed some of the early critics of the deal to allege that there were serious flaws in the agreement or even that secret negotiations were still being carried on. It would, in fact, be several more weeks before a text would be released, a crucial period of time during which doubts and suspicions about the process and the agreement itself would begin to surface. Public opinion polls conducted in those first few weeks showed significant declines from the initial high levels of support, and large increases in the percentage of undecided voters. While an organized opposition was in place only in Quebec, the weaknesses in the strategy of the YES side were already becoming visible.

Gradually, opposition outside of Quebec began to surface. Preston Manning, after some hesitation, announced that the Reform Party would oppose the agreement and would campaign against it nationally. Later, his extensive TV spots denouncing the "Mulroney deal" would become a hallmark of the NO campaign. At about the same time, several prominent Quebec Liberals came out against the proposals, revealing the split in Premier Bourassa's own party, which had begun with the Allaire Report, and indicating that the agreement was in more serious trouble than initially thought in Quebec. About a week later, Deborah Coyne, a constitutional lawyer and former adviser to both Pierre Trudeau and Newfoundland Premier Clyde Wells, presented an articulate critique of the agreement and said that she would oppose it. A few days later, Judy Rebick, President of the National Action Committee on the Status of Women, announced her organization's opposition. Momentum suddenly seemed to be shifting away from the poorly organized and over-confident architects of the agreement.

This gradual forming of opposition lines set the stage for a dramatic intervention by Pierre Trudeau about three weeks into the campaign. In essays published in *Maclean's* and *l'Actualité*, the former prime minister denounced any concessions to Quebec.[14] Then, in a widely publicized speech in Montreal about ten days later, Trudeau called directly for a NO vote. While it was perhaps not surprising that Trudeau, also a critic of Meech Lake, would oppose the agreement, his views commanded wide attention. His comments, timed for maximum effect, managed to dominate the news media during a critical ten-day slice in the middle of the campaign.

While the NO campaign, disparate as it was, was effective, the YES side was often its own worst enemy. Early campaign advertisements by the YES side came across as too strident, reflecting what many saw as "scare tactics" and reinforcing some of the feelings of manipulation by elites that hung over the referendum from the beginning. Business groups published dubious analyses forecasting serious economic consequences arising from a failure to approve the agreement. Such tactics seemed increasingly counterproductive as the campaign progressed. The NO side pulled ahead in the polls during the first week of October and stayed there throughout the remainder of the campaign (Figure 7.4). There were still three weeks to go, but the contest was effectively over even though the public opinion polls continued to show large numbers of undecideds until the very end.

Because there was really no "long campaign" in the sense that one occurs in the run-up to an election, and no long-term basis of opinion on many of the specific issues, the formal campaign held the potential for even greater volatility and uncertainty about the outcome than would be found in a federal election. Some voters, of course, would have been able to make up their minds quickly on the basis of partisan cues or familiarity with one or more of the long-standing issues in the constitutional debates. Strong supporters of either the Parti Québécois or the Reform Party would hardly have needed a campaign in order to make up their minds about the agreement. And some issues, such as the distinct society or the equal Senate were already well known, and may well have shaped some voters' views of the entire agreement. In addition, there were the cues provided by political leaders such as Trudeau, Mulroney, Bourassa, or Manning, personalities about whom many voters had strong opinions.

The differing character of the dialogue across the country also had an effect on the dynamics of the campaign. Information travelled rapidly via the media from one part of the country to another. When a British Columbia provincial cabinet minister (supporting the agreement) claimed that Quebec had been outmanoeuvred in the constitutional skirmishes, his comments were quickly picked up by the Quebec media. Similarly, statements by Bourassa and others trying to promote the agreement in Quebec often made headlines in Vancouver or Edmonton the very same day. In theory the agreement would have had to obtain a YES majority in *every* province, since an overall national YES vote had no intrinsic meaning. If only one province

Figure 7.4

Public Opinion Polls During the Referendum Campaign (Selected Dates)

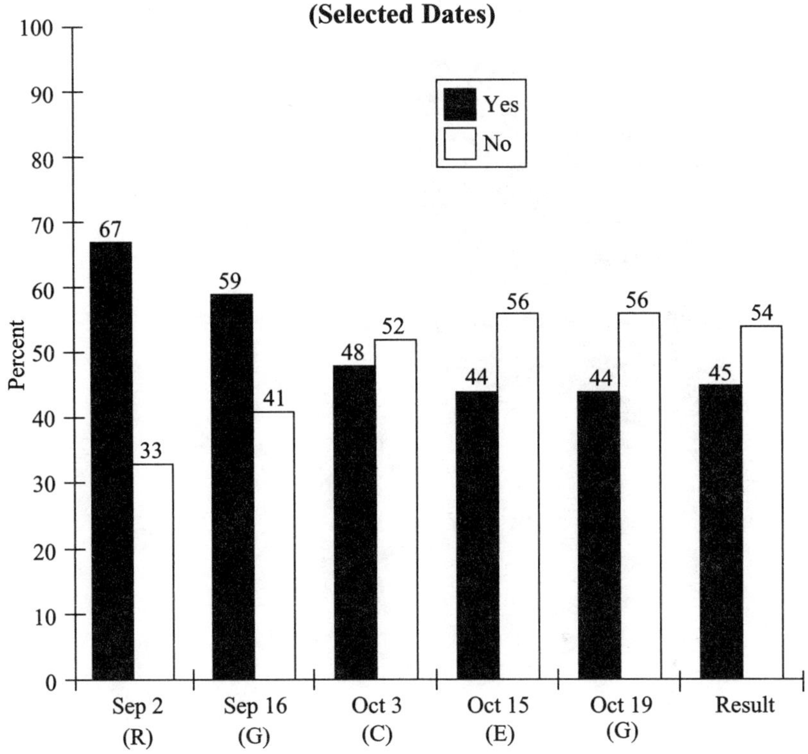

Source: C – ComQuest Research Group/CBC/Globe & Mail;
E – Environics Research/CTV/Toronto Star;
G – Gallup Canada;
R – Angus Reid/Southam News.

voted against it, thereby causing that province not to ratify, the deal would have been dead. Once it became likely that Quebec would vote against the agreement, a vote against it elsewhere could not as easily be seen as "anti-Quebec" or threatening to "national unity." Likewise, as opinion in Western Canada hardened against the agreement over the course of the campaign, the potential risks inherent in a NO vote declined for Quebec voters.

Levels of voter interest were high, with nearly half of the survey respondents reporting that they were "very interested" in the referendum, and another third indicating that they were "somewhat interested." Turnout, at just under 75%, was comparable to the average in federal elections. The pattern of voter decision making was very similar to that which occurs in an election campaign (compare Figure 4.5, p. 88). Thirty-eight percent

Figure 7.5

Reported Time of Referendum Vote Decision

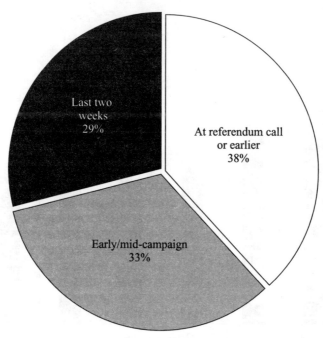

Last two
weeks
29%

At referendum call
or earlier
38%

Early/mid-campaign
33%

Source: CRS.

indicated that they made up their minds early—at the time that the
agreement was announced or even before (Figure 7.5). The percentage of
early deciders was slightly higher among YES voters, possibly reflecting a
view held by some that *any* agreement that might bring constitutional peace
was worthy of support.[15] But about a third of those sampled decided on their
vote during the early or middle part of the campaign. And a nearly equal
number (29%) reserved their decision until the final two weeks.

As in elections, the referendum campaign saw an intense competition
to control the agenda, with all of the actors trying to channel discussion
along their preferred lines. Brian Mulroney proclaimed that the purpose of
the exercise was saving Canada, while Pierre Trudeau argued that it was to
appease the nationalists in Quebec. Preston Manning appealed to anti-
government sentiment, the provincial premiers pointed out the benefits for
their provinces, and the women's movement criticized the agreement's
failure to advance equality rights. The story of the campaign was in many
ways the marginalization of the mainstream politicians from the contest.
The extent to which the NO campaign had managed to tap an "anti-politics"

or "anti-establishment" streak of opinion became increasingly evident in the final two weeks.[16] Numerous endorsements of the YES side by politicians and by notables from every sector of society did little to sway opinion back toward the YES camp. The various groups and individuals supporting the NO side had little in common, ranging widely across the political spectrum and often holding contradictory views on many other issues. But arrayed against them were the pillars of the Canadian establishment: business, government, academia, and seemingly much of the press and media. For many, the referendum campaign seemed to have become a battle of the people against the establishment. Seen in this light, it is perhaps more surprising that 45% of Canadians ultimately voted *for* the Charlottetown agreement than that it went down to defeat.

Explaining the Results

The outcome of the referendum was decisive. In the country as a whole, 54.4% voted NO compared with 44.6% YES.[17] Six of the ten provinces voted NO, with strong majorities against the agreement in all of the Western provinces and the Yukon (Figure 7.6). The NO majority in Quebec was 55.4%, only slightly higher than in the country as a whole. The Atlantic provinces, with the exception of Nova Scotia, supported the YES side by fairly substantial majorities. In Ontario, the result was a virtual tie, with 49.8% voting YES and 49.6% NO.

There were thus clear regional patterns to the results, which partially obscured others. Within Quebec, francophones were more likely to oppose the agreement, while francophones in other provinces were more likely to support it.[18] There was a noticeable urban/rural divide, as a disproportionate amount of the YES support came from the larger cities. Older voters and those with higher incomes were slightly more likely to vote YES. Otherwise, there were only modest demographic correlates to the vote, as the national trend against the agreement crosscut potential divisions along the lines of social class, gender, age, education, or even party affiliation.[19]

Specific provisions of the agreement or perceived group interests were more important as reasons for a NO vote than for a YES. Sixty-four percent of NO voters cited a specific reason for their vote, while only 11% of YES voters did so.[20] For those who supported the agreement, "national unity" was most important, along with the simple desire to resolve the long-standing constitutional impasse. These were also the main items that had been stressed by the campaign committees for the YES side, by the prime minister, and the premiers. The fact that NO voters were more likely to cite a specific part of the agreement that they disliked similarly reflected the campaign themes of the coalition of groups opposed to the deal.

In the aftermath of the referendum, various explanations were advanced to account for the decisive rejection of the agreement. Among these were:

Figure 7.6

Referendum Results: Percentages Voting NO

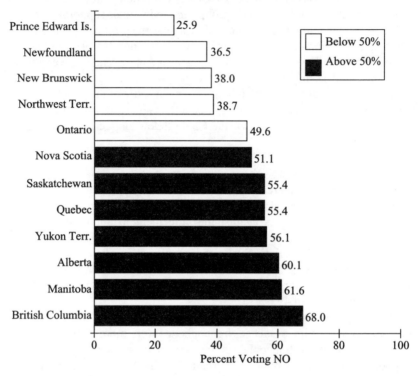

| | Below 50% |
| | Above 50% |

Prince Edward Is. 25.9
Newfoundland 36.5
New Brunswick 38.0
Northwest Terr. 38.7
Ontario 49.6
Nova Scotia 51.1
Saskatchewan 55.4
Quebec 55.4
Yukon Terr. 56.1
Alberta 60.1
Manitoba 61.6
British Columbia 68.0

Percent Voting NO

Source: *Report of the Chief Electoral Officer* (Ottawa: Supply and Services, 1993).

1. *The substance of the agreement,* including specific provisions such as the "distinct society" clause, Senate reform, or Aboriginal self-government, as well as more general "issue" concerns.

2. *Groups and benefits,* including perceived gains or losses by particular provinces and regions and/or particular groups such as women, Aboriginal peoples, or linguistic minorities.

3. *Dissatisfaction with politics,* namely the lack of trust in parties and their leaders, and/or the distrust of some of the political processes associated with Canadian constitutional politics more generally. As well, the unpopularity of the Conservative government, and in particular the prime minister, along with the recession and unpopular government policies such as the Free Trade Agreement and the Goods and Services Tax provided a long list of grievances to feed the climate of general political and economic discontent in which the referendum took place.

4. *Reinforcing cleavages*, meaning the tendency to associate the agreement or some of its specific provisions with long-standing divisions in Canadian society based on region, language, or social class. Let us examine each of these possible explanations in greater detail.

Looking first at the substance of the agreement, we see that the distinct society provision and the 25% guarantee seemed to engender among some voters a reaction based on the perception that Quebec might be gaining too much or too little in the way of constitutional powers. Perceptions of gains or losses by particular groups and regions also bore some relationship to the vote, as did dissatisfaction with politics and politicians, or with the economic performance of the government.[21] Voting behaviour in the referendum was also modestly related to the public's increasingly negative verdict on free trade, as well as to its feelings toward Brian Mulroney, Jean Chrétien, Audrey McLaughlin, some of the provincial premiers such as Robert Bourassa or Clyde Wells, and a variety of federal government institutions. The idea that a class cleavage may have been present in the voting is given some support by the finding of a significant negative relationship between income and NO voting, and by the fact that blue-collar workers were less likely to support the agreement than those in higher status occupations.[22] Younger voters tended to oppose the agreement, and there was no significant difference in the voting patterns of men and women. Majorities of *both* federal Liberals and Conservatives supported the YES side in nearly equal numbers, a finding perhaps to be expected since the leadership of both major parties campaigned actively for the agreement. Those identifying with the other federal parties were more likely to turn the agreement down. Perhaps most significantly, voters in Quebec identifying with the Parti Québécois were overwhelmingly likely to vote NO.

Overall, however, there is no single explanation for the defeat of the Accord. All of these factors played some role in the result, but no single one of them provides a compelling explanation. Rather, as is generally the case in elections, several elements contributed in some measure to the outcome.

The complexity of factors at work may be seen in probit analyses of voting behaviour in the various regions, and in the country as a whole (Figure 7.7).[23]

Public feelings about the substance of the agreement contributed substantially to its defeat. This was true in all parts of the country, although the regions differed on which specific items were objectionable. Resentment of the "distinct society" provision was most pronounced in the West, but the effects of dissatisfaction with this provision were also evident in Ontario. The decision to offer Quebec a guarantee of 25% of the membership of the House of Commons was likewise significant in Ontario, and was also important in motivating NO voting in Quebec itself, where some voters felt that such a guarantee did not provide enough assurance that

161

Figure 7.7
Probit Analysis: Predictors of NO Voting in Referendum

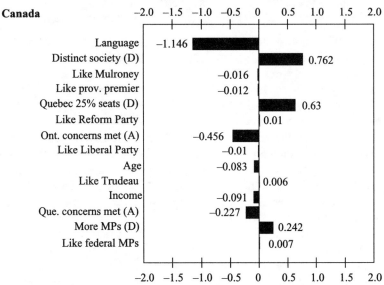

Canada

Language	−1.146
Distinct society (D)	0.762
Like Mulroney	−0.016
Like prov. premier	−0.012
Quebec 25% seats (D)	0.63
Like Reform Party	0.01
Ont. concerns met (A)	−0.456
Like Liberal Party	−0.01
Age	−0.083
Like Trudeau	0.006
Income	−0.091
Que. concerns met (A)	−0.227
More MPs (D)	0.242
Like federal MPs	0.007

Estimated R^2 = .36; percentage correctly classified = 79.5; PRE: lambda = .57
Note: significant predictors only, p < .05
(A) agree   (D) disagree

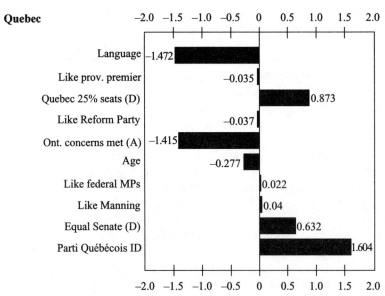

Quebec

Language	−1.472
Like prov. premier	−0.035
Quebec 25% seats (D)	0.873
Like Reform Party	−0.037
Ont. concerns met (A)	−1.415
Age	−0.277
Like federal MPs	0.022
Like Manning	0.04
Equal Senate (D)	0.632
Parti Québécois ID	1.604

Estimated R^2 = .56; percentage correctly classified = 85.5; PRE: lambda = .70
Note: significant predictors only, p < .05
(A) agree   (D) disagree

Figure 7.7 (CONTINUED)

Probit Analysis: Predictors of NO Voting in Referendum

Ontario

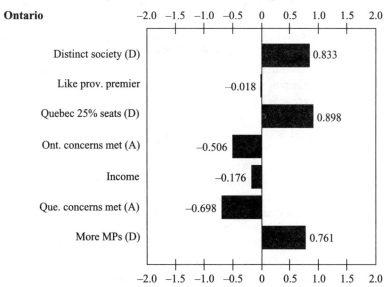

Estimated R^2 = .47; percentage correctly classified = 88.5; PRE: lambda = .56
Note: significant predictors only, p < .05
(A) agree   (D) disagree

West

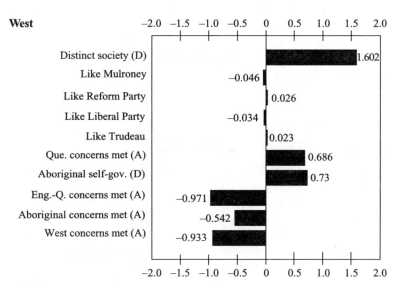

Estimated R^2 = .58; percentage correctly classified = 80.7; PRE: lambda = .67
Note: significant predictors only, p < .05
(A) agree   (D) disagree

Source: CRS.

Quebec would be able to offset the potential effects of a more powerful and equal Senate. Group concerns were important in Ontario and Quebec in a reciprocal fashion. In Ontario, those voters who believed that most of Quebec's concerns were met by the agreement were less likely to vote NO than those who felt otherwise. Quebec respondents who agreed that Ontario's concerns were met were similarly less inclined to reject the Accord. Feelings about particular political leaders were also of some importance in explaining the result. For example, those Westerners who liked Mulroney were less likely to vote NO than those who did not, a pattern similar to that for the country as a whole. The support of Premiers Bourassa and Rae for the deal was important in generating some votes for the YES side. In the West, liking for Pierre Trudeau was weakly associated with NO voting, but feelings about him were not significant in Ontario or Quebec.

A significant demographic variable in the countrywide analysis (and in the one for Quebec) is language, suggesting that the linguistic cleavage was reinforced by the referendum. Class voting, as a hypothesis, fares less well. Only in Ontario did the relationship with income persist, with higher income voters being less likely to vote NO net of other factors. In Quebec, older voters were less inclined to vote NO, and there was also a negative relationship between age and NO voting for the country as a whole. PQ party identification was an important variable in explaining the NO vote in Quebec, and the independent effect of this item controlling for other variables such as language and the specifics of the agreement testifies to the role of the party in mobilizing its supporters to reject the agreement. The Reform Party played a much more ambiguous role in the campaign. While Preston Manning was featured in advertising for the NO side, it was not clear at the time whether adherence to the party itself was important in translating that message into votes. Thus, even though Reform (in 1992) claimed relatively few actual identifiers with the party, liking for Reform was associated with NO voting in the West, and also in Quebec.

Indicative of their collective explanatory power, the variance explained by this combination of factors is substantial: about 50% in each of the regions and slightly lower for the country as a whole. However, the regional variations in the significance of various factors are important, both in explaining the outcome of the referendum and in identifying the factors that best account for the result. In Quebec, language, partisanship, and feelings toward Premier Bourassa were significant; in the West, it was feelings toward Mulroney and the Reform Party. Demographic factors such as age seemed to be of more importance in Quebec, while class-related differences such as income loomed larger in Ontario. In all regions, however, the substance of the agreement and the perceived benefits accruing to certain groups were significant, although not always the same items. In Ontario and the West, the "distinct society" clause was significant, as was the provision to add members to the House of Commons. In Quebec, the equal Senate issue carried more weight. Although group benefits in some fashion figured in the result in every region, the particular configuration of groups whose concerns were felt to have been either met or ignored by the agreement varied from one part of the country to another.

Alternative Futures?

Under what circumstances, if any, might the outcome of the October 1992 referendum have been different? Clearly, the demographics of Canadian politics are relatively unchangeable. Thus, to the extent that factors such as age, region, language, or social class best explain the outcome, perhaps no agreement, no matter how carefully crafted by the politicians, could have overcome the formidable obstacles presented by conflicting group and regional interests. But important as these fundamentals were, there is considerable evidence that the campaign itself *did* matter. The substantive issues of the agreement, together with the way in which it was perceived as affecting group interests, also mattered. So did the role of individual political leaders, particularly that of the unpopular prime minister who tried to sell the agreement to a sceptical public in the depths of an economic recession. So just as powerful short-term forces such as issues, leaders, and events dominate Canadian elections, and are often capable of overwhelming longer-term socio-demographic or partisan factors, so too comparable issue and leader variables combined to seal the fate of the Charlottetown Accord in the referendum. Given that many of these elements are themselves subject to change, it is worthwhile to consider whether the rejection of the Charlottetown Accord was inevitable. What might the referendum result have looked like with a slightly different agreement, for example, or if the referendum had been held under more favourable political or economic circumstances? While such an exercise requires the admittedly unrealistic assumption that all other factors can be held constant, it does allow us to assess the relative impact of some specific elements of the campaign.[24] By assuming different values for some of the key variables in the multivariate analysis discussed above (Figure 7.7), it is possible to consider some possible alternative scenarios for the referendum.

We have seen that attitudes of the Canadian public toward parties and leaders played a significant role in the overall results. Feelings about Brian Mulroney were positively correlated with a YES vote. Nonetheless, his massive unpopularity with the public as a whole actually cost the agreement votes. Behind the public's dislike of Mulroney lay grievances accumulated from a variety of sources—failed policies, a weak economy, a public disenchanted with politics and politicians. A prime minister whose standing with the public exerted a positive rather than a negative pull on public opinion might have been able to carry the YES vote above 50% in the nation as a whole, although perhaps not in every province. Driven partly by the negative economic and political conditions existing at the time, Mulroney's personal unpopularity exerted a significant drag on the agreement. While some of the policies of the Mulroney government such as the Free Trade Agreement or economic policies associated with the recession were also negative factors, their effects on the outcome tended to be indirect.[25] A more popular prime minister *might* have been able to sell an agreement to the Canadian public, even under the difficult economic and political conditions that existed in the country in October 1992.

But could a different leadership have succeeded in selling *this* agreement? The evidence here is much more complex. Overall, the attempt to broker major group interests in the negotiations was not unsuccessful, and the satisfaction of group interests such as those of Aboriginal peoples had some positive effects on the outcome. But the substance of the agreement itself, and particularly the two items most directly associated with Quebec, were major negative influences on the overall result. Public opinion on the distinct society component of the agreement was about evenly divided, with 45% expressing agreement with this principle and 43% opposed. Even so, the distinct society clause exerted a significant negative pull overall, because those who disagreed with it were much more likely to vote NO on the total package. In the aftermath of Meech Lake, the powerful symbolism of the distinct society clause all but assured that in some form it would have to be part of any plausible agreement. But the other major item, which was equally important to the referendum outcome, might have been avoided. Brought in at the final stages of the negotiations to balance the equal Senate provision, the guarantee of 25% of the seats in the House of Commons to Quebec attracted considerable public hostility. Given that such a provision had not been a part of any of the predecessor agreements, one could well imagine the question of "compensation" to the populous provinces, particularly Quebec, for agreeing to the equality of representation in the Senate being handled differently. While the evidence suggests that the agreement did not stand or fall on any single item, the 25% guarantee and the symbolism associated with it was nevertheless a powerful negative force for the proponents of the accord to overcome.

Following the referendum, leaders of all parties sought to put it behind them as quickly as possible. There was a prevalent feeling that the Canadian people had passed judgment not merely on the Charlottetown Accord, but on the political class of the country as a whole. The leaders of the Parti Québécois and the Reform Party were among the few politicians that even wanted to talk about the result, believing that it would prove favourable to their respective political movements. And indeed it would. Almost exactly a year later, Reform won a stunning 52 seats in the federal Parliament, claiming the support of almost one in five Canadian voters, and the Bloc

Figure 7.8

Referendum and Federal Election Voting

A. Percent Voting NO: By Vote in 1988 and 1993 Federal Elections

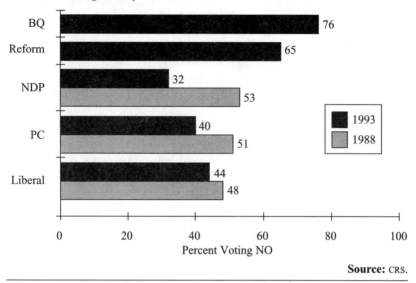

Source: CRS.

B. Vote in 1993 Federal Election: By Referendum Vote

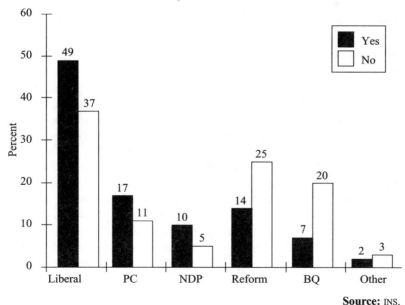

Source: INS.

167

Québécois became the official opposition. Less than two years later, the Parti Québécois returned to power in Quebec, renewing its quest for Quebec sovereignty. While it would be overstating the case to argue that the referendum result foreordained any of these events, it is nevertheless clear that the events and issues surrounding the referendum had a number of lasting effects. For at least some of these, the full implications may still not yet have been realized.

As is seen in Figure 7.8, how people voted in the referendum was related to their behaviour in the dramatic federal election that took place in 1993. The referendum and its aftermath became in effect a part of the "long campaign" of 1993 (see Chapter 4). Both Reform and the BQ were able to use the referendum result as a springboard for their campaigns in the election that followed. Voters successfully mobilized behind the NO side in the referendum could be mobilized again. The Liberals, sensing the public mood following the referendum, resolved not to talk about constitutional matters at all, but rather to concern themselves only with the economy. Although the party leadership had supported the YES side, the coalition of voters that returned the Liberals to power in 1993 had been more sharply divided in the referendum (Figure 7.8A). Unlike Reform or the Bloc, the Liberals could not derive any direct electoral benefits from their stance on the Charlottetown Accord.

It was perhaps for the Conservatives and NDP, however, that the referendum ultimately had the most serious consequences. The NDP leadership, which supported the YES side along with its three provincial premiers, found itself seriously offside with many of the voters who had supported the party in past elections but voted NO in the referendum. In the 1993 election, support for the party was reduced to a mere 7% of the electorate, barely a third of the level that it had obtained in 1988. The support that it did retain was heavily concentrated among those who agreed with the party leadership by supporting the YES side in the referendum. For a party that had long made its reputation by *opposing* what it considered the agenda of the political establishment in Canada, the position taken by the party leadership was a particularly stark reminder of the extent to which the party appeared to have lost touch with its roots. It had seemingly become a part of the very political establishment that it traditionally had opposed.

The Conservatives found that the referendum defeat had exhausted perhaps the most important resource that the party still possessed, the ability to set the agenda for the election. Had the referendum initiative been successful, Mulroney might have been able to structure the election campaign to follow in a way more favourable to his party. But in the aftermath of the referendum defeat, time quickly ran out on the Conservative government. Headed into the fifth year of its term with no coherent election strategy, a faltering economy, and a discredited leader, the party's prospects were truly dismal. Four months after the referendum, the prime minister submitted his resignation and the Conservatives commenced the process of electing a new leader. But, as we have seen, the selection of Kim Campbell to lead the party raised the Tories' hopes of survival only for the briefest period. In retrospect, it is evident that the referendum defeat set the stage for the Conservatives' subsequent electoral disaster. At a minimum, it diverted the party's diminishing resources away from the critical task of fighting the election. And it had ceded crucial electoral ground to the party's most dangerous opponents in Quebec and the West.

Conclusion

Because the 1992 referendum was such an unusual event in Canadian electoral politics, it is difficult to generalize from it. Yet many of the forces that were present in the referendum campaign were the same ones found in elections. Just as elections act to legitimize the process of government in a democratic society, the referendum was needed in order to legitimize the final stages of the constitutional project. Shut out of most parts of the long and arcane constiututional negotiations, it became clear after Meech Lake that "the people wanted in," and that the architects of the Charlottetown agreement ultimately had little choice but to seek a popular mandate for their project, even though they might well have preferred not to do so. But once begun, any electoral campaign takes on a life of its own and can only be managed in limited ways by those who set it in motion.

As the question was framed, only the crudest of mandates could have been delivered by the electorate in the referendum. Virtually all of the parties interpreted the outcome as a negative judgment on at least some aspects of the constitutional project as it had been pursued over the years through the processes of elite negotiation and consultation. Each party however had its own spin. Reform and the Bloc saw the outcome as a negative verdict on the constitutional project more generally, while the Liberals preferred to interpret it as a mandate to move on to other issues. The referendum had also provided Canadian voters with a rare opportunity to pass judgment on the nation's entire political establishment, together with one of that establishment's most cherished projects. And they voted, as citizens never can do in an election in this country, for "none of the above."

Notes

1. See, for example, Patrick Boyer, *Lawmaking by the People: Referendums and Plebiscites in Canada* (Toronto: Butterworths, 1982). See also David Macdonald, "Referendums and Federal General Elections in Canada," in Michael Cassidy, ed., *Democratic Rights and Electoral Reform in Canada*, vol. 10 of the Research Studies of the Royal Commission on Electoral Reform and Party Financing (Toronto: Dundurn Press, 1991).

2. See, for example, Anthony King, *Britain Says Yes: The 1975 Referendum on the Common Market* (Washington, D.C.: American Enterprise Institute, 1977). There are a number of studies of referendums in countries where they are more frequently employed, notably Switzerland, Ireland, or Australia. See, among other sources, David Butler and Austin Ranney, eds., *Referendums: a Comparative Study of Practice and Theory* (Washington, D.C.: American Enterprise Institute, 1978); Austin Ranney, ed., *The Referendum Device* (Washington, D.C.: American Enterprise Institute, 1981); and John T. Rourke et al., *Direct Democracy and International Politics: Deciding International Issues Through Referendums* (Boulder, CO: Lynne Rienner, 1992).

3. We will not attempt here to summarize the long history of struggles over the constitution. On these issues, see Peter H. Russell, *Constitutional Odyssey* (Toronto: University of Toronto Press, 1992); Robert C. Vipond, *Liberty and Community: Canadian Federalism and the Failure of the Constitution* (Albany, NY: State University of New York Press, 1991); and Alan Cairns and Douglas Williams, eds., *Disruptions: Constitutional Struggles From the Charter to Meech Lake* (Toronto: McClelland & Stewart, 1991).

4. Michael Stein, for example, notes the "tensions" that have existed in Canada between elite negotiations conducted within the structures associated with "executive federalism" and more direct types of democratic consultative processes. Stein, "Tensions in the Canadian Constitutional Process: Elite Negotiations, Referendums, and Interest Group Consultations," in R. Watts and D. Brown, eds., *Canada: The State of the Federation: 1993* (Kingston: Institute for Public Policy Research, 1993), pp. 87-116.

5. Citizens' Forum on Canada's Future, *Report to the People and Government of Canada* (Ottawa: Supply and Services, 1991).

6. Government of Canada, *Shaping Canada's Future Together* (Ottawa: Supply and Services, 1991).

7. Special Joint Committee of the Senate and House of Commons on a Renewed Canada, *Report* (Ottawa: Supply and Services, 1992).

8. See Russell, *Constitutional Odyssey* for a summary and discussion of these, including Quebec's Belanger-Campeau Commission, whose report resulted in the passage of Bill 150 in June 1991, committing the province to hold a referendum on either a federal proposal or on sovereignty no later than 26 October 1992.

9. Despite the involvement of other groups in the complex processes of negotiation that led to the agreement, it was the 11 first ministers who signed the accord at Charlottetown and who took the decision to hold a referendum. See Leslie Pal and F. Leslie Seidle, "Constitutional Politics 1990-92: The Paradox of Participation," in Susan D. Phillips, ed., *How Ottawa Spends: 1993-94: A More Democratic Canada?* (Ottawa: Carleton University Press, 1993), pp. 156-58.

10. On the issue of Quebec sovereignty, see André Blais and Richard Nadeau, "To Be or Not to Be Sovereigntist: Quebeckers' Perennial Dilemma," *Canadian Public Policy* 28 (1992): 89-103; or Stephane Dion, "Explaining Quebec Nationalism," in R. Kent Weaver, ed., *The Collapse of Canada?* (Washington, D.C.: The Brookings Institution, 1992), pp. 77-121.

11. This is suggested in the results of a survey question employed by Johnston et al. The question posed *three* options—the status quo, the Charlottetown proposal, or abolition of the Senate. Although their data show that there was greater support for the Charlottetown proposal than for the status quo, it also indicates that a plurality of Canadians would have preferred outright abolition. See Richard Johnston et al., "The People and the Charlottetown Accord," in Watts and Brown, eds., *Canada: The State of the Federation: 1993*, p. 23.

12. A factor analysis of opinion on the substantive provisions of the Accord shows that these two items were closely connected for many respondents. See Lawrence LeDuc and Jon H. Pammett, "Referendum Voting: Attitudes and Behaviour in the 1992 Constitutional Referendum," *Canadian Journal of Political Science* 28 (1995): 1-33. See also Harold D. Clarke and Allan Kornberg, "The Politics and Economics of Constitutional Choice: Voting in Canada's 1992 Constitutional Referendum," *Journal of Politics* 56 (1994): 940-62.

13. An interesting comparison is found in the attitudes of Canadians to the distribution of costs and benefits of the federal system, tending to believe that *their* provinces paid the costs, while others reaped the benefits. Harold D. Clarke, Jane Jenson, Lawrence LeDuc, and Jon H. Pammett, *Political Choice in Canada* (Toronto: McGraw-Hill Ryerson, 1979), pp. 80-85.

14. "Trudeau Speaks Out," *Maclean's,* 18 September 1992.

15. Among YES voters, 41% report having their mind made up from the beginning of the campaign, compared with 36% of NO voters.

16. For evidence on the attitudes of Canadians toward the mainstream parties and politicians, see Harold D. Clarke and Allan Kornberg, "Evaluations and Evolution: Attitudes Toward Canada's Federal Political Parties," *Canadian Journal of Political Science* 26 (1993): 287-312.

17. With approximately 1% of the votes cast being spoiled or otherwise invalid ballots.

18. Sixty-three percent of francophones in Quebec were found to have voted NO, while 79% of francophones outside Quebec supported the YES side [CRS].

19. At least with respect to the mainstream parties. Both Liberal identifiers and Conservatives were about equally likely to have voted YES (57% and 60% respectively). Of course, those identifying with Reform or the Bloc Québécois were almost entirely NO voters. LeDuc and Pammett, "Referendum Voting," p. 24.

20. The question employed was an open-ended question inviting respondents to give reasons for voting the way they did [CRS].

21. For a more detailed discussion and analysis of the role played by economic factors, see Clarke and Kornberg, "The Politics and Economics of Constitutional Choice," pp. 952-59.

22. Data not shown. See LeDuc and Pammett, "Referendum Voting," p. 23.

23. Because of the small number of cases, a separate analysis is not reported here for the Atlantic provinces.

24. See the analysis of possible alternative scenarios in Clarke and Kornberg, "The Politics and Economics of Constitutional Choice," pp. 955-59; see also LeDuc and Pammett, "Referendum Voting," pp. 29-30.

25. Clarke and Kornberg, "The Politics and Economics of Constitutional Choice," pp. 952-59.

The Politics
of Discontent

Canada entered the 1990s with a redesigned economic strategy and new thinking about social questions. Political elites' restructuring projects had generated a neoconservative consensus to replace earlier verities about economic growth and social equity. The country was thereby launched on the path of using more market-oriented mechanisms for distributing income and power, as well as reducing governmental responsibility for creating greater social and economic equality. A new trading relationship was forged within North America, reflecting the decision to scrap earlier efforts to develop a more autonomous location for Canada in the international economy. Conservative governments from 1984 until 1993 had presided over many of these changes. When the Liberals returned to office in 1993, they continued on the same track, despite their Red Book promises to provide an alternative.

In this book we have revealed the tenuous links between these fundamental shifts in governmental projects and the behaviour of parties and voters in the elections held during these years of fundamental change. Restructuring *has* occurred. Nonetheless, competing projects or even alternative versions of neoconservatism were not clearly debated in electoral politics. Constitutional politics was also avoided in the electoral arena, to be debated and decided elsewhere. The electoral discourse of the mainstream parties did not serve as the primary source of ideas about restructuring the future. Consideration of these economic and constitutional projects happened elsewhere, within the bureaucracy and the institutions of executive federalism, in the deliberations of the Macdonald Commission and other appointed bodies, and in the political activities of the newly mobilized popular sector. Even the 1992 referendum, which *did* provide an opportunity for democratic decision making, actually unfolded in such a way that the political parties were sidelined and debate was provoked and organized by other institutions and other actors.

If we are about to enter the next century with an economic and social project that is very different from its predecessor, we cannot say that the people of Canada have clearly endorsed this new direction through the mechanism that liberal democracy makes available for such decisions, namely elections. Ordinary Canadians were not asked for, nor did they provide, an electoral mandate for the political and economic restructuring undertaken by elites.

This absence of mandates from electoral politics is not new. For well over three decades electoral studies have documented a Canadian electorate that is flexible in its partisanship and fickle in its commitment to parties and their programs. For their part, the parties have behaved as classic "brokers," pragmatic organizations adept at smoothing over conflicts and spreading benefits among competing interests, areas, and social groups, and skilled at tacking with changes in the political winds.

Therefore, it is the behaviour of both voters and parties together that has produced the current "crisis" of Canadian politics and the increasingly frequent diagnoses of democratic malaise. Our federal politicians are certainly not the world's only leaders to confront angry and cynical electorates who exhibit little faith in their elected officials' abilities to solve the dilemmas we face at the dawn of the 21st century.[1] Voters everywhere are discontented about the present, and are angry with the politicians who have presided over the politics of the last several decades. Nonetheless there are particularities in the Canadian situation, which are the legacy of decades of absent mandates and brokerage politics and these set the parameters within which our future will be made.

Absent Mandates and Their Legacies

The echoes of partisan flexibility now resound through the electoral process, having an impact well beyond the moment when voters mark their ballots. Given that parties fear the costs of placing long-term projects or principled positions before an electorate that is fickle in its allegiances, it is hardly surprising that the issue agenda of electoral politics has lacked imagination. Electoral discourse has been stunted in content and has fluctuated widely, even as neoconservative restructuring has moved steadily forward.

For their part, parties have learned that they may manipulate the issue agenda to their advantage. Appeals to the public follow one of two strategies. The one most often favoured is to portray problems in very general terms, while trumpeting their importance. Each party attempts to identify itself as best able to resolve the country's most pressing problem.

This first strategy reflects a pragmatic consensual approach as parties present a case for their own definition of the problem and then argue that only they can be trusted to provide a solution. While the party in government has commonly used this strategy to defend its record, opposition parties also have made such general arguments and asked the voters to give them a crack at solving problems. Campaigns organized around the themes of "inflation," "unemployment," or "time for a change" represent this style of general problem definition. With this strategy, parties base their claim for a mandate on a general ability to govern effectively.

The second campaign strategy is quite different; it involves parties trying to distinguish themselves by proposing specific policy packages. This is an attempt to persuade the public that concrete policies, often narrow solutions to big problems, are good ideas and that the party deserves a mandate to govern precisely because it has demonstrated its seriousness by coming up with something definite. Thus the Liberals claimed in 1993 that their Red Book held the answers. Parties adopting this second strategy claim that they are the ones really tackling the issues, while their opponents simply speak vacuities.

All parties over the years have utilized both strategies. Yet neither strategy was likely to produce a real policy mandate. Emphasizing a general problem and trying to foster the image of being best able to deal with it ran into difficulty precisely because everyone did the same thing and voters had no real way of choosing among the alternatives. Therefore, electoral choice tended to respond to other factors that differentiated the parties, such as the images of leaders or campaign-related incidents or events. While voters might have been motivated by real concerns with these general issues, few clear patterns of change or cumulative benefits for one party were observable. Neither the inflation issue in 1974, the energy issue in 1980, nor unemployment in 1984, was identified solely with one party. It was therefore difficult to conclude precisely what the mandate conferred by these elections was, beyond the need to "do something" about the particular problem.

The alternative strategy, of making specific policy promises, however, often fared no better, since there was a strong likelihood that such issues would split the electorate—as happened in 1988—or that any specific policy would be abandoned or changed quickly after the election, as happened in so many areas after 1993. Thus, although these elections may have appeared to produce a mandate to do—or not do—something, the government's willingness to alter its policy stances made voters sceptical and even cynical about the meaning of even seemingly concrete policy promises. Such cynicism has now become a significant factor in Canadian federal politics.

Figure 8.1

**Percentage Believing "Politics is Too Complicated to Understand:"
1965–93**

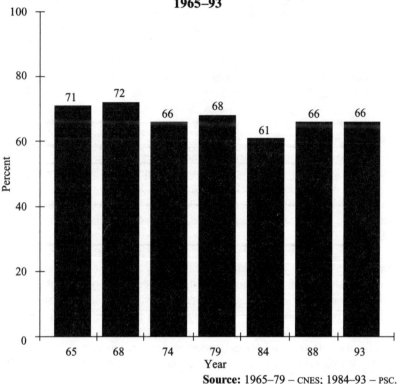

Source: 1965–79 – CNES; 1984–93 – PSC.

An Angry and Cynical Electorate

For a number of years politicians have been the target of a dissatisfied citizenry, which feels left out of the political process and unhappy about its outcomes. Chapter 7 documented the rejection of the Charlottetown Accord in the 1992 referendum by an angry electorate. Other popular consultations, such as those carried out by the Spicer Commission after the defeat of the Meech Lake Accord, turned up high levels of public grumpiness, which fed into the whole subsequent discussion of constitutional politics. In addition, in the 1993 election campaign, much was made by the Reform Party of its promise to make politicians more responsive and more responsible. The populist agenda of the new party resonated for many voters who were dissatisfied with old-style politics.

Canadians do not believe that the problem is of their own making. They place the blame squarely on politicians and the political process. The public remains interested in elections and most citizens cast a ballot when given the opportunity to do so. Yet voters give the parties exceedingly low

Figure 8.2

Electorally Related Activities: 1988, 1993

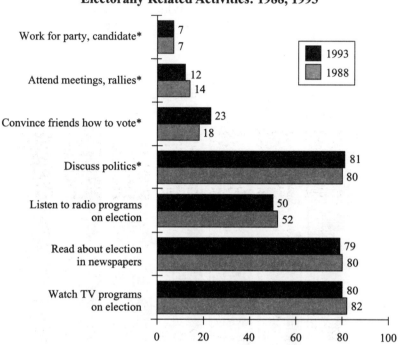

* Responses include percent responding "often" or "sometimes."

Source: 1988, 1993 – PSC.

marks for their contribution to democratic debate and the presentation of alternative futures. Figure 8.1 shows that, despite the array of new issues and long-running controversies that crowd the agenda, citizens do not exhibit any growing tendency to feel that politics is too complicated for them to understand. Indeed there has been a slight increase in feelings of subjective political competence. If anything, voters feel more rather than less capable of understanding politics, despite the abandonment of the familiar discourse of postwar Keynesianism and the adoption of unfamiliar neoconservative frameworks.

Nor are Canadians turning away from politics. Many of them take an interest in elections. In 1993 a majority (52%) of the voters reported that they were "very interested" in that election, while an additional 32% said they were "fairly interested." Levels of interest in elections have remained high over the last decade, therefore providing no evidence that the years of political and economic turbulence have caused the voters to withdraw their attention or concern.

Figure 8.3

**Percentages Believing MPs Lose Touch With Constituents,
Government Doesn't Care What They Think, and
People Like Them Have No Say: 1965–93**

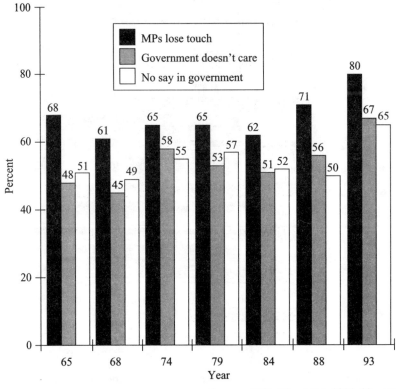

Source: 1965–79 – CNES; 1984–93 – PSC.

Election interest also translated into rates of participation in campaign-related activities, which were generally as high as in the previous election in 1988, which was itself an election that provoked a great deal of attention. In spite of the slightly lower voting turnout in 1993, Figure 8.2 shows that the various other dimensions of political participation remained at or near the same level. Many people continue to discuss politics with others, and the percentage of the population that reported attempting to influence their friends' vote jumped from 18% to 23%. Four-fifths of the electorate had watched a television program about the campaign, while similar numbers reported reading about the election in a newspaper or hearing about it on the radio. The portrait of the voters that emerges from these data is one of a reasonably interested, active group, not discouraged by the complexity of the issues or fearful of discussing the new economic schemas.

178

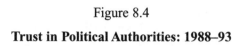

Figure 8.4

Trust in Political Authorities: 1988–93

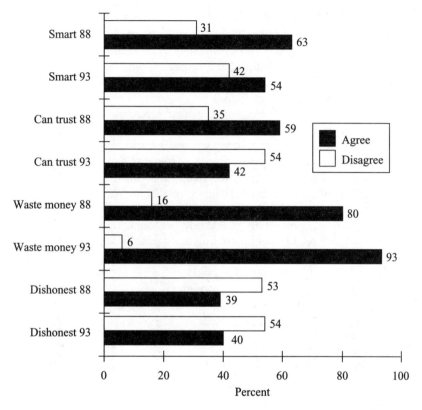

Source: 1988, 1993 – PSC.

' Yet, voters are not happy, and they place the blame for their distress squarely at the door of politicians, especially those practising brokerage politics. If we examine additional measures of voters' sense of external efficacy as well as of their sense of trust, we see that all these indicators have moved in the direction of greater dissatisfaction. As Figure 8.3 shows, the percentage of people feeling they had no say in government hovered in the range of 49% to 57% from 1965 to 1988, but in 1993 it shot up to 65%. Two-thirds of the electorate, rather than a half, now report strong feelings of being ignored. Over the same period the perception that the system itself was unresponsive showed a steady increase, reaching even greater heights in 1993 than the already elevated levels of 1988. In 1993 four-fifths of the voters said they believed that their elected representatives, the members of Parliament, quickly lose touch with their constituents. Two-thirds felt that the government did not care about people like them. In both cases, the reported levels of external political inefficacy in 1993 were the highest on record.

Many voters also believe that the political authorities are untrustworthy, and survey evidence suggests that these beliefs have become more widespread in recent years. Between 1988 and 1993, the size of the group considering authorities to be "smart" dropped by 9%, while that which thought them trustworthy declined by 17% (Figure 8.4). When asked about authorities' stewardship of the taxpayers' dollars, fully 93% of the voters in 1993 believed that money was being wasted, climbing to that level from an already high 80% in 1988.

In giving such evaluations the Canadian electorate is not expressing a generalized cynicism to all things political, however. Both post-election and inter-electoral public opinion surveys reveal a capacity and a willingness among voters to make choices about *where* to direct their criticisms. Voters do recognize that political parties make a significant contribution to democratic politics. As Table 8.1 shows, parties are most often valued as facilators of representation and participation.[2] Levels of approval of activities such as representing "everybody," encouraging people to become politically active, and finding consensus are substantially higher than other characteristics of parties, even if they remain distressingly low in absolute terms (only about a third of the population, after all, gives parties high marks on these general democratic activities).

But voters are profoundly and almost universally dissatisfied with brokerage politics. Almost two-thirds of respondents consider that the parties do not offer real choices, while 69% think that the parties fail to tell the voters about the really important problems facing the country. Moreover, there is virtual consensus that political parties pay too much attention to winning elections and not enough to governing afterwards (81%) and to gaining partisan advantage rather than solving important problems (89%). The most dramatic result in Table 8.1, and the one that most clearly indicates that the practices of brokerage politics contribute to the public's cynicism, is the 91% of the respondents who report that they anticipate a "big difference" between "what a party says it will do, and what it actually does if it wins an election."

Other surveys confirm this finding. In a 1991 study, André Blais and Elisabeth Gidengil found that the highest level of political cynicism over 12 different measures was recorded in response to a statement that "most candidates in federal elections make campaign promises they have no intention of fulfilling."[3] They also found that the electorate reserved its harshest judgment for the parties' capacity to provoke meaningful consideration of the issues. Fully 87% of their respondents agreed with the statement that "the parties confuse the issues rather than provide a clear choice on them" while 81% thought the parties "squabbled" too much.[4]

Table 8.1

Evaluations of Political Parties: 1991

	Agree	Disagree	Don't Know
Parties spend too much time bickering and quarrelling rather than solving important problems facing the country	**89%**	6	5
In elections political parties don't tell people about the really important problems facing the country	**69%**	21	11
Political parties and democracy always go together—no parties, no democracy	50%	**26**	24
Political parties generally try to look after the best interests of everybody and not just the interests of those who vote for them	33%	**57**	10
Parties give people a say in politics that they couldn't have as individuals	44%	**41**	15
There is often a big difference between what a party says it will do, and what it actually does if it wins an election	**91%**	4	5
Parties usually are more interested in winning elections than in governing afterwards	**81%**	12	7
Parties do a good job of encouraging people to become active in politics	31%	**51**	18
Political parties do more to divide the country than to unite it	**56%**	28	17
Parties don't offer voters real choices in elections because their policies are all pretty much the same	**63%**	26	10
Parties generally do a good job in helping groups reach agreement about what government should be doing	29%	**50**	21

Note: Boldface percentages indicate negative response.

Source: 1991 – PSC.

In commenting on such findings, the Royal Commission on Electoral Reform and Party Financing indicted the parties and their behaviour, saying that "feelings about confusing issues and squabbling may... partly reflect the limited efforts by parties to engage in political education and discussion of policy issues."[5] Indeed, the message is quite clear. Canadian citizens are not "turned off" electoral politics per se. They are interested and they want to be involved. Yet, they feel that they do not have access to the political process and that politicians and governments are neither sufficiently responsive nor reliable. Oftentimes, voters behave as if they feel they have no choice but to "throw the rascals out," even if the replacements are not likely to be very different. Thus, the electorate is not simply cynical. It is angry and exhibits high levels of dissatisfaction with brokerage politics.

The Legacy of Brokerage Politics: Permanent Dealignment

Each of the chapters of this book contributes to a portrait of Canadian voters and the contexts within which they act. Crucial to the story is the long-standing legacy of a party system characterized, from the beginning of the 20th century, by a style of politics that has minimized real debate about alternatives. It is a system that has frequently focussed more on leaders and image politics, and in which parties have taken over each other's policies. Thus, the economic and social positions adopted by the two main parties have often been indistinguishable from each other. Moreover, when there were policy differences, it was often hard to predict on the basis of its past actions which position any party would adopt. That the Liberals carried on much of the neoconservatism of the Tories after 1993 is only the most recent example of policy flip-flops and convergence over the years.

Accompanying the pliability in programmatic stances and policy positions of parties has been a high level of flexibility in the responses of Canadian voters when elections invite them to make choices. As we might expect in a party system in which much of the public has not developed enduring ties to political parties rooted in ideology or group loyalties, Canadian voters exhibit few qualms about switching from one party to another as the winds of approval change. The electorate has been willing to abandon earlier decisions on short notice and it has become accustomed to shifting easily among alternative parties, candidates, leaders, and party policies once it decides that it is time to try something new. Few voters have been patient enough to wait out an extended stretch of time before abandoning a position, person, or party. This unwillingness to think long term has been encouraged by parties that have promised quick-fix solutions. As such it has now become a real constraint on any party's ability to experiment with proposing alternative projects for the future.

Moreover, in part because of the fluidity of issues, leaders and their ability to stitch together policy stances have become an important factor accounting for voting choice, especially among flexible partisans. When parties emphasize leadership and voters focus on the leaders, discussion is deflected toward general considerations of public confidence in these individuals. Popular evaluations of the leaders are, of course, based partly on their stance on issues and partly on their perceived personal characteristics. Nevertheless, the prominent role frequently accorded the

182

leaders during election campaigns ensures that any policy discussion occurs around the public utterances and personal skills of these few persons, and that their character and public confidence in their ability to carry out policy becomes inextricably intertwined with the consideration of the electoral issues themselves. This emphasis on leaders and leadership may enable parties to avoid discussion of conflict-creating or unpopular policy alternatives that might damage their fortunes during the campaign. Yet, it also ensures that leaders bear the brunt of public displeasure when the quick-fix policies produced in this way do not work. Individual party leaders have become both the anchors of the brokerage system and its major casualties. The fate of former Conservative prime minister Kim Campbell in the 1993 election is only the most recent, and perhaps most dramatic, manifestation of this aspect of brokerage politics.

Whether the behaviour of the parties or the flexibility of partisan ties in the electorate is the ultimate source of brokerage politics is a question that can never be answered satisfactorily. Indeed, any question about ultimate cause is incorrectly posed. The process over time has been one of learning by both voters and politicians. Political parties have learned that their electoral coalitions are fragile creations, requiring constant and careful tending. For their part voters have learned that they will not be offered clear choices about the future in elections and therefore often seek only to bring about a "change."

The impact of this interactive learning process has been clearly visible in elections since the mid-1960s. Canadians have been fickle in their attachments to political parties, changing not only their votes but also their party identification. Such a situation can be characterized as one of *dealignment*. A dealigned party system is one in which volatility is paramount, where there are frequent changes in electoral outcomes as well as lots of individual flexibility. The 1993 election, which decimated the Conservatives' parliamentary delegation at the same time as it fractured the House of Commons into five parts, is an obvious result of such dealignment. It is, however, only the most recent manifestation of what has been a long-standing characteristic of federal electoral politics, revealed earlier in the big swings of 1958, 1968, and 1984.

An alternative kind of party system is one that is *aligned*. Where alignment exists, large numbers of people believe that their interests and those of others like them are best served, over the long haul, by a particular party that offers something different than its competitors. Voters in an aligned party system consider that a particular party advances the cause of specific social groups and espouses readily identifiable ideological positions. Moreover, parties can be differentiated by their ties to *particular* groups and commitments to *specific* alternatives. One result is that in an aligned party system voters settle into recurrent patterns of political thought and behaviour.

As these patterns begin to break down a process of dealignment takes hold. A variety of factors may give rise to dealignment, including shifts in the parties' links to social groups, abandonment of ideological commitments, or changes in the composition of the electorate. Thus, the retreat from postwar Keynesian economics in many countries has been associated with a dealignment of party systems, as social classes and other social groups found themselves bereft of allies or abandoned by their previously favoured party. Other analyses have identified a dealignment following the "new politics" preferred by the baby-boom generations first voting in the 1970s and 1980s in Western Europe and North America.[6]

We have already seen that configurations of support for Canadian parties have not been adequately explained by long-term forces such as social class, religion, or other group characteristics. Nor has ideology been a strong correlate of either partisanship or voting, and the party system has long defied a simple left/right depiction.[7] Moreover, if federal politics has always been characterized by strong regional patterns of party and electoral support, these have never been stable over time. For example, the Liberal "stronghold" of Quebec crumbled before the Tories led by their new leader from Quebec, Brian Mulroney, in 1984. Only two elections later, that party virtually disappeared from that province's electoral map following the overwhelming victory of the Bloc Québécois. The map of the West has been similarly reconfigured since the Reform Party came on the scene.

The analysis in this book has not presented a portrait of an aligned party system at the federal level. Rather, we have seen that parties are not able to call on loyal electorates and instead have attempted to harness a variety of less predictable short-term forces to achieve victory. It is the predominance of short-term forces that has led us to be sceptical about whether 1993 marks any realignment, despite the dramatic changes and the appearance of new parties. For a party system to be realigned, changes would have to be more than temporary and patterns would have to begin to jell into a stable shape. The specific circumstances of the 1993 events as well as the history of earlier elections suggest a cautious assessment.

First, the Bloc Québécois, despite its success in becoming the official opposition, has publicly proclaimed that it has little intention of being a contender in the next election. Thus, federal politics in Quebec is destined to undergo another major shift. History gives us even more reason to expect continued instability. For example, before the Conservatives were returned to power in the turbulent election of 1988, three successive governing parties had gone down to defeat—the Liberals in 1979, the Tories in 1980, and the Liberals in 1984. Indeed, prior to 1988, the only post-1945 federal election to produce consecutive majority governments was that of 1953. Moreover, if the Tories' back-to-back victories in 1984 and 1988 led to speculation about a realignment in which the Conservatives would replace the Liberals as the "government party," their spectacular defeat in 1993 quickly put paid to that proposition.

Another possibile suggestion is that the Tories' electoral successes in the 1980s simply started a process of dealignment that became evident in 1993. The data presented throughout this book make it difficult to sustain such a hypothesis. Over the last two decades, at least, there is abundant evidence of widespread flexibility in partisan attachments and volatility in electoral behaviour and results. Thus, unlike other party systems in which a convergence of specific events and changes in the electorate in the 1970s and 1980s triggered a dealignment, it is quite likely that the current dealignment of the Canadian party system is rooted in now distant events and conditions.

Election results over several decades reinforce the story told by the survey evidence; the Canadian situation is one of *permanent dealignment*. Whatever its sources, the consequences of this ongoing phenomenon are very visible in the contemporary volatility of electoral politics. Nonetheless, a situation of permanent dealignment does not imply that nothing has changed. Rather, it means that change itself is a key strand of the fabric of federal politics. In 1993, as in previous years, we have seen that levels of partisan identification remained high, at the same time that large numbers of voters shifted the direction of their allegiance. They moved to the new parties and thereby produced the 1993 successes of the Bloc Québécois and the Reform Party. It is far too early—and on the basis of past experience quite unlikely—that these voters will be any more than the "fair-weather friends" that they have already been for the Liberals, Conservatives, or NDP. Massive shifts from party to party from one election to another are not unusual, nor have they proved to be a reliable indicator that a realignment had occurred or was in the offing.

Into the Future

Despite the change in government in 1993, the project for restructuring the Canadian economy and its place in the world continues. Continuity may be observed in both the Liberal government's willingness to pick up the neoconservative torch passed to it by the soundly defeated Tories and its decision to do so in ways that will contribute little if anything to lessening the electorate's dissatisfaction with brokerage politics. A number of policy reversals as well as dramatic initiatives hardly hinted at in the campaign have been documented in several chapters of this book. The Liberal government has acted in this way despite the exceedingly high levels of dissatisfaction with such party behaviour already evident in the various public opinion data we have discussed throughout this book.

The Liberals of course are not the only party that has been criticized for failing to live up to its campaign promises. In the aftermath of its 1993 success, some observers chastised the Reform Party, which had pledged a new approach to politics, for accepting the perks of office and softening some of its policy positions. Although Reform leaders insist that the essentials of their agenda will remain intact, the forces that encourage parties, new or old, to play the traditional brokerage game did not disappear in 1993. As we have argued throughout this book, one of the most important of these forces is the flexibility of voters' partisan attachments. This continued flexibility will continue to generate a strong potential for electoral volatility in the years ahead, and parties ignore it at their peril. If the party system fragmented in 1993, past experience gives us little guide as to whether the patterns yielded by this fragmentation will endure. Rather it encourages a good deal of scepticism about their durability. All parties will continue to face the challenge of building winning coalitions in elections, and dramatic reversals of fortune for *any* party can readily occur.

We have also insisted throughout this book that despite these continuities there have been changes. The most dramatic and consequential is the consolidation of the restructuring project. Over the two decades upon which this book has focussed, the postwar commitment to Keynesian economic policies and constitutional reform has given way to neoconservative economics and constitutional stalemate. These have produced their own responses among the electorate. High levels of dissatisfaction with traditional political forms have not led to alienation or demobilization. Rather, as the events of constitutional debate in the early 1980s first demonstrated and then as the conflicts over free trade and Meech Lake confirmed, Canadians have been seeking new routes to representation. Sometimes this has led to demands for forms of direct democracy, such as the constitutional referendum in 1992. Sometimes it has been expressed in support for a political party, such as the Reform Party, which promises to change the old ways of doing things. And sometimes it has generated new routes to representation, which by-pass the party system and channel energy in the direction of interest groups and social movements.

All of these are signs that there is a serious public thirst for maintaining and extending the spaces of democratic politics. Whether the party system and electoral politics will quench this thirst remains the great unknown as we face the next century. The challenge put to parties and elections, the traditional institutions of democratic governance, is to rise to the occasion and finally begin to fulfil their assigned task of organizing choice and mobilizing change.

Notes

1. In its final report the Royal Commission on Electoral Reform and Party Financing (RCERPF) argued that levels of dissatisfaction were higher in Canada than in the United States, although the trends were in the same direction in both countries. See Royal Commission on Electoral Reform and Party Financing, *Reforming Electoral Democracy* (Ottawa: Supply and Services, 1991), vol. 1, pp. 224-25.

2. Harold D. Clarke and Allan Kornberg, "Evaluations and Evolution: Public Attitudes Toward Canada's Federal Parties, 1965-1991," *Canadian Journal of Political Science* 26 (1993): 292.

3. André Blais and Elisabeth Gidengil, *Making Representative Democracy Work: The Views of Canadians*, vol. 17 of the Research Studies of the Royal Commission on Electoral Reform and Party Financing (Toronto: Dundurn Press, 1991), Table 3.1, p. 35.

4. Blais and Gidengil, *Making Representative Democracy Work*, Table 3.5, p. 42.

5. RCERPF, *Reforming Electoral Democracy*, vol. 1, p. 226.

6. For a detailed overview of this literature, comparing Western Europe to Canada, see Maureen Covell, "Parties as Institutions of National Governance," in Herman Bakvis, ed., *Representation, Integration and Political Parties in Canada*, vol. 14 of the Research Studies of the RCERPF (Toronto: Dundurn Press, 1991).

7. See Harold D. Clarke and Marianne Stewart, "Canada," in Mark Franklin et al., eds., *Electoral Change: Responses to Evolving Social and Attitudinal Structures in Western Countries* (Cambridge: Cambridge University Press, 1992), and Janine Brodie and Jane Jenson, "Piercing the Smokescreen: Brokerage Parties and Class Politics," in A.-G. Gagnon and A.B. Tanguay, eds., *Canadian Parties in Transition: Discourse, Organization, Representation* (Toronto: Nelson, 1988).

Data
Sources

The analyses of Canadian electoral behaviour presented in this volume employ data from a number of different surveys spanning the 1965-93 period. Some of these surveys were conducted in conjunction with the 1965, 1968, 1974, 1979, 1980, 1984, and 1988 Canadian national election studies (CNES). The 1965 and 1968 surveys were national cross sections; the 1974, 1979, and 1980 ones included cross-sectional components together with two-wave (1974-79, 1979-80) and three-wave (1974-79-80) panel components. Field work for the 1965 through 1984 CNES was conducted by Canadian Facts, Ltd. A 1988 reinterview of respondents from the 1984 CNES carried out by the Carleton University Survey Centre is designated separately as the Carleton Panel Study (CPS). The 1988 CNES was a pre-election cross section survey with a pre/post-election panel. Field work for the 1988 and 1993 CNES was conducted by the York University Institute for Social Research. The 1993 CNES was not available for detailed analysis at the time of the writing of this volume.

Another set of surveys utilized here were conducted by Harold Clarke and Allan Kornberg in the Political Support in Canada studies (PSC). PSC surveys were administered at the times of the 1984, 1988, and 1993 federal elections, as well as in several non-election years (1983, 1985, 1986, 1987, 1989, 1990, and 1991). All of these surveys have cross-sectional components and several include interlocking panels. Adjacent panels include: 1980-83 (the 1980 data were gathered in the 1980 CNES), 1983-84 (post-election), 1984-88 (pre-election), 1988 (pre-election)-1988 (post-election), 1988 (post-election)-1990, 1990-93 (post-election). Field work for these studies was carried out by Canadian Facts, Ltd.

Other studies employed here include a national cross-sectional survey organized by Harold Clarke, Lawrence LeDuc, and Jon Pammett (with Alan Frizzell and Allan Kornberg) and carried out by the Carleton University Survey Centre at the time of the 1992 constitutional referendum. This study, denoted as the Carleton Referendum Study (CRS) provides the data for our analyses of public attitudes toward the Charlottetown Accord and voting in the October 1992 referendum. Data from a study conducted by Insight Canada Research Ltd. (INS) following the 1993 federal election is also utilized in this volume. Federal party identification in 1981 is measured using the Quality of Life: Social Change in Canada Survey (QOL), which was conducted by the York University Institute for Social Research.

The CNES data, and the 1983-84, 1988, and 1990 PSC data may be obtained from the Institute for Social Research Data Archive, York University, and the Inter-university Consortium for Political and Social Research (ICPSR) Data Archive, University of Michigan. The 1974, 1979, and 1980 CNES data and the 1983-84, 1988, and 1990 PSC data also are available from the European Consortium for Political Research (ECPR) Archive, University of Essex. The QOL data are archived at the Institute for Social Research, York University. Information concerning sample designs and weighting schemes used to ensure representative national samples accompany these several data sets. Technical information concerning the other data sets used in our analyses and the surveys upon which they are based are available from the authors upon request.

Sample Sizes

Sample sizes for different analyses vary depending upon the incidence of missing data for the variables being considered. The basic Ns (weighted as appropriate to yield representative national samples) for the several surveys are as follows:

CNES: cross sections: 1965 = 2729; 1968 = 2767; 1974 = 2445;
1979 = 2670; 1980 = 1786; 1984 = 3380; 1988 (pre-election) = 3396;
1988 (post-election) = 2769; panels: 1974-79 = 1353;
1979-80 = 1786; 1974-79-80 = 866; 1988 (pre/post-election) = 2671.

PSC: cross sections: 1983 = 2117; 1984 = 1928; 1985 = 1853; 1986 = 2000;
1987 = 2000; 1988 (pre-election) = 2215; 1988 (post-election) = 2010;
1989 = 2000; 1990 = 1967; 1991 = 1828; 1993 = 1496;
panels: 1980-83 = 882; 1980-84 = 623; 1983-84 = 1395;
1984-88 (pre-election) = 868; 1988 (pre/post-election) =
1516; 1990-93 = 1019;
1988 (post-election)-1990-93 = 696.

Others: CRS: 1992 cross section = 1115;
CPS: 1984-88 panel = 1201;
INS: 1993 cross section = 1200;
QOL: 1981 cross section = 2948.

Table A1

Election Results By Province: 1993

		Liberal	Reform	PC	BQ	NDP	Other
Newfoundland	Vote (%)	67	1	27	–	4	1
	Seats	7	0	0	–	0	0
Prince Edward Island	Vote (%)	60	1	32	–	5	2
	Seats	4	0	0	–	0	0
Nova Scotia	Vote (%)	52	13	23	–	7	5
	Seats	11	0	0	_	0	0
New Brunswick	Vote (%)	56	8	28	–	5	3
	Seats	9	0	1	–	0	0
Quebec	Vote (%)	33	–	14	49	1	3
	Seats	19	–	1	54	0	1
Ontario	Vote (%)	53	20	18	–	6	3
	Seats	98	1	0	–	0	0
Manitoba	Vote (%)	45	22	12	–	17	4
	Seats	12	1	0	–	1	0
Saskatchewan	Vote (%)	32	27	11	–	27	3
	Seats	5	4	0	–	5	0
Alberta	Vote (%)	25	52	15	–	4	4
	Seats	4	22	0	–	0	0
British Columbia	Vote (%)	28	36	13	–	16	7
	Seats	6	24	0	–	2	0
Yukon/N.W.T.	Vote (%)	50	10	17	–	20	3
	Seats	2	0	0	–	1	0
Total Canada	Vote (%)	41	19	16	14	7	3
	Seats	177	52	2	54	9	1

Percent turnout: 69.6%

Source: *Report of the Chief Electoral Officer* (Ottawa: Supply and Services, 1993).

Table A2
Election Results by Province: 1974–88

		Liberal					PC					NDP					All Other				
		1988	1984	1980	1979	1974	1988	1984	1980	1979	1974	1988	1984	1980	1979	1974	1988	1984	1980	1979	1974
Newfoundland	Vote (%)	45	36	47	38	47	42	58	36	31	44	12	6	17	31	9	X	X	X	X	X
	Seats	5	3	5	4	4	2	4	2	2	3	0	0	0	1	0	0	0	0	0	0
Prince Edward Island	Vote (%)	50	41	47	40	46	41	52	46	53	49	7	6	7	7	5	1	X	X	X	X
	Seats	4	1	2	0	1	0	3	2	4	3	0	0	0	0	0	0	0	0	0	0
Nova Scotia	Vote (%)	47	34	40	36	41	41	51	39	45	47	11	15	21	19	11	1	X	X	X	X
	Seats	6	2	5	2	2	5	9	6	8	8	0	0	0	1	1	0	0	0	0	0
New Brunswick	Vote (%)	45	32	50	45	47	40	54	33	40	33	9	14	16	15	9	5	X	1	X	11
	Seats	5	1	7	6	6	5	9	3	4	3	0	0	0	0	0	0	0	0	0	1
Quebec	Vote (%)	30	35	68	62	54	53	50	13	13	21	14	9	9	5	7	3	5	10	20	18
	Seats	12	17	74	67	60	63	58	1	2	3	0	0	0	0	0	0	0	0	6	11
Ontario	Vote (%)	39	30	42	37	45	38	48	36	42	35	20	21	22	21	19	3	1	X	1	1
	Seats	43	14	52	32	55	46	67	38	57	25	10	13	5	6	8	0	0	0	0	0
Manitoba	Vote (%)	36	22	28	24	27	37	43	38	44	48	21	27	34	33	24	5	8	X	X	1
	Seats	5	1	2	2	2	7	9	5	7	9	2	4	7	5	2	0	0	0	0	0
Saskatchewan	Vote (%)	18	18	24	20	31	36	42	39	42	36	44	38	36	37	32	1	2	1	1	1
	Seats	0	0	0	0	3	4	9	7	10	8	10	5	7	4	2	0	0	0	0	0
Alberta	Vote (%)	14	13	21	21	25	52	69	66	67	61	17	14	10	10	9	17	4	3	3	5
	Seats	0	0	0	0	0	25	21	21	21	19	1	0	0	0	0	0	0	0	0	0
British Columbia	Vote (%)	21	16	22	23	33	34	47	41	45	42	37	35	35	32	23	7	2	2	1	2
	Seats	1	1	0	1	8	12	19	16	19	13	19	8	12	8	2	0	0	0	0	0
Yukon/N.W.T.	Vote (%)	30	24	37	33	28	30	47	32	37	39	37	23	31	29	33	3	4	X	1	X
	Seats	2	0	0	0	0	0	3	2	2	1	1	0	1	1	1	0	0	0	0	0
Canada	Vote (%)	32	28	44	40	43	43	50	33	36	35	20	19	20	18	15	5	3	3	6	6
	Seats	83	40	147	114	141	169	211	103	136	95	43	30	32	26	16	0	1	0	6	12

	1988	1984	1980	1979	1974
Percent turnout	75	76	69	76	71

X Less than 1%

Source: Reports of the Chief Electoral Officer (Ottawa: Supply and Services, 1974-88).

191

Author Index

Subject Index